College After 30

It's Never Too Late to Get the Degree You Need!

Sunny & Kim Baker

BOB ADAMS, INC.
PUBLISHERS
Holbrook, Massachusetts

Published by Bob Adams, Inc.
260 Center Street, Holbrook, MA 02343

ISBN: 1-55850-167-3

Printed in the United States of America

C   D   E   F   G   H   I   J

This publication is designed to provide accurate and authoritative information with regard to the subject matter covered. It is sold with the understanding that the publisher is not engaged in rendering legal, accounting, or other professional advice. If legal advice or other expert assistance is required, the services of a qualified professional person should be sought.
— From a *Declaration of Principles* jointly adopted by a Committee of the American Bar Association and a Committee of Publishers and Associations.

COVER DESIGN: Peter Gouck

This book is available at quantity discounts for bulk purchases.
For information, call 1-800-872-5627.

Dedication

This book is dedicated to the countless students who, against all odds, go back to school to improve themselves, their communities, and the world. It is also dedicated to the many faculty members and counselors in universities who encourage mature students to complete their college education and who consider age no barrier in the pursuit of knowledge.

Contents

Chapter Eleven

Introduction

It's Never Too Late to Get the Degree You Want and Need

Education makes a greater difference between man and man
than nature has made between man and brute.

—*John Adams*

If you're over thirty and considering college as an option, you're not alone Hun
dreds of thousands of mid-career adults decide to return to college each year. Here
are some facts to ponder if you are among the countless adults who are still thinking about starting college for the first time or pondering a return to college to complete an unfinished degree:

- The number of adult students in colleges has increased steadily over the
  last ten years and is increasing even faster now as recessions and new
  technologies eat into once-secure careers.
- According to the National Center for Educational Statistics, more than
  fifty percent of the college students in the United States today are over 25.
  In addition, over 80 percent of these adults are employed and have more
  experience than the traditional college student.
- At many colleges the average age of the students is over 30. In fact, there
  are accredited universities and graduate schools that won't admit students
  who don't have significant work and life experience or who are under 30.
- Hundreds of colleges offer accelerated-degree programs for part-time students.
- More than half the students in many colleges work full time in addition to
  attending school.
- There are no age restrictions on most federal financial aid programs. Financial aid is also available for part-time students.
- Many accredited distance-education programs allow working students to
  get degrees at home via computers, satellites, and television—without
  ever setting foot in a classroom.
- Many colleges and universities offer free or low-cost day-care programs
  for parents who want to attend school.
- There is an adult-oriented support and counseling center, a continuing
  education program for working adults, or an adult-programs office on al-

most every major college and university campus.
- Senior centers—for adult students over fifty—are now common on the campuses of colleges, universities, and community colleges.

Adults in college are no longer the exceptions—they are becoming the norm. Adults who finish college enjoy financial rewards, increased job security, and new career opportunities. And besides the obvious financial gains and career opportunities, adults enjoy expanded intellectual skills, new personal relationships, and increased self-esteem as a result of their college experience. Millions of people with different motivations and diverse goals have realized significant personal benefits as a result of completing their college education later in life. So, if you are still just *thinking* about college, what's holding you back?

Why Adults Are Afraid to Go to College

Even though millions of adults go to college each year, and programs for adult education are expanding rapidly, many adults remain uninformed about college as an option. Many adults are terrified at the prospect of starting college for the first time or returning to complete a degree after fifteen or more years away from a classroom. Mature adults in pursuit of a degree are intimidated by both the bureaucracy of the programs and their own fear of failure.

Few mature adults feel comfortable attending classes filled with "kids" the same age as their children or grandchildren. After years running a household full time or working in business, becoming a student again can threaten both identity and self-esteem. People who have settled into predictable daily patterns find adjusting to student life difficult if they are not prepared for the changes and commitments demanded by college.

If you are one of these adults—with questions, fears, and anxieties about returning to college at this "later" point in your life—this book was written for you. We wrote this book because we want to help the millions of adults—like you—who would benefit from getting a degree but are confused by the options, intimidated by the requirements, or afraid to try because they think they are too old to succeed.

How This Book Will Help You Succeed as an Adult in College

As educators with fifteen years of experience counseling adult students in college programs, we have heard countless and predictable excuses from adults who want to go to college but are afraid to try. This book provides an experience-based process that works, so you can overcome the obstacles that block your college goals. The step-by-step methodologies and comprehensive information in *College After 30* will give you the confidence and insights you need to make informed decisions about schools, programs, finances, schedules, studying, and managing your new life as a student.

College After 30 includes information on adult-oriented degree programs coupled with unique survival tactics for mid-career students. Worksheets and checklists offer adults direct vehicles for assessing, planning, and ultimately completing any college degree program—whether the goal is an associate degree from a junior college, a bachelor's degree from a state university, an M.B.A. from an alternative school that uses computers and modems to present the courses, or a traditional Ph.D. from a prestigious graduate school.

You may ask why *College After 30* is different from other books that advise on choosing, getting into, and surviving in college. Why is another college guide necessary? *College After 30* is different because it is geared to the needs of *adult* students. With a few exceptions, the audience for almost all other college resource books is young students (and their parents) who need to choose a college directly out of high school. Though some of the information in these widely read books is applicable to adult students, much of it is not.

The real-life obligations of working adults are different from those of younger students. The unique attributes of adult learners make the advice in most college guides only marginally useful to mid-career college students. These adults have different priorities, concerns, and financial problems than the younger and more traditional audience for college handbooks. Unlike the majority of "how-to-go-to-college" books geared to full-time students in their teens and twenties, *College After 30* explains the ins and outs of getting a degree from the working adult's viewpoint and reveals the prerequisites to finding success as an adult student.

College After 30 is a comprehensive guidebook for mid-career adults thinking about returning to school or already involved in completing the degrees they need to get ahead or to survive in turbulent financial times. As a one-of-a-kind reference, it fills the long-ignored needs of millions of adults who are thinking about college as a way to either secure their careers or enhance their options in life—or both.

We hope you find *College After 30* a valuable resource in meeting your life and educational goals. We want you to succeed and prosper. Let us know how *College After 30* helps you. We would like to hear your stories of life as an adult college student, including the challenges, successes, and accomplishments you experience. If we have missed some of the problems you encountered or failed to identify some of the resources you needed, tell us. Then we can fill the gaps in our coverage in the next edition of our book.

Please write to us c/o:

College After 30
Bob Adams, Inc.
260 Center Street
Holbrook, MA 02343

Chapter One

What Will a College Degree Do for You Now?

What kind of people return to college in mid-career or later in life? Consider Joanne and Oscar, two mid-career adults who returned to college and reaped significant personal benefits as a result of more education.

Joanne quit graduate school seventeen years ago and never finished the master's degree she had started. It always bothered her that she hadn't gone back—but her career, family, and financial requirements always seemed to get in the way. She never felt she had the time to go back to school and, at 42, she thought she would be out of place at a traditional university where students are the same age as her daughter. But Joanne discovered Keller Graduate School in Chicago, a night program for working adults, which meets only one night a week and on Saturdays. In only six more months she'll have finished her dream of getting her M.B.A. As a result of the degree, she has been offered a part-time position as an instructor at a local community college. The new opportunity comes at just the right time, too, because the company where she currently works full time is projecting massive layoffs next year, and now Joanne will have a teaching career to fall back on.

Oscar is 37 and a self-taught computer technician with fourteen years of experience at a computer company. Tonight, he is working on a human relations course on route to his B.A. in Management at the University of Phoenix. He is attending class on line, using a computer and modem in his own den while his six-year-old twin sons are in bed upstairs. Even when he's on the road supporting customers, he can still attend class by connecting his laptop computer to the phone jack in the hotel room. Earlier in the year he was informed that without a degree further advancement was not possible, despite his superior work performance—it's just company policy. But now that his degree is only a few months away, his company has promised him a promotion and a hefty raise. With two sons and his wife expecting again, he can really use the extra money.

Are Joanne and Oscar typical of the adult students in college today? Well, yes and no. Like Joanne and Oscar, most adults who choose to attend college are people who want to prosper both intellectually and financially—but the specific motivations and desires behind the return to college are as different as each person is different.

Beyond the fact that most adults return to formal education after a period of time devoted to other endeavors, there really is no such thing as the "typical" adult college student. Adult college students include mothers with babies, grandmothers, divorced folks seeking a new outlook, displaced workers who need new skills, executives and professionals who want career growth, disillusioned retirees who need more to do in life, people who dropped out of high school or college but always regretted it, and a wide variety of people who simply want a new challenge or additional education to fulfill their potential. In other words, adult college students are people just like you who want to do better in life and learn new things.

The one thing we have discovered is that there are more people choosing college as an option later in life than ever before. Like Joanne and Oscar, adults around the country have discovered that it's never too late to reap the benefits of a college education.

Why Are College Campuses Changing to Accommodate Adults?

In a recent survey, the Bureau of the Census counted 3.3 million full-time college students aged 30 and older in the United States. That's double the number of adults in college recorded in a similar survey fifteen years earlier. An estimated 25 million adults were involved in formal higher education activities in 1990, and more are getting involved each year. So why are all these adults going back to college, and what can they expect to gain from a college education attained later in life?

The reasons for the growth in the number of adults in college are diverse. First, there are economic pressures to remain competitive in a shrinking job market. Also, the growth in the number of adult college students is being fueled by the millions of workers who must improve their credentials just to stay employed in today's layoff-prone business world. Many positions that once required only a high school diploma now demand a degree. Some companies are refusing to promote employees who lack degrees. Superior performance and dedicated effort are no longer enough for security and advancement. When it comes to new jobs, raises, and promotions, mid-career adults with experience but no college diploma are losing out to younger degreed upstarts. It all adds up to the fact that higher education is a ticket to security and job advancement, even late in life.

Most of the job growth in the United States is in managerial and professional jobs, which is contrary to the popular wisdom that says more low-paying service-oriented jobs are being created than professional positions. By and large, these higher-paying professional and managerial opportunities are available to those with college degrees. And it is only the people with advanced degrees who fill the openings for these new management and professional jobs that have a growth path to senior management positions in today's competitive business environment.

By the way, for those of you who think you know just as much as a college graduate already, you may be correct. Many studies show that there is little actual connection between the attainment of a degree and actual job performance. Ivan Berg of Columbia University documented the results of his research in this area in *Education and Jobs: The Great Training Robbery.* Berg looked at various jobs in which people with degrees and people without were doing identical jobs. He often found there was no difference in performance between the degreed and non-degreed people. In fact, in a few jobs (notably air traffic control) the people without degrees were doing a better job! Berg also found that the bosses in these companies either ignored or refused to believe the evidence that had been collected in their firms. In a chemical firm where the laboratory workers without degrees were out-performing those with degrees, the management steadfastly maintained its policy of promoting only those employees with degrees.

You should know that it is actually illegal to discriminate against people based on degrees, unless it can be proven that the degree is required to do the job. Following the 1971 Supreme Court decision in the case of *Griggs v. Duke Power Company,* employers must now prove that a degree is required before they can require one as a condition of employment or advancement. This ruling applies to everything from high school diplomas to doctorates.

You may feel it is unfair that personnel decisions are based on degrees, especially if you have already learned as much or more in other ways than the average college graduate learns in school. The fact remains, whether it is "unfair" or "illegal," companies prefer promoting degreed people. The career market is simply closing its doors to those without degrees. Personnel practices are not likely to be changed in the foreseeable future, because employers demand diplomas for "justifiable" reasons. When the personnel managers of major airlines were surveyed by Dr. John Bear, for example, almost all stated they required an accredited bachelor's degree, but they didn't care whether the degree was in aviation, psychology, or Chinese history. The important thing was the discipline of being able to complete a degree program. As Dr. Bear points out, "You may have been flying for ten years for the navy or the air force. But that doesn't count." It's the degree that takes precedence. Conformity to the dominant culture and the "ability" to stay in school for four or more years is often more important to employers than the ability to do the job. This on its own is a valid reason to get a degree.

Recently, we have seen many senior executives, vice presidents, and even CEOs return to college to complete graduate degrees in order to maintain their competitive edge and secure their jobs. Some of the executives in our classes told us that they can't afford to be less educated than the up-and-coming managers in the ranks—they don't want there to be any reasons for getting rid of the old to bring in the new. Thus, the need to stay competitive is stoking the fire under adult college students, and staying competitive means having a degree.

Technological change provides another source for the growth in adult education. Technology and society are changing too fast for many people to keep up. Ongoing education and skill-renewal programs are the only way to stay on top of technological changes. Alvin Toffler said it years ago in the best-selling *Future Shock* (New York: Bantam Books, 1970):

> The rapid obsolescence of knowledge and the extension of life span make it clear that the skills learned by youth are unlikely to remain relevant by the time old age arrives. Super-industrial-

ized education must therefore make provisions for life-long education.

Toffler's observations are even more true today than they were twenty years ago. The rapid changes in technology and business methods and the evolution of a global society are fundamental reasons more adults are returning to school. People need more education on an ongoing basis just to stay informed, not to mention to remain employable. Note that more than 60 percent of the more than 25 million people participating in adult education activities last year reportedly returned to school to advance a career opportunity, to improve a job-related skill, or to get a job.

Changes in the structure of our society are also fueling the adult-education movement. Women are entering the workplace in droves, and are demanding prosperous, high-paying careers. They aren't satisfied with the low-paying positions they were forced to take in the past. The changes in women's roles and their new expectations for careers account for the fact that more than 50 percent of the people in college in general are women—more than 55 percent of the adult students in college are women—and these numbers are climbing still.

The growth in college-bound adults also is supported by the recent development of new educational delivery systems (such as cable TV and computer communications), expanded program offerings, and more-flexible degree options. It's now entirely possible to get a degree while living in a remote farmhouse, far from any college.

Twenty years ago, colleges were being filled by what seemed like a never-ending supply of baby boomers. But the number of eighteen-year-olds decreased steadily, because of declining birth rates in the 60s and 70s, and won't start growing again until after 1995. As a result, many innovative programs were started in the 70s and 80s in response to the declining population of young college students. In an effort to survive and prosper, colleges began developing programs geared to the needs of adult learners to help fill their empty classrooms. The availability and flexibility of these programs has made college a viable option for working adults, where once it was only an impossible dream.

Perhaps the most important impetus for the growth of college-bound adults is our changing views as a society regarding education. Education is becoming more widely recognized as a lifelong process and a lifetime requirement for success and happiness. People live longer. Things change faster. People want better things to do with their time. Ronald Gross summarized these changes in society some years ago and defined the lifelong-learning phenomenon in his book, *The Lifelong Learner* (New York: Simon and Schuster, 1977):

> Colleges, which once spurned adult students, are, as we have seen, now bending over backward to welcome free learners back to the campuses, and more important, offering them help in learning on their own terms . . . . Most important of all, we Americans as individuals seem to be developing a fresh hunger

for experience, for growth, for personal cultivation. Men and women of all ages today feel the urge to seek more in life—to shape a larger self, the quest I call "lifelong learning."

Why Do Adults Go Back to College?

We've probably convinced you that lots of people are going back to school as adults and that there are many good reasons why this is happening. But what *personal* reasons motivate adults to go to college in the middle of their careers? Why do adults decide to take on the extra work, the long hours, and the complexities of higher education in mid-life? We interviewed adult college students around the country to find the answers to these questions.

The responses fell into three general categories: financial gain, personal satisfaction or personal growth, and a need for fellowship and enhanced relationships. In addition, according to our research, some single and divorced students went back to college for another reason: to meet a mate. And, according to our data, a fair number succeeded in their matrimonial goals—in addition to gaining a college degree.

When Carol Aslanian, Director of the Office of Adult Learning Services for the College Board, asked in a recent study why adults return to college, she found that most people were motivated by the need to cope with changes in their lives. The majority of these changes (about 56 percent) were job-related and included finding a new job, gaining new skills to remain competitive at the same job, and the desire for career advancement in general. Sixteen percent cited changes in family situation as a motivation to return to college, including getting married, getting divorced, retirement of a spouse, death of a family member, the rising cost of living, and buying a new house. Thirteen percent of the people surveyed stated that changes in their approach to leisure motivated their return to school. And four percent pointed to a change in their level of spirituality as the trigger to gaining more formal education. A few students stated that it was their desire to be better citizens which motivated them to go back to school.

Education and Income

Many studies reinforce our own conclusions about adults in college: Most adults who decide to get more formal education consider college or a degree a ticket to a better life, to financial independence, or to increased job security and as a vehicle for raising personal satisfaction in general. Of course, the value of an education in financial terms is well documented. According to the Bureau of the Census, the potential lifetime earnings of average men and women can be related directly to the level of education they obtain.

In addition to the financial benefits of finishing college or obtaining an advanced graduate degree, job security and career flexibility are associated with more education. The job market has been moving away from secure manufacturing or office-based jobs. Our society is changing into one that buys services and depends on advanced, information-based technologies. Many service-oriented jobs pay less than the union-mediated manufacturing or white-collar careers of the past. High-paying jobs today require more education than in the past. And, as more people—including women, minorities, and immigrants—enter the employment market, employers can demand a higher level of formal education, even for entry-level jobs that once required only minimal skills. According to the Department of Labor, minimum education levels are rising for almost every occupation. Quite simply, your chances of being unemployed are greater if you don't have enough education.

College and Early Retirement

A recent class of returning students are "early retirees" or "voluntary retirees." Early retirement has become a euphemism for being laid off in some circles. Sometimes these retirees are as young as 40 and not ready to leave the working world. Many of these people go back to school to learn a new profession and actively jump back into the job market in search of a new career. Often at the prime of their intellectual lives and highly motivated to achieve, these people expand their options by completing a degree or beginning study in a field or profession unrelated to their previous line of work.

In general, the students in their 30s and 40s that we spoke with were more focused on career development and financial gain in their choice of a college program. Of the students in our study who were more than 50 years of age (and yes, there are many!), we found that career opportunities still were important for some, but generally less significant in their decisions about school. Older adults emphasized reasons of fulfillment, attainment of dreams, meeting friends, staying in touch, or meeting new challenges in life to make "retirement" more rewarding.

Retirement has negative connotations for some people. They view it as a time for growing old while sitting around with not enough to do. But for adults who return to school after retirement, life is anything but sedentary and boring. People are simply living longer than they used to, and they want something meaningful to do with their lives in later years. Many "retired" students discover new second careers, meet stimulating friends, write insightful books, explore engaging subjects, travel to exotic places, and become involved in other significant and rewarding endeavors. College increasingly is important in realizing the fulfillment of lifelong dreams for retirees.

Even for younger adults, however, not all the benefits of higher education can be counted in terms of dollars and cents. Less tangible benefits of a college education that our contacts espoused included meeting new people and gaining new perspectives on life. In fact, personal satisfaction almost always was expressed as one of the motivations for returning to college, even if people indicated other primary goals such as financial gain or career development. In college you can expect to get the technical background, experience, and skills you need to succeed. But you also meet new people, challenge yourself intellectually, and broaden your possibilities.

Many of our students commented that they gained confidence and improved self-esteem after completing college courses. The profound satisfaction that comes with achieving something important is another major benefit of higher education for most people. Most adults consider these additional benefits of higher education to be as important as the specific skills and knowledge gained in the courses.

You Have the Right to a College Education

The intellectual wealth and experiences of adults are at least as important to society as the untapped potential and energy of youth. Because of this, our educational institutions and the government need to put more focus than they have in the past on education as a lifelong phenomenon. The attitudes of educational institutions and society toward adult learners are still evolving. Though not all schools have jumped on the bandwagon to embrace the concepts of lifelong learning, many have and many more will. Though governmental support for adult education is still unresolved and poorly focused—as more adult students demand their rights for lifelong-learning opportunities—it is our hope that governmental agencies will listen and become more flexible and innovative in their definition of "adult educational programs."

Higher education, regardless of age, is no longer a privilege. It is a necessity for survival, and it is therefore your right to pursue it. You should demand and protect your rights as an adult learner by going for it—and getting the education you deserve.

In support of the lifelong learning process, the American Association of Community and Junior Colleges developed the following Bill of Rights for adult learners:

Lifelong Learner's Bill of Rights

- Every adult American has the right to continue to learn throughout life;
- Every adult American has the right to equal opportunity access to relevant learning opportunities at each stage of life;
- Diversity and access to educational opportunity are important to democracy in the United States;
- Any index of the quality of life in the United States includes opportunities for growth and self-actualization as a right of the learning society;
- Neither age, nor sex, nor color, nor creed, nor ethnic background, nor marital status, nor economic status, nor disability should create barriers to the opportunity to continue to grow through participation in organized learning activities;
- Coping, living, and working are dimensions which exemplify the range of learning needs of the learning society;
- Public investment in the learning society is an investment in human capital and in the human condition.

As more adults like you fill the classrooms and return to school for degrees, renewed skills, and enriching experiences, the lifelong-learning phenomenon will become even more widely understood and accepted. Clearly, lifelong learning represents a significant current in our society, and by reading this book you are part of the flow. As you begin or continue belatedly your college program, recall this Bill of Rights. No matter what others may say as you pursue your goals, remember that as an adult you have the right to be in college and the right to succeed in life.

A College Degree Doesn't Guarantee Success

To this point, we've painted an exciting picture of a prosperous, fulfilled adult college graduate who has the desire and opportunity to continue education throughout life. But we don't want to mislead you into thinking that everything will be wonderful just because you complete a degree. In spite of the many benefits foreseen by the adult students we interviewed, you can't expect a college education to transform your life overnight. If you start college with unrealistic expectations for immediate wealth, exciting relationships, special recognition, and status, you probably will be disappointed.

The long-term benefits of higher education are well documented—but the results are not always immediate. And in some cases, going to college can create new problems in your life. Couples have been divorced because relationships are stretched to the breaking point when one partner spends too much time studying and working on assignments. People who don't plan their finances properly may incur inordinate school-related debts and then not realize immediate financial gains to pay them off after graduation. If not anticipated and managed, the problems that college creates can overcome the benefits.

A degree is not magic nor a guaranteed ticket to unbridled happiness. College is not a panacea. A degree offers new opportunities—but you still have the responsibility for taking advantage of them. Make sure you explore your alternatives before you commit to college, and make sure an education is important to you even if you don't make more money or get a better job. College can't guarantee the job and financial reward—it will only open doors that didn't even exist before. It's still up to you to walk through those new doorways to make things happen.

What Benefits Can You Expect to Receive if You Go to College?

So what does this all mean to you? What benefits can you expect to gain from going back to school? Well, what you actually get out of college largely depends on you. Your own motivations, goals, and desires significantly influence the benefits you receive from higher education. Your work and dedication will determine the amount you learn and the amount you gain from the process.

In their own words, here are what some of the successful adult students we interviewed said about the benefits they gained in returning to school later in life:

"I received a raise almost immediately and was asked to apply for a management job they never would have considered me for if I hadn't finished my degree."

"My boss gave me a 12-percent raise just for completing my degree—and now I can apply for new jobs within the company to make even more money."

"Before getting my B.A., I was desperate. I couldn't get a job, and every company I went to wanted someone with a degree. Now when I read an ad for a great job that requires a college degree, I send out a resume with confidence. The opportunities available seem limitless now."

"My confidence and self-esteem have more than doubled since I started school. It feels great."

"At first I was scared to go back and work on my master's degree, but now I can't believe all the new things I have learned. I didn't realize what I didn't know. It's broadened my whole perspective on my career and my life."

"I am divorced and really felt lonely before I went back to the university. I can't believe all the new friends and contacts I've made in school."

"There are benefits no one tells you about. A college education totally revitalizes you. Though it wasn't easy at first, going back to college is the best thing I ever did."

Can you expect similar benefits? Absolutely, but you'll have to decide which benefits you want and be willing to work for them. If you want a new career, college can be part of the answer. If you want to enhance your skills, college offers many options. If you crave new ideas, more social contacts, or increased self-esteem, college can contribute to these goals as well. Going to college is an exciting challenge with many potential benefits. But a college education—whether your goal is general knowledge, a bachelor's degree, or an advanced graduate degree—ultimately takes hard work, planning, and perhaps some personal sacrifice.

The good news is the many resources and services available to help you meet your college goals as an adult—and we reveal many of these in *College After 30*. But only you can say if your goals include college and if your motivation is adequate to finish a degree. In the next chapter we provide guidelines and suggest resources to help you decide if college is the right answer at this point in your life. If you find the timing isn't right just now, it's likely it will be later—so what you learn from this book still will have value and relevance. And if you *do* have the motivation, desire, and dedication to succeed at college now, you have wonderful opportunities and adventures ahead of you.

COLLEGE AFTER 30

Adult College Students in Their Own Words
Valerie Deacon

I'm a 48-year-old transplanted Canadian female, living with my husband, Jim, in a suburb of Seattle, Washington. In January, 1992, I began coursework with Antioch University in pursuit of an M.A. in psychology with a focus on human resource development. My husband's career as a corporate trainer keeps him on the road a lot. Jim's being away from home base so much gave me both the time and the space for personal reflection. The last four years have spurred some lengthy ruminations about what I want to do with the rest of my life. I've also come to realize that I'm the one that has to look after my own financial needs for my elder years and that I need to put things in motion now if I'm going to meet this need.

I also think my drive to go back to the university is my way of coping with specific life-change events: for example, my need for a career change, aging; moving to a new city. To quote Ron and Susan Zemke in their article "Thirty Things We Know for Sure About Adult Learning" *(TRAINING Magazine, June 1981):* "The more life-change events an adult encounters, the more likely he or she is to seek out learning opportunities. Just as stress increases as life-change events accumulate, the motivation to cope with change through engagement in a learning experience increases. Since the people who most frequently seek out learning opportunities are people who have the most overall years of education, it is reasonable to guess that for many of us learning is a coping response to significant change." I chose to return to school in order to get both the degree and certification which will allow me to do the work I truly want to do—namely guiding others to prosper both privately and within the workplace.

I chose to study at Antioch University because its core values reflect my own philosophical approach to life and learning. These core values include systems thinking, experiential learning, whole-person learning, social justice, and empowerment of the learner. My initial experience as a returning student to the university environment is probably best reflected in the following excerpts from the personal journal of my first few weeks back at school: Jan. 18/92 I've been feeling somewhat buffeted over the weeks since the start of classes. The high-level buffeting is happening for a number of reasons. First, there is the change in personal timetable due to starting my studies. Then there is the change in personal timetable due to starting my job with the Antioch Computer Lab two days a week. The next level of buffeting comes from my re-entering the outside world after a two-year self-imposed retreat. During this time I didn't work or have a social life. I didn't want to have to explain my past or my present to anybody. I hunkered down at home trying to mentally/emotionally sort through what I was experiencing as the rubble of my life. "How did I get to this point? Why do I feel so miserable? Where do I go from here?" Thursday, Jan. 22/92 Well, I've been feeling even *more* buffeted over the last four days. Jim was laid off on Monday morning. I have alternated between functioning in class, doing my work in the Computer Lab, and experiencing anxiety and sadness about our personal situation. I'm trying to be there for Jim while continuing to bring focus to my work and energy to the numerous assigned academic projects I have before me. I have to admit to feeling overwhelmed at this point, and to entertaining thoughts of postponing my studies.

So, why did I continue my school work despite such a rocky start? Well, I remember being told as a child that I was stubborn—a judgment which was always portrayed as a negative. However, stubbornness has its positive side, too! I looked at my personal situation as it had suddenly evolved and I realized that after two years of personal 'composting', my decision to return to school was just too important for me to walk away. Despite my apprehension about our fiscal security and the relentless 'administrivia' of life, I've encouraged myself to stay in the present and to take each day as it comes.

I'm reluctant to give advice, but I will share a few of my reactions to going back to school. For instance, the admissions process and first semester at school, after an absence of 12 years, had me feeling pretty bewildered, scared, and somewhat overwhelmed. If you are considering going back to school, the admissions process will seem obsessed with details, relentless in its attachment to deadlines, and mysterious in its intent. If you also apply for student financial aid, all the aforementioned conditions apply, plus the added feature of anxiously waiting to see if you get the funding in order to afford the education you applied for. My approach is, *don't fight the system.* Just do the paperwork (keeping a complete set of reference copies for your files), pay the admission/ administration fees and await the response. This waiting can be an education in itself—a true test of your faith in a system!

I have found the emotional support of others to be an essential factor in my success in the university. It doesn't have to be a large number of people; just enough identifiable individuals who you feel are in your corner as you go through your learning process. I've found that being able to talk with people about the variety of issues and reactions that I've been experiencing as a returning student has helped me to keep things in perspective. For example, I can share with my husband the lurking fears and apprehensions I sometimes feel about my future as a student and a practitioner in my chosen career. He's someone I trust with these thoughts and feelings because he doesn't put me down and he doesn't go into 'panic mode.' When I'm feeling anxious or frustrated about the university's administrative or educational process, I now know a number of fellow students whom I can talk to in order to get their perspective on an issue and potentially some feedback about how they might deal with it.

As a returning student, there is another issue that I have noted; namely, the pace. I find that younger people tend to think and talk quickly rather than contemplatively. I also suspect that this pace may be generated by the competitive nature of most group discussion in this society. When I feel pushed by this faster pace, and I allow myself to realize that I can choose not to compete, I merely adopt the response, "Can I get back to you on that?" In other words, I acknowledge the faster, younger pace around me but I work at *my* pace—not theirs.

Chapter Two

Is College Right for You Now?

First decide you are going on the journey, then begin the figuring of how to get there.
—*Chinese proverb from the province of Shanghai*

For most adults, the decision to return to college evolves over several years. Studies by the New York University School of Continuing Education reveal that adult students there can take three to seven years to finally make the decision to return to school—though not all adults take this long. Unfortunately, when many adults finally decide to return to school, they want to enroll immediately. They wait until the last minute and then, when they can't get in, they use their lateness as an excuse: "Oh, well, I would have gone, but they won't let me in because it's too late." Adults often set up these situations because they fear failure and use the excuses to protect their self-esteem.

The choice to go to college later in life is important. The decision and the commitment required to complete a college or university degree program successfully should not be made without planning and carefully weighing the impact of college on your life. If you want to reap the potential benefits that a college education offers, the decision to return to college is not one that should be made impulsively—but it doesn't need to take years. And you don't need to set yourself up for failure by waiting until the last minute to get ready.

If you want to succeed in college, the timing, resources, and motivations must be right. You must also understand your reasons for returning to college so you can evaluate whether your motivations are strong enough to get you through a complete degree program. Dropping out without graduating may be tough on your self-esteem, especially when one of your friends or coworkers ask, "When do you graduate? We're going to have a big party for you."

Choosing the correct college program or degree program for yourself must start with an understanding of your own desires, lifestyle, skills, and priorities. As the Greek philosopher Socrates said, "Know thyself." Self-assessment and self-knowledge are critical to your success in college as an adult. The better you know yourself, the more likely it is you will achieve your goals in life and in school.

The Seven-Step Process—
Is College Right for You Now?

- Step 1. Put aside your fears about going back to school
- Step 2. Remove the obstacles from your life so you can attend college
- Step 3. Understand your college trigger
- Step 4. Evaluate your lifestyle and your family situation
- Step 5. Evaluate your career and your current skills
- Step 6. Define your goals and dreams for the future
- Step 7. Evaluate your motivations and commitment level

In our work with prospective adult students we've identified seven basic steps (as specified in the chart above and described in this chapter) that can help you understand yourself and let you decide if college is the right decision at this point in your life. And, even though the decision to go to college ultimately should be yours alone, there is no reason you can't ask for help along the way as you go through the steps. We recommend that you talk to family, friends, and other adult students before you make up your mind.

If you follow the steps and complete the worksheets provided in this chapter, you should be able to determine if your motivations are sufficient to justify a commitment to college at this time. At the very least, you will learn a lot about yourself and this information will be useful in other aspects of your life and career—whether you decide to go to college or not.

Step 1. Put Aside Your Fears about Going Back to School

In spite of the benefits of more education, adults almost always start their educational programs with a list of reasons why they won't succeed at school. It's no surprise that adults who fail in college believed from day one they would fail. Belief in failure is a self-fulfilling prophecy. How can you succeed at college if you already *know* you'll never finish?

The first step toward college success is to understand your fears and then put them aside. If you can't put aside the fears, you're probably not ready for college. Many of your "fears" are simply excuses for not trying. Adults often are more afraid of failure than anything else. Many adults feel that if they don't try, they can't fail. In reality, the ultimate failure is the failure to try. You'll never know what you missed, and you'll never get to enjoy the benefits of success if you don't make a decision to try to make something happen.

Following are the fears we hear most often from the adults we work with when they start thinking about college or a degree program. Do any of these excuses sound like the ones you are using for not going back to school?

"I'm not smart enough to do it. I'm afraid I will look stupid to others."
This simply is not true. You are smart enough to have made it this far in life.

You are smart enough to have picked up this book, which means you are smart enough to want to do better in life. Motivation, drive, and persistence are more important in obtaining a degree than your IQ. If you have the desire, the motivation, and the persistence, you are smart enough to get any degree you want.

"I will feel out of place with all the young students in the classes. I don't fit into the college scene anymore."

The reality is that more than fifty percent of students on college campuses today are over 25, and over one-third are over 30. In graduate school, the average age is much higher. And, if you don't want to attend a traditional school with younger students, you don't have to. Many schools cater exclusively to adults—schools where the average student is age 40 or higher. If you don't want contact with classmates at all, there are the degree programs offered through television, computers, and satellites that don't require attendance at classes—so no one will ever see you or know your age. In the next few chapters you'll learn about all of these options and be able to choose the program that fits your personal needs and lifestyle.

"My study skills are obsolete and rusty. My old brain is too tired to learn all the new information."

There is no evidence that brains wear out as people get older. In fact, research performed during the 1980s showed that IQs actually *increased* as adults got older, up to about 70 years of age. And though you may slow down physically as you get older, all your mental capacities remain in top form. It may be that your intellect is not getting enough exercise, but with only a little effort on your part, your study skills and memory will be better than they ever were. For many people, the skills they acquire just doing their day-to-day jobs are actually a new set of study skills superior to the ones they relied on in high school or college. Keep in mind that, unless you do nothing but watch television all day, you actually get better at learning new skills and coping with change.

Your capacity to learn and cope with new experiences is actually a set of skills honed over time that can help you learn much faster than you did as a teenager or young adult. You have also acquired a lot of knowledge in life that reinforces what you will learn in college. You don't need to learn everything from the ground up as you did when you were younger.

If you do feel rusty or insecure about your academic abilities, this book will show you how to get your study skills up to speed and your brain in gear with only a few minutes of effort each day. As with any exercise, the more you do it, the easier it gets. The first step is simply getting started.

"My work will suffer, and I'll lose my job."

This will only happen if you let it happen. With appropriate time management and an appropriately scheduled program, you should be able to manage work and college. Thousands of other people do. And, over time, the new skills and knowledge you gain in your classes should improve your job performance, not hinder it. If you already are employed, a progressive employer or boss may even encourage your college activities and make it easier for you to attend school. This may take the form of flexible work hours to allow you time to commute to school on class days, financial support for your program, or just positive encouragement to "keep at it."

"I can't attend full time, so I'll never be able to graduate."

Just like there are programs that don't require any attendance in classrooms, there are programs that don't require full-time attendance. There are accelerated programs like those offered by the University of Phoenix that require attendance only one night a week for 13 months to finish the last two years of a bachelor's degree program. And, even traditional part-time programs can be finished within a reasonable time if you plan in advance. Success in college doesn't require full-time attendance—it requires commitment and motivation.

"I never finished high school, and I wasn't very good in school anyway. Why should I be any better this time?"

First, the lack of a high school diploma is not a barrier to attending college as an adult. There are junior colleges and community colleges around the country that accept adult students (people over 21) without high school diplomas. In fact, it doesn't even matter if you finished elementary school in most states. And, for colleges that require a high school diploma as a condition of acceptance, there are equivalency exams and study programs that can get you a diploma in short order. These options are covered in Chapter Six of this book.

If you're worried about your past performance in school, keep in mind that many of the brightest students do poorly in public schools. Perhaps you were bored in high school or lacked focus. Attending college is nothing like the tedium of sitting through Mr. Smith's history class in high school. You're older now. You have more direction. If you lack background or requisite skills, there is a wide variety of support programs to help you gain the knowledge and develop the study habits you need to succeed.

"Younger people are more resilient and flexible than I am, and they learn things faster than me. I won't be able to keep up."

Again, there is no compelling evidence that younger people in college are better equipped to learn or that they are more flexible in their approach to studying. In reality, many younger students lack maturity, experience, and self-esteem. Young students often view older students as their toughest competition, because adult students have more experience to draw on and are often more committed to their education. In most mixed-generation classes, it is the older students that set the standards of excellent performance, not the younger ones often less interested in learning than in just getting through the program.

"I have a job and a family. I won't be able to do it all."

Well, other people have found the time and energy to manage work, family, and school, so you probably can as well. Yes, it will take some time management, some adjustment of priorities, and some changes in your lifestyle—but it *is* doable. Later in the book, we'll give you some guidelines for making it all work.

"My friends will laugh at me for going back to school."
In most cases your friends will be supportive, proud, and maybe even envious. If your friends *do* laugh, perhaps you should consider their motives. Maybe they have thought about school, but are too afraid to try. Maybe they want you to fail to make themselves feel better. If this is the case, maybe you should talk to them about their own desires and fears. If they still are unsupportive, perhaps the friendship isn't what you thought it was. College provides the opportunity, if need be, to find new and sympathetic friends.

"The professors and instructors don't like older students. They punish them by grading them harder."
There is absolutely no truth to this sentiment. Most faculty want students to succeed. Four-fifths of the people in colleges and universities share a genuine desire to help students get their degrees. (The others are simply working there because they have to, and you can find such people in any profession, not just at colleges.) People generally become educators because they want to teach people—they *want* you to learn and prosper. They don't care if the people they teach are twenty years old or sixty years young. In fact, most college faculty welcome the experience-based insights and dedication of adult students in contrast to the less mature efforts of younger students.

"I'll be almost 40 (or 50, 60, or 70) by the time I graduate."
Well, you are going to be 40, 50 (or 60 or 70) anyway. The question really is: *Do* you want to be that old *with* the degree and the education or *without* it? Colleges and universities regularly graduate students who already collect their Social Security and pension checks. Age is not a reason to deny yourself a college education or anything else. So quit worrying about how old you are, and start thinking about how educated you want to be.

The usual fears about going to college are real to each person but are without substance. Most of the fears stem from a general lack of self-esteem. This is normal. Ultimately, however, these fears are only excuses for not trying. Don't let these concerns block your opportunity to achieve something. If anxieties about college seem to dominate your thinking, try taking a class in something that interests you at a local community college, or get a buddy to go to school with you to support you emotionally through the first few courses. In almost every case, you will find your fears to be completely groundless as you get caught up in the challenge and pleasure of learning.

You can also start to remove your fears by identifying them and then dealing with them rationally. We've provided a space to identify your fears on the *College Readiness Worksheet* in this chapter. After completing the relevant section of the worksheet, compare your list with the concerns we've discussed in this section. Almost everyone has fears that match one or more of these "reasons" for not going back to school. Then, reread our comments about each fear, and decide if that fear has any basis in reality or if it is simply an excuse that can be dropped by the wayside on your way to getting the degree you want. This process won't eliminate all the anxiety. But once you identify your concerns, you'll find that you can overcome the anxieties about college and move forward. It helps to know that millions have done it before you—so you can, too.

Step 2. Remove the Obstacles from Your Life so You Can Attend College

In addition to fears, adult students create artificial roadblocks and imaginary obstacles in their minds that make attaining a college degree seem impossible. The most commonly voiced obstacles in the adult's path to college are quoted below. Again, these "obstacles" provide convenient excuses for not starting and later become excuses for not finishing. There are ways to remove every obstacle in the list—and in this book we've documented the methods and resources to do so.

"I don't have enough money to go to college."

The big question—whether you are employed, unemployed, or looking for work—is not, "Can I afford to go to college?" but instead, "Can I afford *not* to go to college?" First, there are no age restrictions on most financial aid from the federal government. Financial limitations often can be worked around with student loans, by choosing inexpensive state-sponsored community colleges and universities, and with employee financial assistance. Some schools offer monthly payment programs that make tuition fees more palatable. In fact, the less money you have, the more grant and loan possibilities are available to you as an adult student. Millions of dollars in scholarships go unclaimed every year. And there are industry, government, and organizational grants specifically for adults pursuing more education. In spite of inflation and recessions, many employers still pay for college costs. You can finish college without depleting your life savings if you plan for the expenses and know the resources available. Chapter Seven details all the options for getting money for college. The money for school is out there if you know how to find it.

"There aren't any colleges within driving distance."

It is no longer necessary to attend traditional classrooms to get a college degree. Just as our workforce has changed as technology has advanced, so the options available for obtaining a college education have evolved and expanded over the years. There are a wide variety of accredited college programs for undergraduate and graduate degrees that require no classroom attendance at all—and many more that require only a minimal amount of classroom contact. We have listed re-

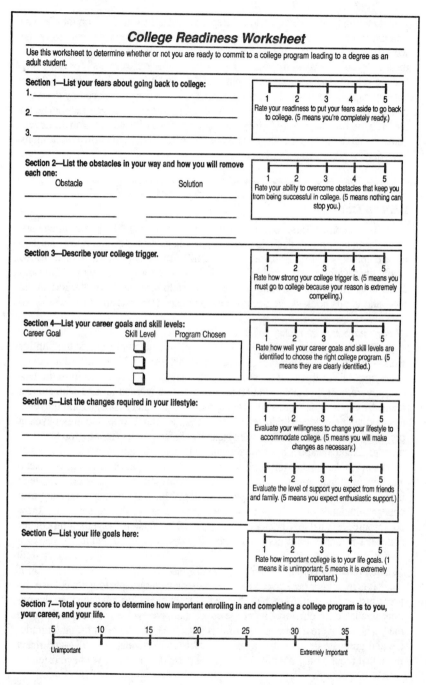

College Readiness Worksheet

Use this worksheet to determine whether or not you are ready to commit to a college program leading to a degree as an adult student.

Section 1—List your fears about going back to college:

1. _____

2. _____

3. _____

| 1 | 2 | 3 | 4 | 5 |
Rate your readiness to put your fears aside to go back to college. (5 means you're completely ready.)

Section 2—List the obstacles in your way and how you will remove each one:

Obstacle	Solution
_____	_____
_____	_____
_____	_____

| 1 | 2 | 3 | 4 | 5 |
Rate your ability to overcome obstacles that keep you from being successful in college. (5 means nothing can stop you.)

Section 3—Describe your college trigger.

| 1 | 2 | 3 | 4 | 5 |
Rate how strong your college trigger is. (5 means you must go to college because your reason is extremely compelling.)

Section 4—List your career goals and skill levels:

Career Goal	Skill Level	Program Chosen
_____	☐	
_____	☐	
_____	☐	

| 1 | 2 | 3 | 4 | 5 |
Rate how well your career goals and skill levels are identified to choose the right college program. (5 means they are clearly identified.)

Section 5—List the changes required in your lifestyle:

_____
_____
_____
_____
_____
_____

| 1 | 2 | 3 | 4 | 5 |
Evaluate your willingness to change your lifestyle to accommodate college. (5 means you will make changes as necessary.)

| 1 | 2 | 3 | 4 | 5 |
Evaluate the level of support you expect from friends and family. (5 means you expect enthusiastic support.)

Section 6—List your life goals here:

_____
_____
_____

| 1 | 2 | 3 | 4 | 5 |
Rate how important college is to your life goals. (1 means it is unimportant; 5 means it is extremely important.)

Section 7—Total your score to determine how important enrolling in and completing a college program is to you, your career, and your life.

| 5 | 10 | 15 | 20 | 25 | 30 | 35 |
Unimportant — Extremely Important

sources to find these schools at the end of the book. So, if there isn't a school near your home or work, let the school come to you via satellite television, computer-based courses, or the mail.

"My children won't get taken care of properly while I'm in school."

If daycare is a problem for you because you have young children, then attend one of the many schools that offer daycare to their students—sometimes at no cost. And if you are worried about the time you'll have to spend away from your children, just make sure your schedule includes time for them. We'll show you how to make a schedule that accommodates your life, as well as school, later in the book. It's only a matter of time management and planning.

"I don't know how to use a computer."

This is a comparatively new obstacle that we've heard regularly in the last few years. We do recommend that all adults returning to school learn to use a personal computer at least for word processing (useful for writing and revising papers). And personal computers offer a wealth of communication options that make research faster and more productive.

Though there are online and distance-education programs that require the ability to use a personal computer, most college programs have no mandatory computer requirements (yet). Still, the newer generation of personal computers, such as Apple Computer's Macintosh, are so easy to use (even for the computer-phobic adult) that in as little as five minutes you can be word processing along with the best of 'em. If your typing skills are weak or nonexistent, typing can be learned just like anything else—and it's not even necessary to be able to touch type to use a computer. One of us (Kim) bought his first computer at the age of 30 and never has learned to type. Kim is now among the world's fastest hunt-and-peck typists, averaging 45 words a minute with two fingers. There are many self-teaching books, community college courses, seminars offered by computer stores, and even television courses on personal computers to get you started. (If you never learned to type, we recommend you take a "keyboarding" class as one of your first classes at a local community college or get one of the self-teaching books or videotape programs available in bookstores. That way you can learn to type faster and better than Kim does.)

If you think a computer is too expensive, you're mistaken. The prices of personal computers continue to fall. A perfectly adequate, brand-new personal computer system for word processing and communications—complete with printer—can be had for less than $900. A reliable used computer system can be purchased for much less. Of course, you can spend much more for faster, whizzier systems, but it isn't necessary. And if you don't want to spend the money now, most traditional colleges provide computer laboratories for students to use to complete their homework assignments.

"There just isn't enough time to go to school."

Look at the time problem in a new way. Do you think you can find an hour a day that you now spend on unproductive activities, such as watching television, reading *People* magazine, or just plain sitting around with nothing to do? Most people can. You probably can find more time if you try. If you find only one hour every day to study, you can finish a course or maybe even two at the same time. And, if you can finish one course, you can finish an entire degree. To get a degree, you only need to finish one course at a time. You can always take fewer classes rather than a full-time load unless your financial-aid package requires full-time attendance.

The truth is, most people *can* find time to do everything they consider important. If school is important enough to you, you can find the time. We provide information on time management later in the book to help you accomplish all your goals.

"I don't know where to go or what to do to get started."

That's why we wrote *College After 30*. We'll show you the steps, explain the options, and hopefully point you in the right direction. After reading this book you shouldn't have any excuses for not knowing where to start. But it's up to you to actually make it happen.

The first task in removing the obstacles to your college education is to eliminate the word *can't* from your vocabulary. Millions of other adults have succeeded in college—so can you. Successful people are not necessarily those with more brains or more money. Instead, they are those who put themselves wholeheartedly into something they really want to achieve. Thus, if you truly want to finish college, attain another degree, or learn a new skill, you can do it.

Using the same technique you used to analyze your fears, again identify the obstacles you believe exist on the *College Readiness Worksheet*. As you read the book, fill in a strategy for removing each obstacle. You'll find that every obstacle can be overcome if you want to attend college badly enough and are willing to work to make it happen.

Step 3. Understand Your College Trigger

Do you really know what caused you to consider completing college or got you thinking about getting another degree? The answer is critical in evaluating your potential success as an adult student. Adults who successfully return to school almost always point back to a trigger that made college an option where it wasn't an option before. This trigger is usually a major life transition—a transition that gets people thinking about more education as a way to improve or enhance their life situation.

What is your trigger? What motivated you to pick up this book and read it? Divorce? Job change? Children leaving home? General malaise in your life? Illness? Change in financial status? Were you laid off? Did you just turn forty and face the fact that you don't have forever to accomplish your goals in life? The immediate triggers that cause people to consider school are different for each person, but everyone has one.

To find your trigger, ask yourself this revealing question: What is it that makes college (or another degree) seem appropriate at this point in life when it didn't seem important before? Look for your motivations and analyze your life situation for the answer. Be honest. Be specific. Now, write your answer on the College Readiness Worksheet. Read your response. Is this really the reason you want to go to school? If not, expand it, adapt it, change it. Only you are going to see the answer, so be honest with yourself. Get it right. This is the most critical question you will answer in determining if you have the motivation and desire to finish school. And the answer will determine if college (or a degree) is really the right answer for you.

Now, consider this question: Is the reason (or reasons) you've documented for attending school important enough to propel you through the hours of studying, countless papers, and changes in your lifestyle required to complete a degree program? Remember, there are many opportunities and options for going to college as an adult—but getting a recognized degree from a respectable institution still takes work, and it also takes motivation, persistence, and dedication. There will be trials, tribulations, and setbacks. We provide advice for getting you through these in the book—but you must know at the onset that a college degree is not and should not be a trivial pursuit.

Step 4. Evaluate Your Lifestyle and Your Family Situation

To know if you are ready for college at this point, you need to understand your lifestyle—specifically how your lifestyle affects your use of time and dominates your priorities and aspirations.

To succeed in college, you need to be able to devote a significant amount of time to studying, writing papers, doing research, and learning in general. You will need to establish a balance between learning, working, and playing. If you are not willing to do this or to make changes in your lifestyle, your college experience will be fraught with anxieties and stresses.

To understand your lifestyle, complete the *Lifestyle Analysis Worksheet* we have provided. To complete the form, you need to keep a log for a week wherein you will list all your activities in 15-minute intervals. You may want to keep the log for two or three weeks if your activities vary significantly from week to week. Then, when you have completed the log, total the amount of time you spent each day in the activities listed on the worksheet. This will reveal the amount of time you spend in specific lifestyle-related activities. It will show you where your priorities lie and what your habits are. It will also expose how much time you spend in low-priority activities that could be spent in pursuit of a college degree.

After completing the *Lifestyle Analysis Worksheet*, there are some questions relating to your lifestyle in the *College Readiness Worksheet* that you now can answer. The answers you provide should reveal if you have the willingness to adjust your lifestyle to college and the room in your life to introduce another major priority at this time. If the answers to your lifestyle review reveal that your resistance to

Lifestyle Analysis Worksheet

	Sun	Mon	Tues	Wed	Thurs	Fri	Sat	Total
Employment								
Time at work								
Commuting								
Doing job-related tasks at home, job-related dinners, etc.								
Total employment time:								
Family & Leisure								
TV time								
Social time with family & friends								
Reading								
Work on hobby or crafts								
Cultural events and movies								
Sports and outdoor recreation								
Driving for pleasure								
Cooking/sewing for pleasure								
Attending classes/seminars for pleasure								
Volunteer work								
Other leisure activities								
Total family & leisure time:								
Living								
Eating								
Preparing food								
Sleeping/napping								
Personal grooming								
Exercise								
Housekeeping								
House and garden maintenance								
Shopping								
Paying bills and managing finances, taxes, etc.								
Car maintenance								
Other living activities								
Total living time:								

change is low, and you have the willingness to add college as a priority, then move on to Step 5 to discover if college is the answer.

You will note that there is a section in the lifestyle section of the *College Readiness Worksheet* to analyze the support and demands of your family and friends. Because the decision to attend school often affects others, the process requires support from your family, as well as your own commitment. College costs money and takes some of your time away from family members and friends. The support of your family is important in getting through. The demands and complaints of family members are the most frequently cited reasons adults give when they explain why they failed to finish a degree program. With discussion, proper planning, and open communication, it is usually possible to get the support and commitment of your family. If you manage your time properly, you can also give them enough attention to keep them happy.

Step 5. Evaluate Your Career and Your Current Skills

What have you done in your career? Where are you right now in terms of job satisfaction? Where do you want to be in five years? What are your ultimate career goals? Do you want to stay in the same field or change careers altogether? If you are thinking about changing career fields, which direction makes the most sense based on your skills and interests? Questions like these seem deceptively simple, but answering them takes some in-depth analysis of both yourself and the careers available today.

Even if career change is not one of your major motivations for pursuing a college education, it's a good idea to analyze your career aspirations and your skills. Along with the desire for mastery of new technology comes the need to document achievement by means of appropriate credentials. So even a person who has kept abreast of developments in his or her career field may find it advantageous to obtain a degree to certify what has already been accomplished.

Your career analysis will help you focus on the types of degree programs that will best meet your needs and match your talents. We have provided a simple *Career and Skills Analysis Worksheet* to help you analyze your current skills and career aspirations. To complete this form, you will probably need to do additional research.

First, you need to decide what careers interest you. Are you aware of the careers now available? Do you know which occupations are growing and which are declining? Do you know what college preparation or degrees are required for the careers you are interested in? If you don't feel comfortable that you know the answers to these questions, there are a number of excellent career books in the bookstores. Some of these books are listed in the back of *College After 30* as references.

Almost every community college, state college, and university has a career counseling office. These offices offer a variety of individual-assessment instruments to help evaluate your own interests. There are also "vocational guidance" centers sponsored by local and state governments that can help you look into alternate career opportunities. (Look in the *Yellow Pages* of your telephone book under

Career and Skills Analysis Worksheet

Use photocopies of this sheet to analyze several career options.
What career are you interested in?

_____

_____

_____

_____

_____

List the skills you already have for the career you're interested in and check your level of sophistication.

Skill name	Minimal	Level of depth Moderate	Sophisticated
_____	☐	☐	☐
_____	☐	☐	☐
_____	☐	☐	☐
_____	☐	☐	☐
_____	☐	☐	☐
_____	☐	☐	☐
_____	☐	☐	☐
_____	☐	☐	☐

List the new skills to be acquired at college

Skill name

_____

_____

_____

_____

_____

_____

_____

What personal ambition are you looking to satisfy?

_____

_____

_____

_____

List the skills you already have for your ambitions and check your level of sophistication.

Skill name	Minimal	Level of depth Moderate	Sophisticated
_____	☐	☐	☐
_____	☐	☐	☐
_____	☐	☐	☐
_____	☐	☐	☐
_____	☐	☐	☐
_____	☐	☐	☐
_____	☐	☐	☐
_____	☐	☐	☐

List the new skills to be acquired at college

Skill name

_____

_____

_____

_____

_____

_____

_____

"Career and Vocational Counseling.") If you want to stay in the same field but expand your career potential, then talk to other people in your field about their recommendations of schools and programs.

As far as your own skills go, you can have a trained counselor in a career-assessment center evaluate your skills and interests using a variety of research instruments and questionnaires. Of course, if you don't want to take the time to talk to a professional, get one of the self-assessment books available in any major bookstore. But, if you feel you already know your own skills pretty well, just complete the worksheet. Once you know how your current skills and career aspirations stack up, you will have a good idea if a degree is a component in meeting your career goals.

Step 6. Define Your Goals and Dreams for the Future

Now, based on your career analysis, skills evaluation, and the trigger you identified earlier, what goals and dreams do you have for attending college? What do you expect to accomplish? Are there other ways to accomplish these things that don't involve college? Is the college degree a lifelong dream in itself? Are there goals that have more priority than college? Try to picture yourself exactly as you want to be five years from now and then ten years from now. What are you doing? What have you accomplished? What has changed?

With your vision of the future in mind, define your goals and aspirations in the spaces provided in the *College Readiness Worksheet*. And remember: Be excruciatingly honest with yourself and as comprehensive as possible in defining your goals. Again, the more you know about yourself and your dreams, the better chance you have of becoming who you want to be.

Step 7. Evaluate Your Motivations and Commitment Level

Finally, look at the dreams and goals you identified for yourself in Step 6. Try to be entirely objective about what you are reading. Pretend you are looking at someone else's goals. What do you think? Does college fit in? Is college important to this person?

We have put a scale beside each section of the *College Readiness Worksheet* so you can evaluate each aspect of your readiness to commit to a college program. In section 1, answer this question on a scale of 1 to 5: Are you ready to put your fears aside? A "1" means you still are very anxious about school and hanging on to your belief in failure. A "5" means you are able to give up entirely any anxieties you have about college and can move forward to be successful.

In section 2, answer this question on a scale of 1 to 5: Do I feel confident I have a strategy to remove all the obstacles I have identified that might keep me from being successful in college? Give yourself a "1" if you're still not very confident. If you are absolutely sure you can make things happen and remove the obstacles, give yourself a "5."

In section 3, answer this question on a scale of 1 to 5: Is the trigger that motivated me to look into college a compelling one? Is the trigger enough to propel me through the time and effort required to finish a college degree? A "1" means the reason is not too important, and a "5" means you have no choice but to go back to school. Most people's reasons fall somewhere between these two extremes.

Now, in section 4, you need to determine if your career goals and skill levels are clearly identified so you will be able to choose an appropriate college program to fit your needs. If you have a clear understanding of your career goals and your skill levels, give yourself a "5". If you have only a few questions, give yourself a "3" or "4". If you are entirely unsure about what you can do and where you want to go in your career, give yourself a "1" or "2".

Now go to section 5. The first scale evaluates your willingness to change your lifestyle and the second one evaluates the support you can expect from your family and friends. In the first scale in section 4, evaluate your willingness to change your lifestyle to accomodate school by asking yourself the following question: Based on what I know about my lifestyle and priorities, how willing am I to make changes to my activities and schedule to accommodate school? On a 1 to 5 scale, a "1" indicates a strong reluctance to make lifestyle changes to accommodate studying and college activities. "5" means that you're completely willing and confident that your schedule can be modified to accommodate school and your other priorities at the same time.

In the second scale in section 5, evaluate the support you can expect from your family or other people in your support system (such as a significant other or close friends, if you live alone). A "1" indicates that family/friends are entirely unwilling to have you attend school. A "5" indicates a very high level of support from your family or friends (as appropriate) for your educational endeavors.

Finally, in section 6, give yourself 1 to 5 points for the following: College is an important part of achieving my goals and/or dreams in life. A "1" means college is not very important in your life goals. A "5" means a college education plays a very significant role in your ability to meet your life goals.

The totals in each area should give you some idea of where your motivation and commitment levels are right now toward college and in which areas you lack support or have unanswered questions or insecurities. Put the total in section 7. The highest possible score is 35 points. If you get a 35, you are probably not being entirely objective in your answers. Almost everyone has at least a bit of apprehension about going back to school. Remember, this is not a test—it is an assessment. Assessments have value only if you are honest with yourself about your answers. A score of 25 or higher indicates that you are a good candidate for succeeding in college as an adult—with this caveat: If any one section scores below 3, then you need to work on this aspect of your college plan before you jump into a full-time degree program. An overall score below 25 indicates general insecurity overall, and means you should do more research and soul-searching before you decide on a college program.

Of course, a high score on this simple assessment doesn't mean you absolutely must succeed if you go to college. It just means you are probably ready to make the commitment to college at this time. If your score is extremely low, it doesn't mean you should not go to college—it just means you need to do some more work on understanding your options, deepening your motivations, or reanalyzing your willingness to change in order to complete a college program or degree.

The *College Readiness Worksheet* is not a scientific instrument and should not be your only source of advice on going to college. The assessment provides a general framework that will help you understand your own commitment levels and your areas of deepest concern about going to college at this point in your life. If you feel insecure about your readiness to commit yourself to a college program, you should contact some of the support resources we talk about in Chapter Seven, including counseling centers, friends, family, college instructors, and school administrators. You also should find out more about the schools (we tell you how to do that in Chapters Three and Four) before you decide if you're really ready.

What Should I Do If I'm Still Not Sure?

> When you have to make a choice, and don't make it, that in itself is a choice.
>
> —*William James*

After completing the seven steps and the worksheet, even if you find that your motivation score came out high, ask yourself one more question: Do I really *want* to go to college? Your answer should come from deep inside and should be excruciatingly honest. If your answer is, "I'm still not sure," you have other things you should do before you make a decision. First, read the rest of this book and complete the basic research on schools and programs we suggest in the chapters. Then, try once again to complete the seven steps outlined in this chapter.

If you're still not sure, consider the reasons for your insecurity about college. Spend some time researching your motives and your fears. The chart below describes common reasons for indecision when it comes to college, and offers suggestions for gathering the information you need to make a choice:

And if you *still* aren't sure after doing all the things we recommend and any you think of on your own, try college on for size before you jump in full time or invest a lot of money. Take a class. Visit some schools. Talk to more people. It helps if you look at schools and classes related to the kind you are considering. If you plan to major in business administration, sitting in on a friend's graduate chemistry course will be dull and intimidating and potentially dissuade you from attending college.

If you are not fully committed to attending college, a hundred reasons not to go will crop up and provide an easy route to frustration and failure. If you start and then quit, be sure you are able to handle the emotional and financial impact of this decision. If you are fully convinced that you want to attend college, every excuse, obstacle, and roadblock can be overcome, ignored, or circumvented. The choice is yours. Take your time, understand the issues, demands, and options. But, don't put off the decision by ignoring it or avoiding the question. *You* are in control of the decision to attend college. If you want to go, there are ways for you to make it work.

Reason for Indecision	What To Do
I'm still not sure if I can handle the academic requirements.	• Try a class at a local community college. • Ask to see the college work of friends who are taking the same types of courses you are interested in. You'll probably find that it looks easier than you thought it would.
My basic skills are inadequate, and I can't get started until I get my reading, writing, and basic math skills up to speed.	• If your study skills or basic skills are weak, attend a local adult education program in skill development. • Most cities, counties, and states offer programs in basic skills at almost no cost to you—look into them. • Private companies offer literacy and basic-skills training for adults in a variety of formats. • Many colleges offer courses in basic skills to bring you up to speed. • Every bookstore and library has books on skill development. Ask a librarian for advice on books that will meet your needs.
I don't know if college will really make any difference in my life.	• Talk to other adult college students. Most adult-oriented schools have names of students who would be happy to talk to you about their experiences in college and the benefits they gained from their education.
I still don't think I'll have enough money.	• Look into the financial aid options we list in the book. • If you don't want to take out loans for college, start a savings program. • Look into less-expensive schools. • Choose a school that offers a flexible tuition payment plan. • Win the lottery.
I'm not sure my family or friends will approve.	• Talk to your family and/or friends. Explain how important school is to you. • Get your family involved in your selection of schools. Let them review the materials.

Have them visit the campuses with you.
● Schedule time to be with your family (and friends) while you are enrolled in school.

I don't know if I'll like it or can do the work.

● Look at a wide variety of college options. There are so many formats, there is probably one that will suit your preferred learning style.
● Enroll in a community college seminar or a summer course to see what school is like.
● Spend some time talking to school counselors or find some other people who are already attending college, and ask them if you can sit in on a class and look at the kind of work required.

Adult College Students In Their Own Words
Gerry Bedore, Ph.D.

Most likely the beginning of my story is much like that of many others of my era—I left college to participate in the Korean conflict, returned to a job that used skills developed while in the service, and started a family. No time for college—it was always something in the plans for the future.

Ultimately, I faced the fact that I needed more education. I was not ready for my growth to flatten so I put together a plan for my future. The future went beyond just my career in industry—I wanted an alternate career for the time I might not enjoy industry any longer. The plan dictated that I proceed through doctoral studies.

I evaluated 15 doctoral offerings including both traditional and non-traditional options. As before, I needed a program that would provide me with a quality education yet didn't require that I leave the workplace to accomplish this. After exhaustive evaluations I selected Nova University in Ft. Lauderdale, Florida. Nova offers a weekend format which was doable. Their faculty was outstanding—they came from major universities across the United States and were both academically and experientially qualified—a veritable *Who's Who* in their subject areas. I received many opinions regarding the credibility of the institution, but having dealt with traditional biases in the past, I knew that these biases could be overcome by performance.

It turned out that the Nova program was essentially a very traditional program with a non-traditional delivery system. I "enjoyed" the rigors of long hours of study and research, together with the preparation of a dissertation. Even while progressing in the program, my status in the workplace changed from staff manager to knowledge resource. When I completed the program, I felt I had completed a very high-quality educational experience. Nova exceeded my expectations in every way.

About a year before completing my doctoral work, I was presented the opportunity to make a career change. The company was downsizing and offered bonuses to some to leave. I decided it was time to pursue my planned "alternate career." I now consult in several areas as well as teach in both traditional and non-traditional university environments. Every year since leaving industry, I have earned well above the amount I had made in industry and have enjoyed the freedom and satisfaction of being self-directed.

Probably the best evaluation of success one can do is to ask the question: "If I could do it over, what would I change?" My career has been fully satisfactory, filled with opportunities, and fun! If I had written a specification for my career thirty years ago, it would not have asked for as much as I have received. I turned the challenge of obtaining an education into an asset—I was ready for education when I finally placed it high on the priority list. I was fortunate to have good non-traditional colleges available to me for advanced studies and proved to myself, and many others, that this alternative, coupled with a sincere individual effort, opens the door to all opportunities.

Chapter Three

The College and Degree Options for Adults

Many new strategies and programs have been developed by colleges to accommodate the special needs of working adults who want and need to pursue a college education. There are hundreds, maybe thousands, of schools, colleges, and universities that are appropriate for adults considering more education. In this chapter, we will introduce you to the wide variety of programs and schools available to choose from. In the next chapter, we will provide a method to help you select the right school and program for your individual needs, budget, and learning style.

What Degrees Are Available to Adults?

As an adult, you can earn any degree you want. The degree of M.D., awarded to medical doctors, is one possible exception to this, if you are over 40. Becoming a medical doctor is a long process. It starts with a bachelor's degree with good grades and prerequisite courses in the sciences, then four years of medical school, a year or two for an internship, and a few more years as a resident doctor in a hospital—all required before you can practice on your own. And if you want to specialize in surgery, cardiology, or some other medical field, expect even more resident training.

Because of the time required to become a licensed doctor, medical schools frequently use age as one of many highly selective criteria for admission. Medical schools want to make sure that doctors actually enter the community to practice medicine for a reasonable length of time. (As medicine gets better and life expectancy continues to rise, these restrictions, too, may become irrelevant.) Some medical schools do admit students in their late thirties and early forties who meet the other selection criteria—but you've got to put together an extremely good case to be accepted. If you really want to become an M.D., don't procrastinate.

So, aside from a few restrictions like the M.D. degree, your ability to earn a specific degree is not limited by your age. Some of the standard degree designations you will find offered in colleges and universities include the following:

Two-Year (Associate) Degrees

Associate degrees are often referred to as two-year degrees because they typically take two years of full-time enrollment at a traditional college to complete.

A few associate degrees, such as those in nursing or engineering, may take three years of full-time study.

Associate degrees are granted by community colleges and junior colleges, through accredited technical colleges, through distance-education and correspondence programs sponsored by a variety of schools, and by a handful of liberal arts colleges that also offer bachelor's degrees. Many associate degree programs are designed to meet the training needs of a specific vocation, such as nursing, auto repair, electrical maintenance, graphic design, office management, retail management, or whatever.

The associate degree majors offered are too vast to list here. You should refer to the catalogs of community colleges and junior colleges in your area to get an idea of the type of vocational degrees the schools offer. *Petersen's Guide to Two-Year Colleges*, updated annually, lists all the accredited programs in the United States. This guide profiles almost 2,000 two-year colleges and lists more than 450 associate degree majors. It can be ordered from any bookstore. For information on the schools in a particular state, each of the commissions on higher education listed in the resources section of this book will provide a list of community colleges in that state. With this information you can contact the colleges directly and order a catalog.

Associate degrees in general studies, liberal arts, or academic majors (such as anthropology, psychology, history, or mathematics) are earned by students who intend to transfer to a four-year college or university for a bachelor's degree. Thus, the first two years at a community college that results in an associate degree are almost equivalent to the freshman and sophomore years in a four-year college, where no degree is granted for the first two years of study. An associate degree often requires one or two additional courses to meet graduation requirements that would not be required of the student in a four-year school. But, you get a degree for the extra work—and the student in a traditional four-year degree program does not. In our view, any degree (as long as it is from a recognized or accredited school) is better than no degree. So, if you're attending a community college to transfer to a four-year school (and many adults choose this option because it is inexpensive and convenient), we recommend that you take the extra course or two and get the degree. It feels good to be degreed, and the degree provides tangible evidence of your effort and education. Besides, the diploma will look nice on your wall.

Bachelor's Degrees

The bachelor's degree is often referred to as a four-year degree because it typically takes four (and sometimes five) years of full-time enrollment at a traditional college to complete one. In some new non-traditional programs called accelerated programs, a complete bachelor's degree can be earned in as little as two and a half or three years, depending on your life experience and skills coming into the program. Bachelor's degrees (and associate degrees) are also called undergraduate degrees.

A bachelor's degree is what people are usually referring to when they want to know if someone has a college degree. Bachelor's degrees almost always require a major (as do associate and graduate degrees)—and there are hundreds of majors to choose from. To see a list of accredited four-year schools, refer to one of the many college guides in the bookstore or in your library, such as *Petersen's Guide to Four-Year Colleges*. Make sure the edition is current. An edition that is more than a couple of years old will not contain completely accurate information.

Some common designations for bachelor's degrees include the following:

B.A. (or A.B.)	Bachelor of Arts
B.Ed.	Bachelor of Education
B.S.	Bachelor of Science
B.F.A.	Bachelor of Fine Art
B.S.B.A.	Bachelor of Science in Business Administration
B.S.W.	Bachelor of Social Work
B.P.S.	Bachelor of Professional Studies
B.Tech.	Bachelor of Technology

Graduate Degrees

A student normally must earn a bachelor's degree before enrolling in a graduate-degree program. There are two broad types of graduate degrees: graduate academic degrees, for people who want to pursue research and teaching in institutions of higher education, and graduate professional degrees, which are usually less research-oriented and lean toward the practice of a specific profession. Both master's degrees and doctoral degrees are graduate degrees.

Doctoral degrees are the highest degree offered by academic institutions and, in most cases, a doctoral degree entitles the person to use the title "Dr." You should be aware that honorary doctoral degrees are also granted by colleges and universities for significant accomplishments. These are usually degrees with names like "Doctor of Humane Letters" or some other special designation. A doctoral degree attained by attending school is referred to as "an earned doctorate" to separate it from honorary doctorates.

The following graduate degrees are some of those commonly granted:

Academic Graduate Degrees

M.A. (or A.M.)	Master of Arts
M.S.	Master of Science
M. Phil.	Master of Philosophy
Ph.D.	Doctor of Philosophy

Professional Graduate Degrees

M.Arch.	Master of Architecture
M.A.O.M.	Master of Arts in Organizational Management
M.B.A.	Master of Business Administration
M.Ed.	Master of Education
M.F.A.	Master of Fine Art (The most advanced degree granted in the studio arts and performing arts, equivalent to a doctorate in some schools.)

M.L.S.	Master of Library Science
M.P.A.	Master of Public Administration
M.S.W.	Master of Social Work
D.B.A.	Doctor of Business Administration
D.D.S.	Doctor of Dental Surgery
Ed.D.	Doctor of Education
J.D.	Doctor of Law
M.D.	Doctor of Medicine
D.V.M.	Doctor of Veterinary Medicine

Certification Programs

If you need immediate career-oriented skills and don't have time to complete a degree from scratch, another way of making advanced study meaningful and streamlined is to take advantage of certification programs offered by many colleges. In a certification program, a student takes a shortened course of study. All the courses in a certificate program bear directly on the subject to be mastered. Typical certificate programs involve five to ten courses and may require the student to pass a proficiency examination or complete a comprehensive project at the end of the program of study. At the completion of this study, the school issues a certificate that attests to the student's proficiency in the subject area.

There are hundreds of certificate programs available at colleges, universities, and vocational schools nationwide. There are certificates available in almost everything—from computer technology to graphic design to executive management to dog grooming. Most of these programs offer a chance for significant skills development for a relatively small investment of time and money. Certificate programs are often monitored by the college's Office of Continuing Education or by individual departments in traditional schools, and are listed in the school's catalog as well. All of the factors for choosing a degree program and school apply to choosing a certificate program. A certificate program is only as good as its reputation, its curriculum, and its faculty.

There are a number of advantages in obtaining certification. The first is that the time required to earn the certificate is generally quite short (often less than a year). Second, the cost of a certificate is often less than that of a baccalaureate course. Third, the requirements for entry into certificate programs are almost always less stringent than those for entry into bachelor's degree or graduate degree programs.

Not all certificate programs are inexpensive or short-term undertakings, however. Some certificate programs are very competitive, selective, and pricey. Upon completion, these programs provide almost all the prestige and recognition of a traditional degree from the institution. For example, Harvard Business School and other notable institutions offer advanced certificate programs. Typically, people who are lucky enough (and accomplished enough) to be accepted into these programs are granted the prestigious certificates from these schools at the completion of three or more intense summer sessions on campus.

While some certificates don't offer the same acceptance and advantages of a degree, they often are all that is required to get a new job or make a career move or attain the feeling of accomplishment—typical reasons why adults attend college in the first place.

Which Degree or Certificate Do You Need?

The degree or certificate program you choose to pursue is a matter of your own motivations for attending college. The first thing you need to choose is a major. Then you need to decide if an undergraduate or a graduate degree is your ultimate goal. If you want to learn more about specific degrees and what they entitle you to, pick up one of the college reference guides recommended in the reference section of this book or get a catalog from a major university and review the degree descriptions. The specific requirements for the degrees are different for each college—but the same degree with the same major will require similar levels of effort and similar courses and demonstrated proficiencies.

What If I Don't Want a Degree or Certificate? Can I Still Attend College?

Many adults enroll in college courses without a degree goal. They go to college for recreation, expanded skills, and myriad other reasons. We have a friend with more than 240 college credits (equal to almost two bachelor's degrees at most colleges) who has never applied for a degree. He just likes meeting the people in the courses and enjoys learning new things.

Most community colleges encourage adults to attend enrichment and general-interest courses. Colleges also offer non-credit courses through their continuing education and community education programs. And many schools, even the prestigious, competitive ones, allow you to take two or three courses without actually applying to the school. There also are schools that let you sit in on courses. This is called "auditing" a course. You must usually pay the fees for auditing a course but will not need to complete the exams or written assignments and, of course, you will not get credit on your transcript for your attendance. Still, auditing a couple of courses at a major university is a good way to see if you will like a particular school, course, or major.

Traditional Colleges and Universities

Now that you know the degree options, let's look at the schools that are out there, starting with the traditional colleges and universities. Traditional schools include community colleges (formerly called junior colleges), liberal arts colleges that offer four-year degrees, and full-curriculum colleges and universities that offer both four-year and graduate degrees. But what does "traditional" mean in the world of higher education and, more important, to an adult who is thinking about college? Well, it means different things, depending on who you are talking to, but "traditional" schools generally share the following attributes:

■ The majority of students on the campus are between the ages of 18 and

25, and many of the activities and programs on campus are geared to the needs and activities of younger students. This is becoming a less-meaningful definition of "traditional" because so many adults over 30 are now attending these schools—but many uninformed people still consider colleges and universities places where "young people congregate to party first and get an education second." These skeptics should visit traditional campuses to see just how wrong they are.

■ Most of the courses in a traditional college are presented on campus with an instructor or professor lecturing in front of a classroom full of wide-eyed students taking copious notes. Classes typically meet over a period of twelve weeks (in the quarter system) or fifteen to seventeen weeks (in the semester system), though there may be a summer session when some courses are accelerated over a period of six to eight weeks.

■ Grades are usually given for each class based on a traditional 4-point grading scale of A to F: A = 4 points, B = 3 points, C = 3 points, D = 1 point, and F = 0 points in this system.

■ Though a limited amount of credit may be granted for life experience, military experience, or equivalency examinations in some traditional schools, most of the credit required for the degree must be earned in regular courses.

■ A full-time student is enrolled in four to six courses at one time each semester or quarter. Part-time students take fewer courses, and thus take longer to graduate. There also is a limit on the number of courses (usually six or seven) that can be taken during one semester or quarter.

■ Most traditional schools offer a wide range of majors and degree options, though there are some liberal arts colleges and specialty colleges and universities, offering only a few majors, that still meet the other criteria of traditionalism.

■ The requirements for graduation are generally inflexible in each major. There is little opportunity for individualizing a program of study in most traditional schools. Degrees generally are granted based on successfully completing a specified number of courses.

■ Most of the faculty in traditional schools are full-time teachers and/or researchers. Few members of the faculty have significant working experience outside the college or university environment. In addition to teaching, most of the faculty engage in independent research and write books and articles for academic journals in order to maintain their academic rank and tenure. (See the glossary at the back of the book if you don't know what "rank" and "tenure" mean.)

■ Large traditional colleges have a football team, a basketball team, and other sports teams, and they spend a significant amount of energy promoting intramural athletic events. These schools also have a school song, a motto, and a school mascot.

Are traditional schools appropriate for adults? The answer depends on the student and the school. Some "traditional" schools unconsciously (or consciously) discriminate against older students who are applying for freshman status in the school by making it difficult for adults to meet "admission standards." These standards may include specific high school course requirements, test scores (SAT or ACT), and personal interviews with a counselor who makes it clear he or she would rather be talking to someone under twenty. Many of the traditional four-year schools, especially the prestigious, competitive schools, prefer to admit their freshman students out of high school. Still, many of the same universities that discriminate against adults as freshmen will gladly accept adults as graduate students or as juniors or seniors.

Many traditional campuses are changing their attitudes and approaches to adult students. This is because they need the revenue from adult students to survive and prosper, and because attitudes toward lifelong learning are changing in general. Traditional schools are changing to meet the market demands for flexible programs, enhanced educational-delivery options, expanded technologies, and more relevant course sequences. These schools are also expanding their on-campus computer support programs. Even the most established of the traditional schools, including Harvard, Yale, Stanford, UCLA, Columbia, and other well-known schools, both private and state-operated, offer distance-education options (more about these later in the chapter), part-time and evening programs, career-development certificate programs, and other less-traditional educational formats that appeal to adult students.

Many adult students prefer the defined structure and stability of the traditional approach to higher education. A degree from an accredited traditional school is less likely to be questioned as to its validity or merit. If you understand the traditional system and desire the structure of a traditional education, then you should concentrate on the traditional schools in your search for a school. Also, some majors are available only through traditional schools. But before you decide to go to a state university or an Ivy League college, read on. There are many accredited schools offering educational alternatives that you may not know about that may meet your needs even better.

Alternative Colleges and Universities

There has been great growth in the opportunities for people who do not want to follow traditional educational paths to a college degree. Thirty years ago, if you wanted to earn a degree without sitting in classrooms for three or four years and wanted to remain in North America, you had two legitimate alternatives: The University of London and the University of South Africa. Both of these schools still offer non-resident programs, from the bachelor's to doctoral and professional degrees. However, today, you have hundreds of alternatives to get an accredited degree from institutions all over the United States and the rest of the world.

Students who are ambitious or have significant life experience can, through a variety of programs and tests, earn college credits in alternative schools without attending traditional lecture- or classroom-based courses.

Alternative or nontraditional education is "alternative" because it does not share the paradigm of education of most traditional schools. To understand how alternative schools are different, it is important to understand how traditional schools are alike. The following summarizes the key factors in the traditional model of attaining a college degree:

- When you start college, the school treats you as if you are a person without significant knowledge or skills. The school's role then is to "fill" you with information. (We call this the "blank slate" orientation.) Thus, past life experience and accumulated knowledge have little relevance in a traditional educational program.
- Education takes place while sitting in courses and listening to an instructor who may or may not be knowledgeable. You also are required to read textbooks and articles selected for you by someone else.
- Knowledge is demonstrated in each class through essay or multiple-choice tests and by completing term papers.
- After you sit through enough of a predefined sequence of courses and pass the requisite tests, you are granted a degree.

Nontraditional or alternative schools use different methods to educate their students. The models vary based on the school—with some alternative schools being only slightly nontraditional, meaning they may adhere to two or three of the traditional aspects of education, such as tests or preselected textbooks or lecturing professors. Other alternative schools employ completely different approaches to education that use almost none of the features of the traditional paradigm.

First and foremost, alternative schools offer nontraditional delivery methods. A delivery method in education is the way information is presented and the means by which students acquire knowledge from the presentation of information. The traditional delivery method is, as we've stated already, a classroom with an instructor lecturing in front of the room. Students in the traditional model are supposed to learn by taking notes, studying, and ultimately through rote memory. Alternative delivery methods do not depend on the classroom model.

Distance-Education Options

Colleges and universities, and even the traditionally oriented accrediting associations, have become more willing to concede that learning need not take place in a traditional classroom with a professor at the head of the class. Learning can take place at home, in the workplace, and during leisure hours. But some colleges have taken this idea a step further. They have conceived of programs wherein students can do most, if not all, of their learning outside the classroom through *distance-education* options. This belief, coupled with the advancement of telecommunications and computer technologies, has given rise to a rich variety of educational opportunities.

Distance education implies that students live and learn away from the central campus. Some of the distance-education options are offered by traditional colleges and universities, though almost all of them were begun at nontraditional schools. The International Council for Distance Education (ICDE) estimates that about ten million people worldwide study at a distance every year. In a survey of 52 countries, 142 associate or bachelor's degree programs and 61 postgraduate degree programs were offered through distance-education programs. Such programs were found in every region of the world except Eastern Europe, from which questionnaires were not returned, but which is known to have a significant number of distance-degree programs as well.

For good reasons, distance education is primarily an adult activity. Working adults must ration too little time among too many demands, have little time for class, less time for study, and no time to waste simply getting to class. Educating adults at a distance would appear to be a big task, but most adults are continuous learners in an informal way as they adjust to the various role changes that confront them in life—thus, adults are already experienced in learning things on their own and are usually mature enough to manage their own educational program. It follows that distance-education methods are ideal for self-motivated, self-directed adults.

Distance-education programs are successfully delivered to adult learners regardless of their location. The instructional delivery methods for distance-education programs include the following:

Online Instruction via Computers

In an online program you attend class by communicating "on line" through a telephone connection with a remote computer via a modem attached to your personal computer. Sometimes online programs are called "electronic universities" or the like. The remote or central computer is used to store information and provide storage functions and communication links between students and faculty. The computer takes the place of in-class discussion and out-of-class student-teacher communications. Each person has a private "mailbox" on the remote system for messages to be sent or read. Other "conference areas" or "course mailboxes" allow faculty and students to share access to the same information and leave messages for groups of people. When students "log on" to the computer they gain access to the conference and mailboxes that contain information about the course. "Lectures" are sent by faculty on line. Assignments are also sent to the faculty online via the computer. Most online courses require students to interact through online forums. The students in an online environment can be from all over the world but in the same class. Usually students are sent textbooks and other curriculum materials to augment the online instruction and discussions. Online access is typically available 24 hours a day to students and faculty alike. With online programs, students can control the time and place of their individual participation and work at their own pace. All students in an online program have equal access to the instructor and facilities, so the learning environment is not dominated by a handful of students, as it often is in traditional settings.

> You get out of the online program what you put into it. I've worked very hard in this program and feel I can hold my MBA up against any Ivy League MBA and come out a winner.
>
> —*Nancy Hoffman*, Graduate of the University of Phoenix Online MBA Program

Self-instructional or Home-study Courses

The term *correspondence school* got a bad name when a number of unscrupulous schools offered worthless degrees through the mail, so correspondence courses are often referred to as "home-study courses" or "self-instructional modules" instead. Self-instructional and home-study courses are available in a number of formats. These self-instructional, self-paced courses usually consist of lesson materials specially prepared by the school for students who complete the assignments based on their own initiative and schedule. The prepackaged materials may include a text, a workbook, a syllabus, videotapes, audiotapes, and other materials, depending on the school and the course. Students follow the information and assignments in the course materials and submit assignments to an instructor, either through the mail, over the telephone, or during scheduled meetings. The faculty member returns the assigned work to the student with corrections, comments, and further subject-matter guidance. The courses vary greatly in scope, level, and length. Some have a few lessons and require only weeks to complete, while others have a hundred or more assignments requiring three or four years of study. Also, a wide variety of subjects is offered, covering such diverse areas as accounting, robotics, travel-agent training, gun repair, gem identification, and broadcast journalism, just to name a few. Some alternative schools offer complete bachelor's, master's, and doctoral degree programs almost entirely through home-study methods. Many traditional colleges offer credit for their correspondence courses or accept some correspondence credits from resident students working toward a traditional degree.

Self-paced Computer-based Courses

These interactive courses are a form of self-instruction that uses personal computers and programs stored on a computer disk or a CD-ROM like the compact discs (CDs) from which we listen to music. The CD-ROM or disk contains instructional data and programs that can include animation, sound, and assignments for courses. The student works through the computerized course at his or her own pace until the computer verifies that the objectives of the course have been attained.

Televised Instruction

Courses delivered over television are often scheduled during late-night and early-morning hours on cable TV or on local public broadcasting stations (PBS) so they can be recorded with a VCR and viewed at the student's convenience. Televised courses are offered by both alternative and traditional schools.

A Televised College:
Mind Extension University

Mind Extension University® (ME/U), started in 1987, is presented solely on cable television. ME/U is devoted solely to distance education. Programming consists of direct student instruction and staff development for secondary schools, undergraduate and graduate degree programs, and continuing education for personal development. ME/U has formed partnerships with twenty accredited universities that offer undergraduate and graduate telecourses in a variety of subjects. ME/U also offers adult literary programs and test-preparation courses for the GED, SAT, ACT, and CLEP tests.

ME/U offers exclusively on cable television the first fully accredited, televised M.B.A. degree program from Colorado State University, a bachelor's completion program in management from the University of Maryland, and a master's in education program from George Washington University.

According to Glenn R. Jones, the founder of ME/U and a leader in cable television programming, "The Mind Extension University network was created to serve as a distribution channel for educational opportunities, combining the technologies and resources of cable and satellite television with the expertise of the finest education and instructional facilities."

Teleconferencing and Satellite Instruction

Teleconferencing involves the use of special locations from which instructors can communicate with more than one group of people at the same time over ordinary phone lines. Satellite communications use satellite transmissions in the same way. Students either dial a special number on their own phones or meet in special teleconferencing locations where they can view and interact with the instructor. The instructor teaches a class (which may involve more than one remote location) from a central campus. Students respond to instructor queries and query the instructor over phone lines or satellite connections. Course materials and assignments are sent through the mail or by online communication with computers, as described earlier.

Other Educational Approaches Used in Alternative Colleges

Not all alternative schools employ distance education. Some use other educational methods, coupled with traditional delivery methods to meet their educational objectives. These other educational-delivery methods include internships, cooperative education programs, and individualized learning contracts that combine traditional courses with individual projects and special learning activities.

Many of these alternative delivery methods have been adopted by traditional schools as well. Traditional universities and colleges, like Hofstra and Pace University, have responded to the rising number of successful alternative schools with an extraordinary range of their own nontraditional educational programs. Some of these nontraditional programs sponsored by traditional schools have been developed in conjunction with programs set up by the government, the military, and private industry. Most traditional schools provide a few courses each semester in a nontraditional format. Keep in mind that not all traditional schools offer alternative educational options, however. You should get more information from the colleges you are interested in to find out what variations are available. Colleges continue to develop and evolve their nontraditional offerings, so keep an open mind and ear when you look into college opportunities.

Some of the alternative offerings you will commonly find available from traditional and nontraditional schools alike include:

Part-time Programs

Perhaps the most traditional path for the nontraditional student is to attend college part-time. It is possible at virtually all colleges to take less than a full course load (generally four or five courses for twelve to sixteen credits) and still be considered to be working toward a degree (matriculated). This policy is especially true for a college's School of Continuing Education, the administrative unit in a traditional school set up to help the non-traditional and adult students. It is not uncommon for traditional students to take only one or two courses per semester, especially if one of the courses is extremely difficult or has a laboratory section required. Many schools offer accelerated part-time programs that lead to degrees more quickly as well.

Evening and Weekend Classes

Many traditional schools offer their continuing education courses in the evening and/or on weekends. Evening classes generally begin at 6 or 6:30 p.m. and last from 75 minutes to two hours or more, depending on the course and the school. Although it is often possible to schedule a full course load during evening hours at a traditional school, it is not a good idea to do so. Coupled with a full-time job, a full evening course load could be difficult. Alternative schools offer evening programs that are better geared to full-time attendance. For example, some schools offer courses over five, six, or eight weeks. These courses typically meet for four hours once a week or for two hours twice a week.

Courses often are given by traditional schools on weekends as well. These classes commonly meet only once a week and last three hours with a ten-minute break midway through the session. Classes usually are scheduled so that it is possible to attend two different courses on the same day.

In general, the courses offered in evening and weekend programs are of the same caliber as those given during the day. In fact, traditional day courses and alternative night courses may be taught by the same professor and use the same textbook. There is no need for quality to go down with the sun at any school.

Summer Programs

To help part-time students speed up the process of earning a degree, many universities offer evening and weekend classes during the summer. Summer sessions usually start a week or two after the end of the spring semester and continue into early July. A second summer session may be offered from mid-July until the start of the fall semester. While summer course offerings are not as extensive as the selection offered during the regular school year, summer sessions do provide courses that are needed to fulfill degree requirements.

Condensed Courses, Seminars, and Workshops

Yet another way to cover academic ground quickly in traditional schools is to take condensed courses. These courses are offered during intersession (the time between Christmas and spring registration), and generally cover in four to six weeks the information provided in a complete fall semester. Needless to say, the pace is fast, and the eight to ten hours of lecture per week can be overwhelming to some students. There has been, and undoubtedly there will continue to be, a great deal of ingenuity and imagination put into intersession and other condensed courses.

In addition to intersession courses, seminars are offered throughout the school year. These generally take one of two forms. The first involves having speakers from a given field present their thoughts to the class, with the professor acting as moderator. The students are graded on their participation in the question-and-answer period following the presentation and/or on a paper written on topics brought up by one or more of the speakers. The second type of seminar involves the student in a far more active way. After some introductory material is presented by the speakers, the students research and present seminar topics. The students are graded on their written and oral presentations and on their responses to the questions of other students. In addition to seminars, some schools also offer workshops. Though similar to seminars in some ways, workshops stress the interaction of the participants. Workshops are generally scheduled to meet over a few weeks. The sessions can be one or two daylong affairs as well.

Seminars and workshops can be extremely lively offering an interactive dimension and personal contact not often found in traditional courses. However, workshops and seminars are often noncredit activities, so beware if you are trying to graduate. Make sure alternative courses offer the requisite credits for your degree before you pay the fees for them.

Immersion Programs

Immersion programs offer another accelerated option in traditional settings. In an immersion course, the student lives in an environment where he or she eats, drinks, and sleeps a subject for twenty-four hours a day. This can be done for a period of several weeks (generally in the summer) or over weekends. While most immersion-style courses are for learning languages, there are some programs in computer programming and other fields that are attempting immersion techniques to expedite the learning process.

Internships and Study Abroad

Another way to earn credits outside the classroom is to take part in an internship program offered by a university or to take one of the study-abroad programs offered by schools over the summer. An internship involves working in a real business environment in the field that interests you. There are a variety of internship programs in Japan, for example, that are very useful for business majors. In an internship you receive work experience that you can use on your resume and a chance to network in your chosen field. Many internship and foreign-study programs are restricted to younger students, but there are a rising number of these programs for adult learners, especially in the business, education, and science disciplines.

Cooperative Education Programs

Cooperative education (or co-op as it is often called) is offered in one version or another by nearly a thousand colleges and universities around the country. Hundreds of thousands of students and tens of thousands of employers participate in these programs. Once restricted to younger students, cooperative education programs are now opening up to adults as well. Cooperative education programs are available in a wide range of subjects including the natural sciences, education, agriculture, business, computer science, environmental sciences, the health professions, the humanities, and many trade and vocational areas.

Most four-year colleges provide some cooperative education opportunities on an optional basis. The schools make provisions for students to spend two or three semesters or quarters in work assignments over the course of their regular academic programs. Community colleges generally offer parallel programs with part of the day spent in class and part on a work assignment. Several institutions offer five-year programs with cooperative education required as part of the curriculum. Students in these programs graduate with a traditional four-year degree augmented by up to two years of cooperative experiences.

Cooperative training programs are available through both traditional and nontraditional schools. In most programs, students receive academic credit for their work experiences with increasing responsibility in their chosen fields. Cooperative programs are especially appealing to adults who are changing careers or people who aren't clear on their career objectives. For adults with limited finances who are not already working full time, the earnings from cooperative work assignments can help defray college expenses. For all students, cooperative education makes classroom study more relevant by combining it with on-the-job experience.

Internship programs are offered in particular areas by either the school placement office or individual departments. It is worthwhile to check with both these sources to determine the internships available and possible liaisons that the departments in a school might have with businesses or other enterprises.

**A Nontraditional School with Many Options:
Nova University**
Nova University was founded in 1964. The main campus is located in Fort Lauderdale, Florida. In 1991, Nova University enrolled more than 10,000 students, and the number continues to grow.

From the beginning, Nova distinguished itself through its innovate outlook and its unique, nontraditional choices in programs. Though many students attend traditional classes on the main campus or at one of the satellite campuses, like the one in Coral Springs, Florida, Nova also offers degree programs and continuing educational opportunities off campus and across the United States in "learning clusters." There is even a Panama Center that provides undergraduate programs to Panamanians, U.S. citizens, and professionals from other countries. In addition, Nova offers computer-based and online programs, as well as other distance-education options. The University offers full-time, part-time, and self-paced programs of study. Nova is committed to the idea that education should not be timebound or placebound. Part of its mission is to provide educational opportunities to adult students wherever they may be.

The school offers bachelor's, master's, and doctoral degrees in a wide range of subject areas, including liberal arts, marine biology, computer science, education, business, psychology, and family studies, among others.

The Shared Features of Alternative Schools

Almost all non-traditional schools or programs (also called external degree programs) employ one or more of the alternative education methods we just discussed. Non-traditional schools frequently combine the alternative delivery techniques with traditional classroom courses or may use multiple alternative delivery techniques in one course. For example, televised or teleconference courses may use online access for course discussions and submitting assignments. An internship may be combined with an individualized-study program.

In addition to the use of nontraditional instructional methods, all alternative schools share some, if not most, of the following attributes:

- A learning model that regards previous life experience as significant and desirable input into the lifelong learning process. Thus, a significant part of the learning experience in non-traditional schools is attributed to interaction with the environment, life experience, meaningful projects, and/or group process. Textbook studying and memorization are still required, but are not the only way to learn.

- Credit for prior learning through tests and/or a structured portfolio that documents past accomplishments. Almost all non-traditional schools offer diverse and generous programs for granting college credit based on life experience and self-education.
- Flexible scheduling options. Regardless of whether the goal is to improve oneself in general, to catch up on what's new, or to obtain credentials commensurate with what one has already achieved, time is a major logistic problem for adults who want to attend college. Most working adults cannot arrange their schedules so they can attend full-time day classes. They need alternative schedules if their educational goals are to be reached. Non-traditional education offers many ways for adults to attend college without having to pack up their lives for four years to attend day courses. These flexible options may include weekend and evening courses, summer seminars, accelerated courses, distance education alternatives, and other options.
- A belief that students share some of the responsibility for their own education. The role of the instructor or professor in alternative schools often is one of facilitator or mentor, rather than one of lecturer and test-giver.
- Programs can be individualized to meet the learning objectives of the students. Many adults are dissatisfied with what they consider to be the cookie-cutter education of traditional schools. Even some young students prefer a less rigid approach to their degrees. There has been a drive since the 1960s to make degree programs more flexible and more individual, allowing students to broaden their horizons as they choose and to concentrate on a particular aspect of their field of study. Many of the alternative schools for adults and even traditional institutions are giving students more control over the design of their own programs. The "learning contract" is a common component in many alternative schools allowing students to individualize their own course of study with the approval of the school and faculty. (In Chapter Eight, we will discuss the common components of a learning contract since so many adult-oriented schools employ this method of individualizing the educational program.)

The first question adult students ask before they seriously consider alternative schools is almost always: Are degrees from nontraditional schools recognized and accepted like those from traditional schools? With few exceptions, as long as the degree is from an accredited institution, the answer is a hearty "Yes!" Options that were unthinkable only a few years ago are now recognized and accepted ways of obtaining accredited degrees. Employers are realizing that most holders of nontraditional degrees have far more practical knowledge and experience than those who learned a subject in traditional college classrooms. And the person who has both the experience *and* a nontraditional degree based, at least in part, on that experience may be in the best career position of all.

Adult-Oriented Colleges and Universities

Adult-oriented colleges are a special kind of "alternative" educational institution. Most, but not all of the adult-oriented schools use the alternative methods of educational delivery and support alternative views of educational process like those we have just discussed. The difference between "alternative" schools and adult-oriented schools is simply the emphasis placed on the life experience of the students admitted to the programs.

There are a variety of accredited, high-quality colleges that will admit only students with significant work experience. Most of these adult-oriented schools prefer to admit students over the age of 25 or 30 and cater to the learning styles and scheduling preferences of adult learners. Many are specialized in the kinds of programs offered and may focus entirely on one or two major areas, such as business, psychology, or education, instead of offering the broad choice of majors available in other colleges and universities.

Though adult-oriented colleges offer a wide variety of formats and educational opportunities, ranging from traditional to alternative, there are some things exposed in our research that consistently differentiate adult-oriented schools and programs from those in traditional schools.

The first thing that stands out in adult-oriented schools is the philosophy of the school or the mission statement. Here are representative statements describing adult-oriented schools:

> Nova University believes in the unlimited potential of every individual. It stimulates men and women to learn; to make a difference in the world.
> —*Nova University in Brief,* 1991

> We felt it was critical to design programs which built upon the experience of the working professional and which employed a collaborative learning model reflective of the team approach in the workplace. Students are able to take what they learn in the classroom and apply it on the job because we continually update our curricula and only employ faculty who actually work in a field related to the material they teach.
> —*Dr. John Sperling*
> founder of the University of Phoenix

> Walden's mission is to provide high quality academic study for experienced professionals. Walden's programs build upon professional and personal competence and seek to enhance that competence through scholarly inquiry and the advancement of knowledge in matters of societal significance. This century has seen unprecedented social, political, and technological

changes, and more profound changes lie ahead. By seeking a better understanding of the potential and the problems of the future, Walden aspires to contribute to making it a more humane one.

—*Walden University Bulletin,* 1991

Saybrook's focus on helping professionals to understand what it means to be human will contribute significantly to understanding and solving the problems of a highly diverse and changing world.

—*Dr. J. Bruce Francis*
President Saybrook Institute

Antioch's Center for Adult Learning has been designed with a specific set of assumptions in mind. We believe that most adults need: Respect for their autonomy . . . Respect for their maturity . . . Respect for a complex life based on multiple roles . . . Respect for the great self-discipline which adults have developed . . . Respect for their great self-understanding . . . Respect for the valuable experience that generally comes with age . . . .

—Brochure, Antioch University

These quotations, which represent only a few of the adult-oriented schools, were selected because they reveal the common philosophies of these schools. This commonality includes a focus on lifelong learning, social consciousness, and innovative programming for working adults. In addition to the similar philosophies of adult-oriented schools, other shared features of these programs include:

- Significant emphasis is placed on the value of past experience and flexible options for gaining academic credit for documented life experiences.
- Flexible scheduling options are available, which may include one or more of the following: accelerated courses, evening and weekend courses, distance-education options, self-paced correspondence courses, online courses, and other alternative delivery methods.
- Most adult-oriented schools offer special-format programs to accommodate adult students that incorporate night classes, special seminars, televised courses, and other innovative methods to enable adult students to attend college on their own terms.
- Students are predominantly over the age of 30, and often average more than 35 or 40 years of age. For example, the average age of University of Phoenix's online students is 38 and the students in the University's classroom-based programs average 34 years of age.
- The faculty in adult-oriented colleges generally have significantly more experience in business and industry to augment their academic back-

grounds than found in traditional faculties.

An Adult-Oriented University: The University of Phoenix

The University of Phoenix, headquartered in Phoenix, Arizona, has a relatively short but very impressive history of providing educational opportunities for working adults. Originally founded as the Institute for Professional Development (IPD) in 1971, IPD was renamed the University of Phoenix in 1977. The University of Phoenix (UOP) now has campuses in Arizona, California, Utah, Colorado, New Mexico, Hawaii, and Puerto Rico. Through its ACCESS telecommunications and directed-study programs, it offers degree opportunities to students across the United States, in Europe, and even in Asia. UOP's ONLINE division, operated out of San Francisco, California, can provide business education anywhere in the world to students who are able to access the UOP's ALex™ information exchange system with a personal computer and a modem.

UOP offers bachelor's and master's degrees in business, management, nursing, and education, in addition to a variety of professional certification programs. More than 13,000 students were enrolled in UOP's degree and certificate programs in 1991 and another 8,000 students enrolled in professional development courses and seminars offered by the parent company, Apollo Group, Inc. In fact, UOP is now the largest private business school in the United States. In total, more than 60,000 students have completed UOP programs.

Students are accepted into the university only with significant life experience and some college background. Credits for college can be earned through courses, tests, and portfolio assessments. In UOP's campus programs, full-time students take one course at a time. The students work in study groups throughout the campus program. The intensive program enables students with two years of college credit to complete a bachelor's degree in eighteen months and earn a master's degree in two years while attending classes only one night a week for four hours. In keeping with its mission to serve the educational needs of working adults, UOP continues to expand its programs to fit individual preferences for location, timing, and interaction with the faculty.

Of course, the University of Phoenix is only one of the high-quality, adult-oriented schools and programs that serve the hundreds of thousands of adults students who return to college each year. Many of these other accredited, adult-oriented colleges for mid-career adults are presented in the resources section at the end of the book.

There are also a significant number of adult-oriented schools that employ study groups, cluster groups, or learning teams as a central component of the educational experience. These teams allow people to share ideas and exchange information. These teams also provide a support system to assist adult students through their degree programs.

Adult-oriented schools are not for everyone, but they do offer significant advantages over traditional options for many adult learners. The greater age of the students makes the educational experience more comfortable and more relevant for most adults. The acceptance of life experience for college credit enables adults to get their degrees in less time than in traditional programs. And, adult programs offer many flexible scheduling options, delivery methods, and campus locations to enable working people to attend full time.

International Schools

There are many international schools that offer degree programs, in English, to students in other countries. For example, the University of South Africa, which we mentioned earlier, offers a full range of correspondence degree programs that employ prepackaged course materials, tapes, and slides. Villarreal National University, the largest university in Peru, also offers completely non-resident master's and doctoral degrees, in English, to people living in the United States. There are also certificates offered by well-known foreign universities, such as Cambridge, for example, that can be earned by spending an extended vacation in Europe or Japan.

Be aware that foreign degree programs range from credible to extremely flaky—the same range you'll find in the United States. Only certain foreign degree programs are recognized as being the equivalent of accredited degree programs in the United States. If you are interested in foreign-study possibilities or in international schools that offer distance-education options, refer to one of the agencies we list in the back of the book that can verify the accreditation equivalency of international schools.

Trade and Vocational Colleges

There are many trade and vocational colleges in the United States. Some are viable alternatives for adults who want to gain new skills or change careers. Vocational schools usually offer short-term training programs designed to provide specific career-oriented skills. The degrees and certificates offered by vocational schools can be quite useful, as long as you select a legitimate, recognized school. DeVry Institute of Technology, for example, offers accredited degree programs in technical areas such as engineering and computer science in ten cities across the United States. DeVry's accelerated programs enable students to earn a credible bachelor's degree in only three years.

Unfortunately, some technical and vocational schools are simply scams to pry people's money loose. For example, there are phony art schools, incompetent engineering schools, and a variety of other less-than-credible institutions that are licensed to operate as businesses in many states. (A school can be "licensed" or ""approved" by the state and still not be accredited. More on that in the next chapter.) These crooked institutions employ inexperienced instructors, offer substandard curricula, and use outdated equipment and techniques. Some of these schools promise new careers, but fail to inform you that the opportunities in the field are very limited. Other schools imply they will guarantee a job on completion of the program, but this is rarely the truth. By the way, price is not a way to judge the credibility of one of these institutions, because some of the most questionable vocational schools are among the most expensive. If you think a vocational school will meet your needs, check it out thoroughly before you sign on the dotted line.

Graduate School Options for Adults

The options for graduate study are very similar to those for undergraduate work. The traditional, alternative, and distance-education options we have already discussed are available for graduate study, just as they are for undergraduate work. And because many adult students choose to continue their education after getting a bachelor's degree, there are even more adult-oriented graduate schools that provide the flexibility, commitment to lifelong learning, and individualized programs we have described already than there are undergraduate programs.

When there are special considerations for applying to or attending graduate school, we will note them in the book. Otherwise, everything we say about college in general pertains to most graduate degrees and programs.

A Graduate School for Professionals: Saybrook Institute

Saybrook Institute, headquartered in San Francisco, California, is a graduate and research center for adults that offers an innovative, individualized, and rigorous at-a-distance learning program. Saybrook, founded in 1971, took its name from a 1964 conference held in Old Saybrook, Connecticut that launched humanistic psychology as a social movement within psychology. Saybrook currently enrolls about 200 students, ranging in age from the mid-20's to 60's. It offers graduate programs leading to master's and doctoral degrees in human science and psychology, with programs that emphasize organizational inquiry, clinical inquiry, systems inquiry, and other social science disciplines.

The faculty at Saybrook is composed of noted psychologists and social scientists who have practical experience, extensive research backgrounds, and an impressive list of books and other publications in their portfolios. The master's and doctoral programs at Saybrook are characterized by faculty and student discovery of knowledge about human beings, innovative teaching, and the development of new methods of inquiry. Another distinctive aspect of Saybrook Institute is its mode of education. Saybrook uses an at-a-distance format which is an adaptation of the European tutorial model emphasizing one-to-one interaction. Using learning guides, students complete coursework at home. Their progress is guided by faculty members who communicate by phone, letter, or computer. This format works especially well for mature students who prefer to tailor the pace, scope, and process of education to their individual requirements.

This chapter has revealed the traditional, alternative, and distance-education opportunities and the adult-oriented options available for getting an accredited or recognized degree or special certificate. There are degree programs, schools, and options for almost everyone. Adults who feel they won't have time to attend school are offered a number of accredited, innovative, flexible, and affordable options for fitting college into their life. It's only a matter of matching your preferences and goals to the right school. In the next chapter, we give you a step-by-step method to do just that.

Chapter Four

Choosing the Right School to Meet Your Goals

The college options in the preceding chapter may seem overwhelming. However, using the step-by-step methods in this chapter, you'll find it is relatively easy to narrow your choices down to a few types of programs or schools that meet your needs. Then, you should expect to take some time to evaluate the schools and programs before you start school.

Many criteria affect the decisions to be made as an adult learner. Not only must schools be researched and degree goals identified, but learning styles, personal abilities, and finances must all be considered before applying to or enrolling in a program. If you make the right decision about the school, program, and timing of college in your life, you could gain profound personal satisfaction, increased earning potential, and expanded intellectual horizons. If you make the wrong choice, you will probably not succeed in finishing the program—and you may find yourself immersed in feelings of failure. Or, you may work hard and pay good money to achieve a degree from a school that lacks the faculty, reputation, or accreditation to make your expense and effort worthwhile.

We want you to succeed in meeting your college goals. The seven steps described in detail in this chapter will help you make the right choice of school. This chapter also provides checklists, guidelines, and questions to answer to help you make the right choices about a school and a degree program that is right for you.

Step 1. Reevaluate Your Reasons for Attending College

Your choice of a school starts with the reasons you want to attend college. In the College Readiness Worksheet completed in Chapter Two, you described your motivations and needs for attending college. Reevaluate these reasons now and make sure they are accurate and complete.

Most people's primary reasons for going to college fall into two main categories: either to get an education or to get a degree. The two can be quite independent. There are those who care only about the training; there are those who want only the degree; and there are those who want or need both. There are also secondary reasons that revolve around self-fulfillment, social contacts, and entertainment. After reviewing your reasons, check the boxes in the *College Selection Worksheet* that best describes your situation. The worksheet offers suggestions after each box about the type of schools and program that would best meet your needs.

Step 2. Determine Your Field of Study and Degree Goals

This step will eliminate many schools that don't offer a degree or courses in the field you are interested in pursuing. Your degree goals are a function of the previous college work you have completed. If you have no previous college credit, your first goal will be either an associate or bachelor's degree. If you already have a bachelor's degree, you may choose to get a second bachelor's degree with another major, or most likely you will want to pursue a graduate degree—either a master's or a doctorate.

Your choice of a major is based on your interests and career aspirations. For example, if you want to major in business to further your management career, a school that offers only advanced degrees in psychology is probably not one of your possibilities. Refer to the *College Readiness Worksheet* again to review your career goals and personal aspirations. These should help define the major fields of study you are interested in. We have provided a list of common majors in the back of the book to expose you to some of the possibilities. To get more information on degree options, get some college catalogs (in the library, or call schools to get theirs) and start reading about the programs.

After doing some research, most people discover that a number of majors are appropriate or of interest. For example, a major in psychology, education, or human science may all be appropriate to meet your educational goals in pursuit of a teaching or counseling career. Or a major in electrical engineering, computer science, or mathematical physics may satisfy the prerequisites required to undertake advanced engineering research. If you are interested in developing your management skills, you might choose a major in management, organizational behavior, or even social science. Again, if you're not sure of the major that will best satisfy your objectives, talk to a school counselor or pick up some career books (we've listed some in the resources section of this book).

When you have narrowed your major interests down to three or four, fill in section 2 of the *College Selection Worksheet*.

Step 3. Determine the Criteria that Are Most Important to You in Choosing a School

Before you choose a school, you should determine your preferences for educational delivery, scheduling, program flexibility, and timing. Your preferences in these areas will determine the type of program you are interested in pursuing. For example, if you want flexibility in your schedule, you may need to look into programs that offer distance-education options. If you feel that a nontraditional degree would be inappropriate to meet your career objectives, then you need to focus on traditional programs. If you need the degree quickly to meet a job goal, then you need to look into accelerated programs. If you just want to explore possibilities,

College Selection Worksheet (Part One)

Goals for Attending College	School Options

Career Development

❑ Need degree as quickly as possible — Look into accelerated programs

❑ Need real-world knowledge — Adult-oriented schools with experience-based faculty

❑ Want a career as teacher or researcher — Traditional school with traditional faculty

Social Contact

❑ With younger students — Traditional and some nontraditional schools

❑ With adults only — Adult-oriented schools

Academic Pursuits

❑ Interested in a wide range of subjects in various disciplines — Large school with wide variety of course offerings

❑ Want contact with well-known researchers in the field — Check the faculty profiles in catalogs of both traditional and nontraditional schools

Entertainment Goals

❑ Sports are important to me — Traditional state schools are your best bet

❑ I want to learn about art, music, theater — Liberal arts and specialty schools, among others

❑ I want to be able to choose from a wide variety of on-campus events and activities — Large schools

Majors

List three majors that would meet your goals:

_____

_____

_____

List schools offering these majors:

_____

_____

_____

Important Factors

The following are most important to me in my choice of school:

❑ Accreditation — Important to everyone—don't go to a school without it

❑ Flexible scheduling — Distance education programs

❑ Low cost — Community college and state schools

❑ Academic faculty with impressive publications — Check the catalogs

❑ Practitioner-based faculty — Nontraditional and adult-oriented schools

❑ Top ranked school in the field — Check with accrediting agencies and faculty

❑ Structured program without too many options to confuse me — Traditional and some adult-oriented programs

❑ Individualized program that let's me do things my own way — Alternative schools and distance education programs

College Selection Worksheet (Part Two)

Preferred Learning Style   **School Options**

❏ I am independent and I like to learn on
my own   Alternative schools or alternative programs

❏ I feel more comfortable if someone
gives me instruction on what to do   Traditional or structured alternative programs

❏ I like to combine defined direction and
independent effort when learning
new things   Some traditional and most nontraditional schools

❏ I am a procrastinator   Structured school with good advising system

❏ I prefer the support and security of
working in groups   Many adult-oriented and nontraditional schools

❏ I dislike traditional examinations   Some nontraditional schools

❏ I read a lot already   Any school—distance education program may be best

❏ I understand and prefer the traditional
model of education   Traditional schools—private or state operated

❏ I love to use computers and other
technology   Online programs

❏ I like to try new ways of learning things   Nontraditional programs

Constraints on Your Choice of School

❏ I have a fixed time limit to obtain a degree   Accelerated programs

❏ I must go part-time   Nontraditional may offer more options

❏ I can't attend regular classes   Nontraditional or distance programs

❏ I can only attend classes in the evening   Nontraditional or distance programs

❏ I can only attend on the weekend   Nontraditional or distance programs

❏ I require a school with child-care facilities   Most traditional and many nontraditional schools

❏ The school must be within commuting range   Check your phonebook under *Schools*

❏ There are no schools nearby   Consider distance education programs

❏ I need financial aid to attend a private school   Almost all schools offer something

❏ I travel a lot   Online programs or other nonresident programs

After researching schools that meet the criteria you have identified above, list the colleges that meet most of your priorities:

_____

_____

_____

then attending a local community college or state university is a viable alternative. Everyone has different priorities—that's why so many educational options are available. If everyone expected the same thing out of a college program, there would only be one kind of school—and we've already proven that there are almost as many kinds of schools as there are kinds of people.

Step 4. Determine Your Preferred Learning Style

Learning styles of adults are different from those of younger students. In general, adults tend to be more self-motivated and better organized. In widely published studies, adults have been found to be fairly pragmatic learners who emphasize the practical utility of the information learned, usually as it relates to their economic status and proficiency on the job. If you are one of these typical adult students, then you need a program rooted in real-world application and flexible enough to allow you to voice your own opinions. On the other hand, you may be someone who enjoys delving into the theoretical and academic disciplines, with little desire for practical training. The knowledge itself is reward enough for you. If this is your style, then you need a program with a more academic approach. You may be very self-motivated—in this case, an individualized program of study may be more appropriate. But if, like many people, you need the structure of schedules and exams to keep you on track, then you should choose a program with a predefined structure.

To find out what kind of learning style you prefer, answer the questions on section 4 of the College Selection Worksheet. The worksheet offers suggestions for choosing programs based on your style preferences.

Step 5. Determine the Constraints on Your Choice of Schools

All the students we interviewed had practical constraints on the schools and programs they were able to choose. The constraints were defined by lifestyle, financial, family, and timing criteria. These same criteria will likely affect your choice of a college program. For example, if you need to stay at your job full time, you will need a program that can be scheduled around your job. If you must stay in the same city (and most adults choose to do this), you need a program within commuting distance or a distance-education program. If you travel on business, you need a program, such as an online program, that you can complete while you are on the road. Fill in section 5 of the College Selection Worksheet and you'll have a pretty good idea about the things in your life that will need to be accommodated in your choice of a school.

Step 6. Identify Five Colleges That Meet Most of Your Educational Priorities

This is the step that can take some time. There are thousands of schools in the United States. Only a few of them will meet your specific criteria, however, as identified in the *College Selection Worksheet.* You will need to find and match schools and programs to your style, goals, and financial constraints. (If you don't understand your financial constraints, read Chapter Six, which describes the options you have for financing your college education.)

Your search will probably start with obtaining a catalog from the local community colleges (if you are just starting college for the first time) or a nearby state college or university (if you are pursuing a bachelor's degree or graduate degree). You should also get catalogs from the private colleges in your area—many of these you won't even know about. Look in the *Yellow Pages* under *Schools.* The *Schools* listings will be broken into various subsections, such as *Schools—Business and Secretarial, Schools—Correspondence, Schools—Industrial and Technical Trade, Schools—Adult Education,* and the listing that will probably be most relevant, *Schools—Academic, Colleges and Universities.*

If you live in a rural area, where there aren't many schools to choose from, then you need to start your search with the distance-education options and alternative schools. Even if you live in a metropolitan area, you should look into some of the adult-oriented schools that offer distance-education options. Some of the alternative and adult-oriented schools are listed in the back of this book. We have also provided the names of catalogs and other resources that can help you locate traditional and alternative schools we did not have room to include.

If you want some additional help, or don't want to spend the time researching schools on your own, there is a relatively inexpensive college search service available from Degree Consulting Services in Santa Rosa, California. For a $60 fee, the obliging people at Degree Consulting Services will help you find appropriate colleges and will give you critical assessments of their programs. We've provided more information on Degree Consulting Services in the resources section of the book.

When you're done with your search for a school, you should have five potential schools on your list that meet at least some of your criteria: relevant major, appropriate degree, delivery system you can live with, location that is feasible, etc. For comparison purposes, you should include a traditional, an adult-oriented, and a distance-education or other non-traditional option on your list. In this way you will be able to evaluate a wide variety of options and to match the right school to your preferences with more certainty.

Before you go any farther in the process, you should look objectively at the colleges on your list. Are they realistic? Are they affordable? What are your real chances of being accepted into these programs? If part of your life goal is to have a degree from one of the top schools in the nation, this is great—as long as it is realistic. If you have limited your selection to only the obvious prestige schools, reassess your reasons. There are so many excellent schools in the United States with great reputations, it seems futile to limit your choices arbitrarily. Your reasons may be valid, but in most cases, as an adult it is more important to get a degree than to get a degree from a specific school. For example, there is no sense in choosing Harvard as your only choice for a business degree if you know you only have a minute chance of being accepted. And, you may not want to move your life, job, and family to Massachusetts just to attend Harvard. (Of course, if you live down the street in Cambridge, Harvard might make a lot of sense.)

Schools such as Harvard or Stanford are very competitive and highly selective—even though the selection criteria may be considered arbitrary and inappropriate for some, especially adult students. Be aware that it is not only private universities that are selective—some state universities, including UCLA, for example, are highly sought after because of the high standards of their faculty and facilities. In fact, some of the best state schools can be more selective than the prestigious private colleges. More people try to get into these schools because of the lower tuition fees. (Remember, the private schools need the money to survive. The state schools have the tax base to fall back on.)

Don't fool yourself into believing that only the best and brightest get accepted into the competitive schools—they overlook many outstanding candidates every year, just because they have to draw the line somewhere. So if you don't get accepted to one of these schools, it shouldn't be considered an evaluation of either your intelligence, your ability, or your stature. (More on this in the next chapter.) You need to know that the "prestige" schools often accept people that shouldn't really be there, just because they look good on paper (or because a relative went there and donates considerable funds to the school each year).

Sure, go ahead and apply to Harvard or schools of similar reputation if you have adequate scores, grades, contacts, time, and money to go—but make sure you have something else on your list that will also meet your needs. (By the way, in Chapter Six we explain the ins and outs of the application and acceptance process for all types of schools. So, if you really want to go to Harvard, we'll tell you what you need to do to compete.)

Schools that are not as selective or competitive are not necessarily any less difficult. You will still get a good education and a valuable degree in other schools, so make sure your list offers options if you aren't accepted at your first-choice school.

Step 7. Evaluate and Prioritize the Schools on Your List

For each school on your list you should complete a *School Evaluation Worksheet*. To do this, you will need to evaluate the school based on the following factors:

- The school's accreditation or recognition in the outside world
- The quality of the faculty
- The quality of the learning environment and the appropriateness of the learning environment to your own learning style, constraints, and objectives
- The appropriateness of the program in meeting your educational objectives
- Access to library facilities and other information sources
- The overall quality and value of the program in relationship to the cost of the school

School Evaluation Worksheet (Part One)

School _____ Address _____

City/State/Zip _____ Phone number of Admissions (____) _____

Counselor: _____ Phone (____) _____

Department: _____ Phone (____) _____

Other Contacts:

Name   Phone

_____   _____

_____   _____

_____   _____

Requirements for Admission:

❑ Grade Point Average _____?   ❑ Transcripts   ❑ Deadline (if any) _____

❑ Exams: _____   ❑ Letters of Recommendation: Number _____

❑ Essay   ❑ Other _____

Accreditation:

Regional _____

Professional _____

Catalog Evaluation:

❑ Complete Info   ❑ Application Process   ❑ Programs Appropriate

❑ Academic Calendar   ❑ Faculty Background   ❑ Registration Process

Transfer Credit and Restrictions: ❑ Other Schools _____   ❑ Life Experience _____

                              ❑ Examination _____   ❑ Other _____

Financial Aid: ❑ Federal _____   ❑ State _____

                              ❑ Tuition Financing _____   ❑ Fellowships _____

                              ❑ Other _____

School Evaluation Worksheet (Part Two)

Support Services (if applicable):

☐ Health Insurance   ☐ Child Care   ☐ Adequate Parking   ☐ Academic Counseling

☐ Skills Development Program   ☐ Career Counseling   ☐ Computer Lab

☐ Adult Student Center   ☐ Student Lounge   ☐ Medical Center

☐ Gym or Exercise Center   ☐ On-Campus Book and Supply Store

☐ Handicapped Student Support Services   ☐ Restaurant or Cafeteria

---

School Tour

Rate: Libraries and Research Facilities   1 — 2 — 3 — 4 — 5

Rate: People Friendly and Informative   1 — 2 — 3 — 4 — 5

Rate: Counselors Knowledgeable   1 — 2 — 3 — 4 — 5

Rate: Quality of Facilities   1 — 2 — 3 — 4 — 5

Rate: Overall Impression   1 — 2 — 3 — 4 — 5

Comments on tour:

_____

_____

_____

Overall School Rating

Rate: Faculty   1 — 2 — 3 — 4 — 5

Rate: Program Meets My Needs   1 — 2 — 3 — 4 — 5

Rate: Administration   1 — 2 — 3 — 4 — 5

Rate: Cost   1 — 2 — 3 — 4 — 5
Annual tuition $ _____ Annual Fees $ _____

Rate: Facilities (if applicable)   1 — 2 — 3 — 4 — 5

Rate: Location   1 — 2 — 3 — 4 — 5

Rate: Course Delivery Method(s)   1 — 2 — 3 — 4 — 5

Rate: The School Overall   1 — 2 — 3 — 4 — 5

After completing the evaluation of each school, rank the schools on your College Selection Worksheet. Then, following the recommendations we make in the next chapter, apply to the top schools on your list.

So, that's the process. In the rest of this chapter we explain how you can evaluate the above factors so you can complete these worksheets and make a decision on the schools you want to apply to.

Determine the Accreditation and Reputation of the School

It is not titles that honor men, but men that honor titles.

—*Niccolò Machiavelli*

In almost all cases, you will want to earn a degree from a school that is accredited by one of the six regional accrediting agencies or from a school that has equivalent recognition. (For example, foreign schools must be recognized as granting degrees that are equivalent to those from accredited schools.)

While a diploma from an accredited school can be used everywhere, not all employers accept degrees from unaccredited schools. For example, almost any teaching job—from teacher in primary school to professor in a university—requires a degree from an accredited college or university. Jobs in research, engineering, and at certain picky companies require the same. Some unaccredited schools are recognized as being legitimate, and therefore a degree from one of these schools can be valid for some companies and adequate for promotion purposes as well. If you plan to use your degree for a promotion, quietly find out if the company is concerned about whether the degree is from an accredited college. Note that most companies that pay (or reimburse) college expenses require you to attend an accredited college.

Depending on your reasons for attending college, accreditation may not be very important to you. There are thousands of legal schools that are not accredited. Most of these are authorized to grant legal degrees. Some of these schools are excellent—some of them are terrible. Still, the fact remains, in spite of some arbitrary criteria in the accreditation process that tend to favor traditional institutions, that almost all employers specify a degree from an accredited institution when they are searching for new employees. Many nontraditional schools have jumped through the hoops to gain regional accreditation—so accreditation does not restrict your options too severely. In fact, accreditation provides an insurance policy of sorts that your degree will actually be worth something after you graduate.

The issue of accreditation is complex and not without controversy. Accreditation is unique to the American system of higher education. In almost every other country in the world, colleges and universities are approved to grant degrees by their governments. But in the United States, the legality of offering degrees and the accreditation of the school are two separate factors.

Accreditation in the American model is a completely voluntary process, whereby a school submits itself to evaluation by a recognized outside agency. If the school meets the criteria the agency has established, then the school is accredited. The process of accreditation (by legitimate agencies) is complex and time-consuming. Some excellent schools feel that accreditation is too restricting, and they do not apply for accreditation by the traditional agencies.

Of course, for this system to make any sense, the accrediting agencies themselves must be recognized, evaluated, and approved. Two agencies, one private and one governmental, have the responsibility for evaluating the accrediting agencies. The private agency is COPA, the Council on Postsecondary Accreditation. COPA recognizes and reviews the work of its member agencies. COPA determines the appropriateness of proposed accrediting activities, and member accrediting commissions are officially recognized in COPA's membership listing. The government agency responsible for evaluating accrediting agencies is the Accrediting Agency Evaluation Branch of the U.S. Department of Education. This agency also publishes a list of approved accrediting agencies that meet the department's criteria. For the accreditation of the school you are looking for to have validity, the agency must be recognized by one or both of these agencies.

To make the accreditation issue even more difficult to understand, there are three distinct types of accreditation and recognition you need to consider when evaluating a school:

- *Institutional accreditation.* This is by far the most important type of accreditation for colleges and universities. Six regional agencies are approved to accredit colleges in their regions. These are the Middle States Association of Colleges and Schools (MSACS), New England Association of Schools and Colleges (NEASC), North Central Association of Colleges and Schools (NCACS), Northwest Association of Schools and Colleges, Southern Association of Colleges and Schools (NASC), and Western Association of Colleges and Schools (WACS). When people ask for an accredited degree, they usually want a degree from an institution accredited by one of these six agencies. There are also six institutional accrediting bodies for business, trade and theological schools.
- *Professional accreditation.* This level of accreditation is provided by a long list of agencies for specific trade or professional areas. For example, the business department of a school might be accredited by one of these agencies although the school might not have institutional accreditation. In most cases, the criteria for professional accreditation are more stringent than for institutional accreditation. Major colleges have both institutional and additional professional accreditations. Some specialized schools will have only professional accreditation because the curriculum is too specialized to meet the requirements for institutional accreditation. We have provided a list of approved accrediting agencies for professional areas in the reference section of the book.
- *State recognition.* Most states give licenses to schools so they can legally operate in that state. The license also authorizes a school to legally offer

diplomas or degrees. Unfortunately, this recognition may or may not mean anything. For example, many states "approve" colleges. While this may mean that the school actually must meet a set of academic standards of some sort, in some states it means little more than the school applied for and received a permit to exist. This permit may be as easy to acquire as a license to operate a hot dog pushcart at the corner of 5th and Main. In other states, schools must meet some basic criteria in order to be licensed. In California, for example, there are three levels in the accreditation process. A school can be "authorized," which means it can legally offer degrees. A school can be "approved," which means the school has met some established academic criteria. This is a step half way between "authorization" and true accreditation. And, if the school wants to voluntarily submit to the accreditation process, it can apply to be accredited by WACS, if it meets the WACS standards.

In most cases it is easy to tell an accredited school from an unaccredited school because the accredited institutions are proud of the standards they maintain to become and remain accredited. They make no secret of their accreditation(s). Unfortunately, some non-accredited schools claim accreditation by saying things like, "we are an accredited institution of higher education." When a school doesn't mention the accrediting agency's name, beware. There are also a number of phony or unrecognized accreditation agencies—and being "recognized" by these agencies is like having no accreditation at all. The best thing to do if you aren't sure about the accreditation of a school is to write to the legitimate accrediting agencies. They will gladly provide you with a list of their accredited schools.

Stay away from diploma mills at all costs. You may decide you want to go to a legitimate but unaccredited school, and that is fine. But buying a degree from a diploma mill or attending a substandard institution will not gain you anything—except perhaps a pretty piece of paper to hang on the wall, and sometimes it won't even buy that. If you really want a college degree and an advanced education, you have to earn it. The self-esteem, skills, knowledge, and prestige of a college education only come with the effort and learning that go into earning the degree. There are well-publicized reports of public officials, politicians, and others coasting on the strength of a degree that years later was discovered to be fraudulently issued by a less-than-reputable college. These misrepresentations can bring down a high-flying career in a matter of days.

So, how can you recognize a diploma mill or substandard institution? Easy. In most instances the questionable schools won't have adequate facilities and won't have much for you to do to earn your degree, except send them a check and the name you want on the diploma. Or you may have to fill out a few forms and send in some kind of brief paper explaining your credentials, and voilà, you have a degree. Diploma mills take your money, print your name on a degree (if you're lucky), and then move on to another address just before the police and government regulators knock on the door. Get a copy of *Bear's Guide to Earning Non-Tradi-*

tional College Degrees (Tenspeed Press). This comprehensive guide, now in its eleventh edition, and updated regularly, contains amusing descriptions and reports of the antics of diploma mills, and lists many "colleges" you will want to stay away from if you plan to use your degree for anything more than lining the bird cage. Get a copy—it is a definitive guide on the good, the bad, and the ugly in alternative education.

Also, you should talk to businesspeople, graduates and officials of other schools to determine the reputation and overall recognition of the school you are evaluating. After establishing the legality and accreditation of the school, get a copy of the school catalog and read it—from cover to cover.

Evaluate Carefully the Information in the Catalog

The college catalog should be one of your primary resources in reviewing any school. Don't just review the promotional literature, get a complete catalog. (The catalog is sometimes called the bulletin, but be aware that the bulletin is usually not the college catalog. The college bulletin is typically a list of course schedules.) Though it doesn't hurt to review other documents as well, it is the catalog that provides the most comprehensive information for evaluating a school.

The college catalog is a contract of sorts. When there is a question or disagreement, it is the college catalog that forms the basis of arbitration. It is your responsibility to know what is in the catalog before you apply, while you attend, and prior to graduation. The catalog specifies what the school will provide and what you need to do to graduate. You should read everything in the catalog carefully—and should always ask a school official (counselor, advisor, or department chairperson) to clarify any information in the catalog you do not understand.

Beside listing the accreditations the school has been granted, the catalog should contain all the information described below—if it doesn't, find out why. When evaluating a school, you should evaluate the following information in the catalog:

- Background on the school and its mission.
- A description of the application process and acceptance criteria.
- Detailed description of the majors, courses, and requirements for graduation.
- Information on the academic calendar, including when to apply, when school starts, when school ends, etc. For non-traditional schools, there may not be a calendar—courses can be started any time—but this also should be spelled out in detail.
- Information on the faculty, including their degrees, their work backgrounds, and their areas of specialization. Most of the faculty should have master's degrees or doctorates from accredited schools.
- Description of the types of credit the college accepts toward its degrees. The catalog should be very specific about the amount and types of credit that can be transferred as partial credit toward a degree.
- Information on applying for financial aid and other sources of financial support, including grants, scholarships, and teaching assistantships.

- Information on libraries, research facilities, and other data sources. You need easy access to published information in order to finish college. The information in books and periodicals remains and should be a major component of your educational program.
- Descriptions of the support services available. For an adult student, support services in traditional schools are important considerations. For example, are there daycare facilities? Is the parking adequate? Does the school offer mail-in registration (important if you have to work during registration days). What about academic and career counseling? Tutoring services? Computer facilities? Transportation and commuting services? Adult student center or adult-student support groups? Does the school have a reentry program or continuing education programs geared toward working adults? Is there an adult-student orientation program? What about the health center and health insurance? (Health insurance is especially important if you will be giving up your job to attend school full time). Basic skills program? Personal crisis center? The best schools offer all of these support services and more. Other schools offer almost none. If you are apprehensive about your return to school, the support services are important to your success and should be an important component in your evaluation of the schools. Again, if you're not sure about the services after reading the catalog, ask someone.

Visit the School to Experience the Flavor of the Campus

If you are looking at classroom-based programs, visit the campus. Do you feel comfortable on campus? Do you fit in? Are the facilities adequate? And don't just take the school-sponsored tour. After taking the "official" tour if the school has one, walk around on your own. If you live close by, go on different days or in the evening. Talk to people in the departments. Don't be shy. Get out there and ask questions. Meet with counselors, administrators, and some of the faculty. The department chairperson in your chosen major should be willing to meet with you—but call to make an appointment first. And schedule meetings with some of the faculty as well. If the faculty aren't friendly or supportive enough to meet with you, question how friendly and supportive they will be when you are in their classes. Meeting with faculty members is especially important if you are applying to graduate school, where it is often the faculty who make the acceptance decisions for the department.

Talk to Students in the Program

In a traditional school, look for students your own age and in the same program or department. You can usually find people to talk to in the cafeteria or the bookstore. In nontraditional schools, ask for the names of students you can contact for information. If the school is not willing to provide names, you should wonder why and may want to consider another school that is more supportive.

Ask people in business or in your field of study if they have any experience with the school you are considering. Get a reading on their opinion of the quality of the school and the quality of its graduates. Ask enough people to get an overall picture. One person who has a bad experience may paint a biased picture. But if you ask many people about the school and get the same story more than once, your research has more validity. If you mostly hear negative, grumbly attitudes—beware. Even if the school passes all the other evaluation criteria, you may want to consider another school.

Special Considerations for Selecting a Graduate School

Choosing a graduate school is a bit different from choosing a program for an undergraduate degree. In addition to considering the college as a whole, including its faculty, campus, costs, scheduling, and reputation, in graduate school you have to evaluate additional faculty criteria and the research facilities. Graduate education is highly compartmentalized in traditional schools and very specialized in private institutions. Be aware that a very prestigious school may have a very weak graduate department and a smaller, lesser-known school may have outstanding departments in certain fields. The quality of the faculty in the department and the relevance of their work experience, publications record, and research records should be very important in your choice of a graduate school. Of course, the more well known and influential the department, the more selective the department will be in its choice of graduate students.

Schools with large graduate departments (meaning more faculty *and* more students) offer more opportunities to specialize than small departments. However, you may get lost in the crowd in a large graduate department in a large, traditional university. Again, remember that department size and quality of the department are not synonymous. The quality of a graduate department is evaluated only on the sum of the faculty's reputations. A few well-regarded faculty with significant publications and impressive research grants is better than a bunch of unknown, mediocre researchers—especially when you are completing a doctoral degree, where the faculty you work with has a direct influence on the prestige of your own work.

When choosing a graduate program, you will also want to ask about the available teaching assistantships or fellowships. How many are granted and how competitive are they? These programs are usually available from traditional schools but not always from alternative or adult-oriented graduate schools.

After you have evaluated the schools and ranked them, you are ready to apply to those that meet your selection criteria. We'll show you how to do that in the next chapter.

Adult College Students In Their Own Words
Mark Preston, M.B.A.

Like a lot of people in these times of profound changes throughout corporate America, I found myself facing a career transition that would determine my professional direction for many years. As I began to evaluate my professional goals and objectives for the next decade, I knew that in my chosen field, consumer products marketing, I would be competing for career advancement with people who had attained an M.B.A. degree. Without an M.B.A. my career growth would be severely restricted.

Having made the decision to pursue an M.B.A., the next step for me was to research the business school and program that would best fit my needs. I made a list of my priorities:

- Academic Excellence. In order for this education to be of any real value to me (as opposed to just a piece of paper attesting to the fact that I had passed a set of predetermined requirements) I wanted to attend a school that would challenge me academically—one that would provide a learning experience of the highest quality. I also wanted to attend a school that was dedicated to *real-world* learning, not just business theory.
- Strong Accreditation. Because I was in the process of interviewing for a job that might take me away from my home in Phoenix, there was a possibility that I wouldn't finish up my MBA degree at the same institution at which I started. My concern was to make sure that all credits would transfer to another school.
- Program Flexibility. I wanted a program that I could pursue at my own pace. Because my circumstances were likely to change during my studies, I needed a program that would let me take as many courses as possible, as quickly as possible, but would allow me to change the pace if and when conditions changed.
- International Perspective. Because today's firms face tremendous competition in an increasingly global marketplace, I felt that exposure to students from all over the world in an academic setting would help me attain a practical perspective on business practices throughout the world.
- Personalized Learning. The faculty and staff were also important in my choice of a school. The greatest possible student-teacher interaction was my goal. Professors who not only had the academic credentials, but were active in the business community also interested me since they would have the real-world experience to supplement the theoretical information in the courses.

As I evaluated various business schools in the Phoenix area, Western International University stood out as one that met the above criteria across the board. I was especially impressed with the international aspects of classroom work at WIU.

There were students and teachers from literally all over the world, who provided current, real-world, and progressive insights into business practices across a broad spectrum of cultures. It would be difficult to put a value on this type of exposure. Because most of the students at WIU were in their 30s and 40s, and had ten to twenty years of business experience already behind them, the classroom discussions, case analyses, and term papers were all grounded in real-world thinking, which made them far more valuable than discussions based solely on business theory. The backgrounds of the professors at WIU also reflected this real-world orientation, which I felt was conducive to being on the leading edge of business practices.

From my first inquiries at WIU, the staff proved to be sincere in their desire to help me not only enter the graduate program but make sure that my progress through to graduation would be smooth. I also noticed how sensitive the staff was to the varying needs of the international students. Finally, because of the flexibility of the program at WIU, I was able to finish my degree in just 14 months. I believe the concentrated format allowed me to focus my time and energies on each class, helping me get more out of the class than I might have with a traditional format. At WIU, one class builds on another. By the time I finished, the natural progression of courses left me totally prepared to take my comprehensive exam, and I was ready to conquer the business world.

Chapter Five

The College Application Process for Adult Students

Even after selecting a prospective school and program and figuring out how to finance your education, there is no guarantee of acceptance at your first-choice college. Though some programs and schools accept almost anyone, other schools are more choosy. And, for access to most graduate degrees, as well as some undergraduate degrees, admission is required by the department *as well as* the school.

This chapter provides advice for adults who want to gain admission to any type of school, including the more selective institutions. It offers guidelines for completing the application, writing the application essay, getting letters of reference, handling the interview (if required), and taking entrance tests. The chapter also explains how to make and use political allies within college departments to optimize admission chances at colleges with more applicants than openings.

Planning Ahead for Application and Admission Schedules

The easiest schools to get into are community colleges. They rarely require more paperwork than is required to apply for a driver's license, and you can usually apply and get accepted at the same time you are registering for classes. The only exception is getting into computer science, engineering, and special programs that require prerequisite coursework or are traditionally overloaded with students.

Most other colleges and universities require a time-consuming and sometimes complicated admission procedure. Depending on the school you are applying to, admission to an undergraduate program may take as much as two to eight months for the wheels of bureaucracy to come to an admissions decision. For entrance to graduate school, this process can take even longer, particularly at "prestige" colleges.

For that reason, you should apply as early as possible for the best chance of timely admission. At some colleges, early applicants get priority over later applicants in "impacted" (too many applicants) programs. A call to the school's admissions department will tell you how early they accept applications for the semester or quarter you want to be admitted to. Use this information to get your application and other relevant paperwork to the Office of Admissions the first day they accept it. Hand carry your paperwork if necessary to ensure it arrives neither too early nor too late. Alternately, send it using an overnight delivery service such as Federal Express or UPS. These services guarantee delivery dates if you use their next-day or second-day service.

If you are applying for financial aid, you should make a point of applying early as well—even to programs with wide-open enrollment. Since this process often takes even longer then your acceptance into the college, you want to start the ball rolling as early as possible to give yourself the best change of getting both accepted and awarded money to finance your education.

Completing an application and gathering the requisite paperwork is about as complicated and time-consuming at most colleges as applying for a new home mortgage. To complete your application in a timely manner, also make sure the results of required tests and transcripts from other colleges arrive as quickly as possible. Some colleges, will initially accept a photocopy of these items presented with your application. Then, to formally complete your application, have sealed copies sent to verify the photocopies. Transcripts and admission exams are discussed later in this chapter.

Apply Early

At schools short on students, it is possible to get admitted as late as the first week of school, if you're willing to handle the flurry of paperwork. Avoid this last-minute approach at selective schools, because it significantly reduces your chances of being admitted and all but wipes out the prospect of receiving financial aid for the first semester. When applying to a school you need to be aware of the school's calendar, it is the school's calendar that will determine when you should start the application process.

Academic Calendar Options

There is no uniform pattern to the calendar (also called the "school year" and "academic year") from one school to the next. However, most schools follow one of five basic patterns. You need to be aware of your target school's calendar so you can apply at the right time. Adult-oriented or distance education programs may have calendars completely unlike those of any other college. You may plan on starting in the fall, but find out too late that the college's calendar starts on an apparently arbitrary date in early June. Here are the common school calendars:

1. *The Semester Plan.* A semester is usually 5 to 18 weeks long and there are typically two semesters per year, plus a shorter summer session. Many classes are one semester long, while others will last two semesters or longer (e.g., Chemistry I in the fall semester and Chemistry II in the spring). A class that meets three hours a week for one semester is likely to be worth 3 semester hours (or units) of credit. Depending on the amount of homework, additional reading, laboratory time, etc., the actual amount of credit could be anywhere from 1 to 6 semester hours for such a class.

2. *The Quarter Plan*. Many universities divide the year into four quarters of equal length, usually 11 or 12 weeks. Many courses require two or more quarters to complete. A course that meets three hours a week for a quarter will probably be worth 3 quarter hours or quarter units, with a range of 2 to 6. One semester unit is equal to 1½ quarter units.
3. *The Trimester Plan*. A small number of schools divide the year into three equal trimesters of 15 or 16 weeks each. A trimester unit is usually equal to 1¼ semester units.
4. *The Monthly Calendar*. A model popularized by National University, the University of Phoenix, and other alternative schools is that of one course per month. Students can start school in any month—and as a result applications may be submitted at any time.
5. *The All-Year Plan*. Some distance-education programs have no official semesters or other breaks in the academic action. Many non-resident programs have no calendar either. Students can begin on their independent study program as soon as they have been admitted. You simply choose classes and work at them until you finish. A single class must be completed in a specified period, often established through a learning contract. With distance education, a college can be highly flexible in scheduling because the instructors do not need to maintain regular hours or hold formal classes at a pre-specified time.

Some Schools Are Easier to Get into Than Others

You have probably overheard people talking about the difficulty of getting into certain schools. This is true—there are colleges that take fewer than ten percent of their applicants. Usually a school that can afford to be very choosy about its applicants receives far more applications than can be accommodated. To make the selection process easier, the college looks for applicants with the highest grades and the best scores on admissions tests. For really picky schools, entrance exams, personal interviews, and an essay may be added to the usual list of procedures.

Other kinds of limiting factors may be at work as well. At many colleges, while humanities departments may have unfilled openings for students, computer science and engineering may be hopelessly jammed with far more applicants than they can admit.

Graduate work requires superior scholastic abilities compared to undergraduate classes within the same major. Many graduate programs are also relatively unstructured, even in traditional schools. For a student who has not demonstrated exceptional tenacity in his or her undergraduate work, this lack of structure may lead to a lack of productivity. So graduate departments look for self-starters with obviously exceptional academic skills.

A Special Note: If you are applying to a non-traditional education program that requires almost no paperwork and provides fast or instant admission, check the program's accreditation before signing up or paying tuition. You may be applying to a fly-by-night school, or one where your hard-earned degree won't be recognized by your employer or accepted for credit by legitimate colleges and universities.

Should You Apply to More Than One School?

The answer to this question depends entirely on your plans for attending college. Unless you plan to apply to distance-education programs, it also depends on the number of colleges and universities within commuting distance of your home and place of work. If you have one school in mind that takes almost all applicants with the right credentials, then applying early to only that one school practically guarantees your admission. If, however, admission is risky at your college of first choice, consider applying to two or more colleges to improve your odds of getting accepted. The only exception is a state college system that specifically prohibits application to more than one school within the system. This rule still allows you to apply to one of these schools and colleges outside the system at the same time.

The Application Process

The application process varies from college to college, but at most schools it follows a series of steps, although the internal mechanics of the Office of Admissions may be largely invisible to you, the applicant. The steps are as follows:

1. You choose the college you want to apply to and request an admission application. (Many colleges now accept a standardized application as well as their own. You can buy these applications at many bookstores.) You should schedule any standardized tests at this point and take them as soon as possible so the scores can be forwarded to the college as soon as possible. These tests are explained later in this chapter.
2. You fill out the application. This can be a long process at many colleges because the application requires details of many factors including previous college work, work history, financial aid requirements, and even, for state institutions, your residency status.
3a. You submit the application along with an application fee. This fee may be waived for indigent applicants at some schools; check with the Admission Department for details. If the school requires an entrance essay, it usually accompanies the application.
3b. (Optional) You may need to apply for separate admission to the department you plan to major in. The requirements for departmental admission (if required) vary from department to department. Applicants to graduate programs may have significant work ahead of them to gain admission to the department they choose. Submissions of scientific papers, completion of multiple interviews, and even presentations before the faculty are among the things that could be asked for in a departmental application.

4. You submit transcripts, letters of recommendation, a writing sample or essay, and the results of entrance exams. You may need to pay the college or testing agency a nominal fee to mail sealed copies to the school you are applying to. (Never send photocopies of transcripts—you must have official copies sent directly by the school or testing agency.)

5a. The Office of Admissions builds a file around all of the submitted information and evaluates your suitability for admission and whether you are a resident or nonresident for tuition changes. Financial aid information, if included with the application, is submitted to the Financial Aid Department for separate processing. Within the Office of Admission, a document is added to your file that tracks all required information and when it was submitted. Files missing components are usually not processed further until all items required are obtained, although photocopied transcripts may be adequate for conditional admission until the sealed ones arrive. Most colleges notify you of missing information so that you can rectify the matter before admission closes for your intended start date.

5b. (Optional) An interview or personal presentation is scheduled by the school. Not all schools require a personal meeting, but many do. If an interview is required, it is held sometime between receipt of your application and the end of the acceptance period. At many colleges, if you fail to achieve the paper qualification with adequate grades and test scores, no interview will be held. At most non-traditional schools some sort of meeting or preliminary personal evaluation is scheduled to verify your suitability for the rigors of independent study.

6. A Dean of Admissions or other senior person within the department or the college studies your file and accepts or rejects you based on the information within the file. In a few cases, especially in graduate schools, there will be a meeting of an acceptance committee or other team that reviews the applications and makes the final decisions.

Transcripts

In addition to the application form, your transcripts of previous college work are one of the most important components of your application to any school. A transcript is, quite simply, the official, detailed record of all work one has done at a given school. Typically, a transcript is a typewritten (or, more common nowadays, computer-printed) sheet of paper listing in columns all the courses taken, when they were taken, and the grade received. The overall G.P.A. (grade point average) is calculated as of the end of each semester or quarter—if the school uses a number-oriented grading system. (More on that later.)

Nearly all non-traditional schools and programs issue transcripts as well. Sometimes they try to make the transcripts look as traditional as possible, listing, for example, flying experience as "Aviation 100, 4 units," "Aviation 101, 3 units," etc. Other programs offer a narrative transcript, in which the procedures used by the school in evaluating the experience are described.

The original copy of the transcript is always kept by the school. Official copies, bearing the raised seal of the school, can be made for the student, other schools, or employers, at the student's request.

Unfortunately, there is a great deal of traffic in forged transcripts. Sometimes students change grades to improve the G.P.A., or add entire classes. Of course such changes would normally be on the copy only. For this reason, most schools and many employers accept only transcripts sent directly from the office of the registrar of the university. Unfortunately, several scandals in the late 1980's involving tampering with a university's computer, either by hackers having fun or by dishonest employees for a price, raise questions on the validity of any university-produced document.

Grading and Evaluation Systems Used in College and on Transcripts

Most schools, traditional and nontraditional, make use of one of four grading systems. Grades are generally given for each separate course taken. Some schools assign grades to equivalency examinations, learning contract work, and correspondence courses. Life experience credit is rarely graded, but rather is assigned a certain number of units, without further evaluation.

Four common grading systems in use are:

1. *Letter Grades.* This is by far the most accepted grading system. An *A* is the highest grade, *B* means "good," *C* means "average," *D* stands for "barely passing" (or in some cases, "failing"). Some schools use pluses and minuses, so that a *B+* is better than a *B*, but not quite as good as an *A-*.

2. *Number Grades.* Many schools use a system in which students are graded on a scale of zero (worst grade) to 4 (highest grade). The best students get 3.9 or 4.0. Other outstanding students might get 3.7 or 3.8. Average students get grades between 2.0 and 3.0.

3. *Percentage Grades.* A small number of schools follow the European system and grade each student in each class on a percentage score, from 0% to 100%. In most (but not all) schools, a grade of 90% to 100% is considered excellent, 80% to 90% is good, 70% to 80% is fair, 60% to 70% is either failure or barely passing, and below 60% is failing.

4. *Pass/Fail System.* Quite a few universities have a pass/fail option, either for some classes or, more rarely, for all classes. In such a system, there is no specific evaluation of a student's performance—only the faculty's determination that the student has either passed or failed the course. At many schools using this system, a student is given the chance to choose a pass/fail option for one or two out of the four or five courses taken during a given semester or quarter. In this way, a difficult course can be taken without the risk of lowering the overall grade point average.

5. *Narrative Evaluation System.* In some non-traditional schools the pass/fail system may be combined with a narrative review system that provides detailed information on the student's progress and performance. This system may combine comments from the student as well as from instructors and advisors.

The Grade Point Average on Your Transcripts

Your grade point average is an important part of the information on your transcript. Most schools report a student's overall performance in terms of the Grade Point Average (G.P.A.). This is the average of all grades received, weighted by the number of semester or quarter units each course is worth. For example, if a student gets a 4.0 (or an *A*) in a course worth 3 semester units and a 3.0 (or *B*) in a course worth 2 semester units, his or her G.P.A. would be calculated like this: 3 x 4.0 = 12, and 2 x 3.0 = 6. Then 12 + 6 = 18, which, divided by a total of 5 semester units, results in a G.P.A. of 3.6. Pass/Fail courses are generally not taken into account in calculating a grade point average.

G.P.A.'s can be very important. Often it is necessary to maintain a certain average in order to earn a degree—typically a 2.0 (in a 4-point system) for a bachelor's degree, and a 3.0 for a master's degree or a doctorate. Honors degrees (*magna cum laude,* etc.), scholarships, and even permission to play on the football team are dependent on the G.P.A.

Entrance Examinations

Most programs at traditional colleges require you to take an exam or series of exams so that your scores can be used to judge your ability to successfully complete the program. Many people (including us) feel that these tests are simply a measurement of how much studying was done in core classes in high school or college. These tests may actually discourage *really* intelligent students who were bored in high school or in comparatively dull core college classes, but many schools still use them. Scores on most standardized tests can be manipulated by attending special (and sometimes expensive) preparation programs or reading one of hundreds of exam preparation guides that teach students how to get better scores on the tests. Even if you don't believe the courses or preparation manuals will improve your scores, they will help you become familiar with the exams, and this can reduce test anxiety.

For a variety of reasons, some schools have stopped using standard tests as admission criteria, and almost all colleges use the scores as only one part of their admission criteria. Some colleges have also developed their own (sometimes more relevant) tests as an alternative to the standardized examinations.

Basically the standardized examinations break into two groups: undergraduate exams and graduate exams.

Undergraduate Exams

The most popular undergraduate exam is the SAT (Scholastic Aptitude Test), with the ACT (American College Testing) running second in popularity. These tests consist primarily of multiple choice questions that attempt to quantify the depth of your verbal and mathematical capabilities. Some colleges accept scores submitted from only one of these tests. Other colleges accept scores from either. In addition to the basic SAT or ACT, there are also Achievement Exams that specifically test your abilities in natural sciences, math, English usage, social studies, and other subjects. Depending on the college and department within the college you are applying to, one or more of these achievement tests may be required in addition to the regular SAT or ACT exam.

In addition to these tests is one used for non-native English speakers, the TOEFOL exam. This is used to quantify English language ability because students lacking in English skills have a difficult time making it through an American college. Students who perform poorly on this test must study English before starting college or take remedial English classes within the college before taking regular classes.

Graduate Exams

There are a number of standardized graduate exams. The first is the formidable GRE (Graduate Record Examination). The GRE is like an SAT exam on steroids. Designed as a general indicator of prospective success in graduate school, this exam tests core areas of knowledge across a broad range of topics. But like the SAT, it is primarily concerned with verbal and mathematical abilities. You'll also come into contact with exams like the Miller Analogies Test and subject-area versions of the GRE.

The second kind of test is used to judge your suitability for entrance into a specific program, such as business, law, or medicine. The GMAT (Graduate Management Admissions Test) is used by business schools and the LSAT (Law School Admissions Test) is used by law schools. These tests may evaluate your knowledge in the undergraduate core classes required as the basis of a graduate program and/or incorporate general aptitude evaluations, similar to the GRE. For example, would-be medical students who take the MCAT (Medical College Admissions Test) are evaluated on their knowledge and understanding of biology and chemistry—as well as their ability to read and comprehend.

Getting the Most from a Standardized Test

While there is considerable argument as to how much attendance at a test preparation school or practice in a workbook improves performance on standardized tests, practicing for one of these exams is bound to improve your score at least slightly. On the SAT, where a total score of 1600 is possible, scoring 1205 after studying is better than scoring 1190, because the small increase in points puts you in a higher category at most colleges.

In addition to expensive prep programs and the bulky practice books available from bookstores, the range of practice aids also includes computer programs that interactively take you through exam questions. This helps train your thinking to better respond to the kind of questions used and the best ways to choose your answers.

You can also practice on the real thing as well. You can take many of these exams more than once. Unfortunately, the testing agency forwards *all* of your scores to the college. Various colleges use your highest, lowest, or average scores as your actual score. Check with admissions officials to see how they handle multiple score submissions. It may work in your favor, or it may not. However, you can take the test for practice, and if you call the testing agency within the next day, the exam will not be scored at all and will not go on your record.

Unfortunately, you don't want to improve your scores too much. As reported by *The Wall Street Journal*, one high school student improved his scores through a preparation program beyond the amount the testing agency claims is credible. As a result the agency refused to accept his scores and accused him of having a stand-in take the test even though witnesses who personally knew him clearly remembered that he had been there that morning, taking the test.

Other Entrance Exams

Instead of using standard exams such as the SAT or GRE, a few colleges and universities have their own entrance exams, which they create and administer. Because these tests vary as much as the different kinds of college programs available, there's little specific we can tell you about them. Check with the school's catalog or Office of Admissions for more information. Some colleges provide a sample test complete with answers so you will have a better understanding of how to prepare for it. In addition, departmental exams may be required, especially for graduate students. Majors in the arts, cinematography, or graphic design require a review of an applicant's portfolio containing samples of past work.

A second kind of test common in colleges and universities tests your writing, math, or foreign language skills (sometimes all three). This test is usually administered after acceptance but before you register. Should your score on the English test not meet minimum requirements, you'll be placed in a remedial English class known as "bonehead English" to make up your inadequacies before continuing with the normal program.

The GED (High School Equivalency) Test

In most cases, you will not be required to have a high school diploma to enter college as an adult. Some schools consider adults over 25 or 30 exempt from the high school diploma requirements—and if you already have college units completed, you probably don't have to worry about your high school records.

But there are a few schools that do require everyone to provide the equivalent of a high school diploma before they can be admitted. The GED (general equivalency diploma) is a mechanism for getting a diploma equivalent to the one high school seniors receive when they graduate. If you failed to finish (or even start) high school, there is a GED program in every city that allows you to take a comfortable class load and pass the GED exam to earn the equivalent of a high school diploma. If you must have GED equivalency to get into your chosen school, the best way to take advantage of the GED examination program is to take a three-week-long crash course at night and then test out.

If you don't think that you can successfully test out (get one of the GED exam preparation books to see if you feel comfortable with the material), instead of wasting time on getting a high school diploma, you might be better off starting out at a community college that accepts older students without a diploma. Then when you have completed 15 units or more of community college work, transfer to a four-year college, skipping the high school diploma completely. If you choose the GED route, it will take time to complete, time that could be more productively put toward a college degree. And the regular GED classes are usually just as dull as those you remember from high school. Only the presence of other adults makes the proceedings somewhat interesting.

How to Handle the Application Procedures

As with many elements in life, it's not how you do something but also how you look doing it. This is especially true when applying to college and when applying for acceptance into your major. Everything that you supply to the college is carefully reviewed by someone. For that reason, you want to make all your materials look competently completed and provide a good impression in person should an interview be required for admission. You must also remember that most if not all of these reviewers have never met you. They know you only through the materials you submit for their evaluation.

How to Make Your Application Materials Look Professional

Your college application requires careful effort on your part to make it look like it came from a person who is not only meticulous but really wants to be accepted into the college. Fortunately, as a mature student, you probably have far more experience filling out forms and applications than the average recent high school graduate applying to college for the first time. To make your application look its best, get *two* copies of the form and fill out the first one, crossing out errors and rephrasing answers to questions as you go.

Once you are satisfied with the information and have made sure you have answered all the questions, type the answers neatly on the *second* form and use it to apply. Always type all forms, and if you must submit supplementary material such as an essay, either type it or print it out by computer, using a laser or daisy-wheel printer on high-quality white paper. If the essay originates on your word processor, avoid printing it with a dot matrix printer on cheap, tractor-fed papers. The person reviewing your materials may subconsciously knock a few points off your essay if it is hard to read or looks unprofessional.

Here are a few rules for application materials:

■ Make sure that all boxes are completed. Irrelevant ones should have

"N/A" entered in them for "Not Applicable."

■ Never submit false grade point averages, test scores, credits accumulated from other colleges, or financial information used by the college for financial aid eligibility. All of these facts are verified by the college sooner or later, and even minor discrepancies may be grounds to refuse you admission. False financial aid information may require that you pay back any financial aid you receive and in extreme cases may be grounds for criminal action.

■ Never fail to list a college you attended because you received poor grades there. While it may be possible to lose a lousy grade from a single class taken at an obscure college, your transcripts and records are cross-referenced by all colleges that send them. This information is passed on to other colleges every time you request transcripts. Instead, if you dropped out of a program, or the results were embarrassing, it's best to try to provide a convincing written explanation why you were forced to quit the program. This tactic in the form of a carefully worded letter is particularly useful when applying for acceptance to a degree program within a department.

■ Carefully proofread all application materials. If your proofreading (or writing skills) leave something to be desired, have someone else help you with the application. Typos in application materials make you look at best sloppy and at worst illiterate. Don't rely solely on the spelling and grammar checkers available in most word processors to find errors. Most of these programs can't so much as tell the difference between and correct usage of *there, their*, and *they're*.

■ Know when materials are due and get them in as early as possible before the deadline. Most colleges, already busy with many applications, refuse applications for admission or financial aid made after the filing deadline. If you blow the date, it means waiting until the next semester or academic year for admission.

■ Keep photocopies of everything in case a question comes up.

■ You may want to supply a resume in addition to the standard application materials at some schools or for admission to a graduate degree program, and most adult-oriented programs require one. If you do, create a new resume that emphasizes your abilities and past education rather than sending them one you assembled five years ago for another purpose. Unless it's required, don't send a resume if it doesn't add value to your presentation. Admission counselors won't be favorably impressed if your work history consists solely of several stints waitressing or mopping floors.

■ Carefully check the application requirements to ensure you have supplied *everything*. Just one missing form can bring the whole admissions process to a grinding halt.

Handling Application Essays

This is one of the tougher points in completing an application. Essays may be a requirement either for the general college application or as part of a departmental application for admission into a degree program. Essays have become an increasingly important component of most college applications as colleges have began moving away from simple grade point averages and standardized test scores as the sole criteria for admitting applicants. Instead the essay is regarded as a key test of writing ability—a talent very important to completing a college degree successfully. And an essay required for admittance to a graduate program may be the most important part of your application.

If an essay is required for simple admission into the school, study carefully the instructions and sample essay provided with the application. If no sample is provided or you feel left in the dark, visit the college and discuss the requirement with someone in the Office of Admissions to get a better idea of what they are looking for. A really helpful employee may show you a sample essay written by someone who gained admission to the school.

When writing an essay, do the following:

- If you are allowed to choose your own topic, avoid stiff topics such as great philosophers, painters of the Renaissance, or important works of English literature unless you really know what you're talking about. Remember, the admissions people are looking for writing ability, not a demonstration that you don't need college because you already know everything there is to know. Also avoid sensitive topics such as religion and sex, and be careful of very personal topics or explanations of why you want to go to college. This last overused topic sounds to an admissions officer like begging for admission.

- Make your writing clear and crisp and avoid stuffy or overly academic vocabulary. Don't use a thesaurus to choose your words because you may pick a complex but impressive sounding word and then use it incorrectly. Humor can be used to enliven your essay, but be very careful because what's hilarious to you may be offensive, trite, or just plain dumb to someone else.

- Have your essay reviewed by someone who can write. That person may have important pointers that turn a poor piece of writing into an essay that will get you into college. If you work in a fair-sized company, there may be accomplished writers working in the department that handles advertising and PR. Avoid relying on technical or instruction-manual writers unless you want only a check of sentence mechanics.

- Research the topic before writing about it. Unless your essay is *What I Did over Summer Vacation* (a topic not recommended unless you are applying for admission to high school instead of college), research the idea to get background on it as professional writers do. This makes writing easier and creates a more interesting essay. Head for a well-stocked library before sitting down at the word processor or typewriter and check out books that will help or photocopy relevant articles.

- Keep the essay to the length requested or the space provided on the application. Busy admission people prefer to give essays a quick read. Unfortunately, one of the most difficult tasks for the inexperienced writer is saying something clearly while keeping the essay short.

■ Have the essay proofread by a competent proofreader. Keep in mind that the same person who advised you on your writing may not be a good proofreader as well. Very creative writers are often horrendous proofreaders.

Departmental Essays

Along with an essay required for general admission to the college, some undergraduate and most graduate departments require written responses to essay-style questions. Many also require a formal essay on the topic of study to gauge your level of knowledge and depth of understanding before admission.

These essays require more brainpower than general admissions essays because the professors in the department review your writing. They are not looking only for concise prose but also for a grasp of the subject matter appropriate for a student entering the program. Careful research and writing is vital to creating a strong departmental essay.

If you have your doubts about the integrity and persuasiveness of your essay, run it by a sympathetic instructor (maybe one at another school) and take his or her comments to heart.

Handling the Interview and Dealing with Objections

If you must be interviewed as part of the admissions proceeding, this is sweaty palms territory. An interview may be handled by only one or two people either in person or on the phone. Or it may happen in front of as many as four to eight members of a committee. Get ready for the interview by practicing answers to questions such as, "Why do you want to go back to school? You already have a successful career." or, "What do you plan to use this degree for?" or, "What do you know about our program?" Generate a list of difficult questions and then have a family member ask them of you to give you an opportunity to practice answering. Practice several times over a period of weeks to help build your abilities. This activity also helps you think up useful answers that can be used at the interview.

On the day of the interview, dress appropriately without resorting to flashy or obviously expensive clothes and jewelry. (Few admissions people make more than $40,000 per year and many make far less, so your $1,000 suit or four-carat diamond ring may intimidate them.) The kind of garb worn in most offices is about right to wear to your interview. If, however, you are applying to a fashion design program, dress like the faculty in the department, and eschew standard business dress at all costs.

Show up on time. Get there early and hang around, just to be on the safe side. The interviewer or committee may have a busload of prospective students to interview. If you're late, you may blow the interview without so much as opening your mouth.

During the interview, if a difficult question is posed, it's perfectly okay to ponder your answer briefly. A well-thought-out answer after a brief wait is far superior to a glib answer that lacks forethought or that sounds stupid. Never apologize for being nervous, because the interviewers expect that you will be.

Use the think-first-before-answering tactic to deal with the objections. If told that you don't need the degree you plan to work for, explain calmly why you *do* need it and why it's *very* important to you. Make responses to objections clear and succinct. Not all interviewers are serious about their objections; instead they may really be testing your determination. Here are a few suggestions for dealing with interviews:

- Read up on the school and the program you plan to enter. Know why you want to attend this specific school. Interviewers assume that you know something about their program. Otherwise, why would you want to attend? If the interview is for admission into a department, use your spare time to bone up on the current literature on the subject. To do this right, ask for a copy of the department's reading list several months before the interview for suggestions on what to read.
- Skip humorous or sarcastic answers.
- Take the proceeding very seriously, just as you would a job interview.
- Don't ramble. Keep your answers as short as possible unless someone asks you to elaborate on a point. Also avoid curt yes/no answers wherever possible, and never let yourself appear or sound angry in the unlikely event that a question sounds intimidating or insulting.
- Try to look enthusiastic and excited about attending the college. Look at the person asking the question and then spread your gaze among individual members of the group. If you are really nervous about the interview, pick up a book or two on public speaking. Most public libraries are jammed with titles on this topic.
- Keep in mind that you will do fine. Depending on the program, many of the day's interviewees were probably immature high school students with little interviewing panache. Their ineptness will make you look like the seasoned professional that you already are.
- Don't discuss your job extensively unless asked to by the interviewers. Many academics are secretly uncomfortable with the business and corporate world. If your job is extremely senior or sought after or obviously pays very well, tone it down when explaining what you do.
- Avoid questioning your questioners unless you don't understand what they are looking for in a question. Let the interviewers control the procedure and the time. Also let them tell you when they are done instead of watching the clock or your watch.
- When the interview is done, thank the group for its time and calmly walk out. *Never* ask how you did. If the interview is conducted by a group, they won't even know until they compare notes after you leave.

Graduate Interviews

Graduate interviews are fairly standard for admission into an advanced degree program. More than just a personality contest, a graduate interview is also a test to see what you know, how deep your interest is within the major, and whether you are pliable enough to be further shaped as a student.

These kind of interviews may be either formal and held in front of several faculty members, or they may be casual one-on-one meetings held over coffee at the Student Union. For distance-education programs, the interview may take the form of a long-distance telephone conference call.

To make these interviews work, follow most of the suggestions above, but ask in-depth questions to get a feeling for what the program is really about and to let the interviewers know that you know the right questions to ask. You may want to project a particular academic point of view by making the faculty aware of your specific interest in studying or what your primary focus in the field has been. Make a pitch for the kind of work you want to do and solicit interest from the faculty and support for your intent.

Unlike an undergraduate interview, which is used simply to gain admission, a graduate interview is more of a two-way street. The faculty should be interested in you, and you should be interested in them and the kind of academic work they do. In a very academic college (or program), if no obvious or at least tentative match is found within a department for the kind of work you want to pursue, then this may be the wrong school for your pursuits. A bad match of graduate school and student often results in the student dropping out without completing a degree. (The authors have some personal experience with this.) It may also result in a degree program that takes seven years to complete because no one shows any interest in or supports your work.

Letters of Recommendation—Who, Why, Where, and When

One of the most ignored parts of college applications is the requirement for two or three letters of recommendation. It's easy to assume, since you never hear about these letters after they're delivered to the college, that they went into a black hole in the Office of Admissions after someone checked the box on your file showing that they had been received. Unfortunately, these letters can be important to admission, especially at a crowded college or in an impacted program. While it's true that today you can gain access to the letters one way or another because your college file is yours to review, in a tight program, good letters (coupled with good grades, scores, and essays) may tip the balance in your favor over a student with less than enthusiastic recommendations.

There are two facets to letters of recommendation: What the letters say and, more important, who wrote them. Where a three line-letter from Jane Goodall almost guarantees admission to a department involved with primate studies (regardless of your grades and essay), a glowing tribute from your mother, no matter how positive, will do little to help you get into a school. In fact, it may keep you out.

A good letter of recommendation talks very positively about you and may mention one or two of your accomplishments. It may also contain one slightly negative point and explain how you have since worked hard to get around it. What actually goes into a letter of recommendation varies widely. To get the best results, carefully choose someone who knows you fairly well, likes you, and has some standing in the community. It helps if this person is someone such as a past professor or boss who writes letters of recommendation regularly and knows what to put in one. Bland but positive letters are next to useless. The letter writers should also have adequate writing skills. Otherwise, a laughably incompetent letter may make you appear to lack judgment as well as educated acquaintances.

To get someone to write a letter, explain what you need and why and make it easy for the writer by providing a long lead time. State the date when the letter must be at the college. Discuss the kinds of topics you want addressed in the letter, but don't dictate or be demanding about what you want. Provide a stamped, addressed envelope to make the process easier for your letter writer. To reduce the possibility that someone will write a less than persuasive letter and to save prospective letter writers for other occasions, have only the number of letters required by the school submitted. Extra letters add little to your case for admission.

Here are suggestions for people who make credible letter writers:

- Past instructors and college officials who know you. These can be from any college or university
- People with titles in government
- Politicians at almost any level of government
- Senior managers in your company or in other companies
- Your boss
- Important people in your field of study
- Community leaders
- Celebrities (preferably ones who are well-known and respected for their brains as much as their looks)

Avoid letters from this list at all costs:

- Your parents, no matter how important their position
- Your priest or pastor, unless you plan to attend a Bible college
- Other relatives unless a cousin, aunt, or uncle fits into one of the above categories. It helps if the last name is different from yours.
- Your doctor
- Your psychologist
- Your parole officer
- Remote people such as high school teachers whom you haven't seen in twenty years and who know nothing about what you've done since tenth grade algebra
- People you hardly know

■ Anyone who may secretly write a negative letter (a rare occurrence, but it happens)

About a week before the letters are due at school, send all letter writers a thank-you note for their help. People who have sent your letter will appreciate the gesture. Also, the people who forgot all about the letter will get on it ASAP when they receive your thank-you note.

Making Contact with the School

If you are pursuing an undergraduate or graduate degree in a selective or impacted program, you should take your application efforts one step further—become known and respected around the department before applying. Once a large number of the faculty know your name and like you and your work, they will respond more positively to your name during a vote on whom to admit and whom to reject. Handled properly, this may give you a measurable advantage over students with better grades who are still unknown quantities to the department. Here's several ways to build awareness of your worthiness for admission into a overcrowded departmental program:

■ Be an enthusiastic and hard-working undergraduate in the department and then apply for graduate status. At most colleges, unless your grade point average is under a B (the lower limit for accepting grad students at most schools), the admission process will be easier.

■ Take classes in the department if possible to get to know the faculty and help individual faculty members get to know and like you. Volunteer for jobs and assignments that make you visible in the department. Volunteer to help out faculty members with their pet projects if possible.

■ Chat with faculty members about their research or other academic projects whenever possible, but don't overdo it. You don't want to look like you have a brown nose.

■ Have a good reason why you *must* have a shot at an advanced degree that makes sense to the faculty.

What Is the School Looking for in an Applicant?

When you are competing for a one-in-a-hundred spot in a department swarming with worthy applicants, you will be faced with supplemental admission materials including essays, lengthy questionnaires, and possibly additional testing. These extra materials are used to give decision makers more specific information on each applicant in order to choose the best candidates. Instead of wrapping up the admission materials quickly, take the time to understand what the department is looking for in its applicants so that you can tell them what they want to hear—both in writing and in person.

The best way to do this is to schedule a series of informal meetings for "advice" from faculty members. Most faculty members who aren't snowed under with students and research like being asked their opinions, and they will give you their "take" on what the department is looking for in applicants. After talking to several professors, you will begin to get a picture of how to tailor your application to match the wants of the department. This gives you a significant advantage over someone else who completes the materials without first identifying the department's hot buttons.

Other Application Options for Adult Students

If the application procedure sounds like a rough road to travel, depending on your age, life experience, and the college of choice, there may be a Mature Student Policy to make things a little easier. While these vary from school to school, the underlying idea is that older students should be able to qualify to go to college regardless of past school experience or grades. At schools that offer Mature Student programs, they are your *Get Out of Jail Free* card for avoiding tests and a number of other hassles. (The age criterion varies from 50 to 60 to be eligible for the Mature Student privileges at most schools.) Check with your prospective college to see if it has such a program and what the admission criteria are.

Your Options If You Don't Get Accepted the First Time

If at first you don't succeed . . . If you get rejected by all the colleges you applied to there may be several factors at work that are individually or collectively sinking your chances of admission. These include:

- Applying to colleges or college programs that half the world wants to attend. Examples include the computer science program at the University of California at Berkeley or Harvard's prestigious Business School.
- Applying for an advanced program without the right credentials. If you have an undergraduate degree in music and apply to a master's program in Mathematics, the school will likely take your application, materials, and application fee, and then automatically send you a rejection letter at the end of the admissions period.
- Applying with low test scores or a poor grade point average from another program. The way around this is to improve your scores or to take some additional courses to raise your G.P.A.
- Providing a poor image based on application information or really blowing an interview. Apply again the next year—and don't blow it.
- Appearing on paper that you have little chance of finishing the program because you won't have enough extra time for college. Don't exaggerate the difficulties of your working life or pretend on the application that you will be 100 percent dedicated to school.
- If a faculty member or administrator explains you were not accepted to a

public college because of your age, you may have legal remedies available to help you out. Before embarking on a lengthy and certainly choppy legal battle, take the comments verbatim to the department chair, and then to the dean who oversees the department. If neither of these people can help, the college may have an ombudsman's office that you should contact immediately. Tell your story there succinctly and calmly. Put as many people on your side as possible. The ombudsman will mediate for you, and you may need to have a arbitration session or a hearing to get the issue resolved. Age is simply not a legitimate reason to be rejected at most schools.

Can You Look Too Good?

Yes, while it may seem surprising, at some schools, students who already appear as sophisticated in their field of study as the faculty get rejected in favor of someone who can benefit more from the educational opportunity. This is especially true in some traditional colleges with very young faculty. If you want to go to a school where this might be a problem, don't make yourself sound more experienced on paper or in interviews than the faculty who will "teach" you. Be deferential to the faculty. You should be knowledgeable about their interests and their publications (if they have any)—but you should sound as if you want to benefit from the faculty's expertise, not show them where they have gone wrong. (That's for later, after you are accepted.) Be especially careful not to sound arrogant or above the proceedings at hand.

What Can You Do If You Are Rejected?

You may feel frustrated, because even with all the work you put into applying, you got nowhere. But there are several remedies open to you. Here are some of the more useful ones:

- Apply for general admission to the college as an undergraduate or graduate with an undeclared major and then work (worm) your way into the department that rejected you.
- Choose a program specifically geared to adults instead of trying to crack the prestige schools like Stanford. Many adult programs are more flexible in admitting students than traditional colleges. They work with you to remove any educational deficiencies that could block your acceptance. Distance education may be a good option if there are few other adult-oriented college programs available locally. Ultimately, your degree from one of these accredited schools will be every bit as valuable as the one from Stanford—and you'll have a better chance of completing it, anyway.
- Attend community college to hone your skills and grade point average and then transfer to a four-year school. At some schools, transferring from a community college is an easier way to get admitted because you have a

transcript that proves you are college material.

■ Make connections with a professor at the school to help overcome invisible roadblocks.

■ Reapply with a better application packet next semester. Talk to a senior admissions official and ask him or her to "lay it on the line" about why you were rejected. If the rejection was departmental, take the matter up with the department chairperson. Listen carefully to any comments and avoid getting testy over negative ones. If anyone gives you recommendations, such as improving your test scores or taking additional courses, work to remove these deficiencies. If this person takes a liking to you and you make a strong effort to overcome your perceived shortcomings, you will likely find a berth in the department the next semester. Remember—college has more to do with persistence than anything else.

■ Reconsider the kind of program you desire even if it means lowering your initial expectations.

■ Look into re-entry programs specifically designed for older students. Most campuses offer special programs for former homemakers or displaced workers who want to improve their skills in order to reenter college. These programs often advise you how to improve both your academic skills and your chances of getting accepted to the department of your choice.

The process of applying to school can seem tedious if your are a busy, working adult—but it is worth it, because it is your first step toward success in college. Be assured that there are enough schools and enough programs that you will be able to be accepted to an accredited school somewhere, without demeaning or degrading yourself. We hope the steps we provided in this chapter will make it easier for you to complete the application process and get accepted by the college of your choice. In the next chapter we'll discuss how to get the credits you deserve from the college you apply to—so you can receive your college degree.

Adult College Students in Their Own Words
Alan Vandendriessche

I don't think I am in any way special, but because I think there is a real need for alternative education methods in this country, I appreciate the opportunity to tell my story. First, I returned to college after 30 for the personal satisfaction of earning the degree. There really is no other reason; I don't need the degree for my work or any other external reason like that. As Ralph Waldo Emerson said, "The greatness of a thing is having done it."

I grew up in the 1960s and 1970s. I didn't complete my bachelor's degree when I was young because I was having too much fun as a member of the counterculture. School was simply too much work. I was a real estate salesman, and when I needed money I went out and sold a house, and in that way I survived for several years. My father finally decided that enough is enough and got me a job at his place of business as a computer operator. It was there that I began to see the real business world and how important an education could be.

When I was 26, I got married and subsequently returned to the University of Maryland with the intention of completing my degree. I was also working part time at an actuarial consulting firm. As I learned more and more about actuarial consulting I ended up working more and spending less time on school. In addition, my wife and I wanted to buy a house and needed the money. So for the second time I quit college and went to work full time as an actuarial consultant. I moved up the ladder over a 10-year period to become a vice-president and shareholder in my firm. I really learned the "street" side of the business world and became exposed to very bewildering management problems—a domineering majority shareholder, unreasonable and demanding clients, employees who did their best to take advantage of the system, poor marketing, and on and on. In 1986 I saw the handwriting on the wall for our small consulting firm—declining client base and revenues. I went back to school once again and completed my B.S. in Management Technology at the University of Maryland. I wanted to keep going, but I had a problem. I had been told several years before that I had an eye problem that was incurable and progressive and will eventually lead to total blindness. I could no longer drive at night, and continuing an education when I was unable to drive seemed an unsolvable problem.

One day I received an invitation in the mail to sign up for the Prodigy service. While using the Prodigy service I spotted the ad for University of Phoenix Online and the rest is history. The people I have discussed it with have sometimes reacted as though it was not a real degree. There is not universal acceptance of alternative learning yet. Others want to know more about it. The director of human resources in my company looked over the material I had and felt it was a good and worthwhile program. She encouraged me to proceed with my master's degree. I now view this program as a step along the way to a Ph.D. I do not know how I will obtain the Ph.D. or even if it will be possible given my diminishing vision, but that is two years away and I will deal with it then. I'm sure the world will come up with something to make it possible.

Chapter Six

Getting Credits Where Credits Are Due: How to Make Your Life Experience Count at College

One of the biggest obstacles for an adult considering school after fifteen or more years on the job is the prospect of starting from scratch. Adults are vehement in their belief that their lives and job experience are worth something. It doesn't seem fair to be denied college credit for the things learned on the job or through years of personal effort that others with less experience are being given credit for simply by completing a course and reading a book or two.

This chapter explains the options and the ways to get the maximum number of college credits for experience to help you get your degree faster and with less frustration—if you decide to attend one of the schools that is sympathetic to granting credit in this way. For example, in the New York State University system students need earn only 26 percent of their credits at the school they plan to receive their degree from. Therefore, it is possible to either accelerate the degree process or lighten the load by obtaining credits in ways besides attending courses.

There are many legal options, depending on the school and the degree desired, for obtaining valid college credits for life and work experience. Whether you can actually use these methods will depend on the school you choose to attend. Each school has different (and often complex) rules and criteria for granting credit. These systems range from completely inflexible and unreasonable to completely fluid and accommodating.

Getting Credit for Business and Life Experience

Beside taking college courses, you have also learned skills and received training throughout your life. Colleges have recently developed ways of giving credit for these learning experiences. In a traditional school, most credit is earned by taking classes—but even some traditional schools will grant a limited number of credits for documented life experience. Nontraditional schools are more flexible in the number of units and the ways in which credit can be earned for life experience. The most common methods for granting experiential credit are the following:

Documented Mastery and Life Experience

If you can document with credibility, through performance or recommendation or both, that you have mastered specific skills or abilities, then you may be granted credit for what you have learned. This type of credit is granted regardless of how or where the skill or knowledge was learned. In colleges that accept experiential credits, the variety of learning experiences that can lead to college credit is virtually endless. Not only are there the skills that you may have learned on the job, but also the skills you may have acquired through volunteer work and hobbies. For example, a given university might offer six courses in Spanish worth four semester units each. If you can show the school that you speak and write Spanish just as well as someone who has taken and passed those six courses, you will be granted 24 semester units in Spanish, whether you learned the language from your grandmother, from living in Mexico, or from audiotapes played while you were commuting to work each day. The same philosophy is applied to specific business skills, hobbies, and dozens of other non-classroom learning experiences. For example, if you earned a airplane pilot's license, you may be granted units in basic aviation. If you have ten years of business planning experience and can show the school the results of your work, you may be able to get credit in planning, strategic management, and other areas. The documentation of this experience may be formal or informal—but there must always be some kind of documentation. This documentation is often called a "portfolio" of past experience. Some schools even offer a course for completion of the life experience portfolio. The number of units granted for this course depends on the amount of life experience you are able to document with credibility.

Equivalency Examinations

Many schools say that if you can pass an examination in a subject, then you should get credit for knowing that subject. This is one of the easiest non-traditional ways to get credit toward a college degree. Hundreds of standard equivalency exams are offered, each worth anywhere from two to 39 semester units each. If you are unsure of your ability and placement level, the standardized tests can also serve as a sort of diagnostic exam, showing you in which areas you are already performing at college level and where your knowledge or skills may need strengthening.

Be aware that two schools may award significantly different amounts of credit for the same examinations. Before you pay for or take any examinations for credit, ask the school about the types of examinations it accepts for credit and the number of units you can transfer by examination. Though many schools accept credit by examination, they often limit the number of units that can be applied toward a degree in this way.

The most often accepted standardized examinations include the following:

CLEP Examination Program

Offered by the College Entrance Examination Board (called the College Board for short), The College Level Examination Program (CLEP) is open to anyone interested in demonstrating college-level proficiency, including people who are thinking about college and those already in college.

The diagnostic aspect of the tests, especially the tests of general knowledge, can be particularly important to those who are returning to school after a prolonged absence. The tests can be interpreted by the student, of course, but also might be of assistance to counselors at the college. The counselors can suggest specific courses for remediation, if necessary. Also, the experience of taking the test can in itself help acclimate adult students to academic life again.

Depending on the individual institution's policy, students can save time and money by satisfying degree requirements through CLEP exams. The exams can also increase the likelihood that a returning student will be accepted into the college of his choice. Because they are relatively recent, the tests can reduce the negative impact of low high school grades or low test scores obtained so long ago that they no longer reflect the student's knowledge or ability. The fact that the exams are on the college level may have weight even in schools that do not accept CLEP tests for credit.

There are two kinds of CLEP examinations, the General Examinations and the Subject Examinations. All of the exams are 90 minutes long. Most of the exams are solely multiple choice, although there are some that have an essay component as well. There is a $50 (approximately) fee for taking each exam.

If you write to CLEP (we have provided their address in the resources section of this book), you will be sent information on the available exams and information on the content and structure of each. A variety of study guides is also available in bookstores and libraries. Be sure to get a current one, as the content and structure of the examinations change from time to time.

Every college has its own policy concerning CLEP examinations. Some colleges will use them only for diagnostic purposes. Others set limits on the number of credits they will allow for any particular exam. There are minimum score requirements that must be attained in order to receive credit. Unless you just want to find out how you'll score for your own satisfaction, it is important to fully understand your school's policy before taking any exam for credit.

PEP/ACT Proficiency Examinations

The ACT Proficiency Examination Program (PEP) consists of almost fifty standardized tests designed to help adult learners earn college credit for college-level knowledge gained from work, experience, and independent study. The tests cover a wide range of subject areas in business, nursing, education, and the arts and sciences. PEP tests are accepted for credit by hundreds of colleges and universities. The fees for the exams vary from about $50 to $150.

Most PEP exams are three- and four-hour multiple-choice tests. Some include essay or short-answer questions, and a few are entirely essay tests. The tests are administered by the American College Testing Program. Each test is based on a course outline included in the PEP Study Guide for that test. The address for contacting ACT about the PEP examinations is provided in the reference section of the book.

Advanced Placement Credit

Another way to improve your position in college is to establish advanced placement credit toward required courses. Advanced placement means that you do not need to take introductory courses to qualify for a degree in that field. Most often you are granted the credit for the course, but those credits are not figured into your grade point average. (If you are granted advanced placement status, your transcript will normally state that you received X advanced placement credits, and it may list the courses for which you received those credits.) Be aware that you may have difficulty transferring advanced placement credits if you decide to change schools.

Waivers or exemptions are terms used when certain course requirements are dropped in consideration of factors such as related job experience. Because no credits are awarded for courses from which you are exempt, there is no possibility of transferring such advanced placement if you change schools. However, you won't have to go through the drudgery and boredom of taking courses in subjects you have already mastered. As an adult student, the transition from the worker role to the student role at the end of the day can be difficult. To have to walk into a class where everything taught is obvious, simplistic, or redundant puts a weight of tedium on top of the educational experience that is not necessary. This sense of fruitlessness can affect your entire attitude toward school, especially since the classes that are most likely to bore you with overfamiliarity are the very first courses you'll take.

With this in mind, a note of caution should be added. It is not a good idea to get advanced placement for subjects that you do not know very well. While you may save some time and money skipping some of the early courses, the material covered in those courses may be essential to your success in the advanced courses.

The best way to determine if advanced placement is appropriate is to read the catalog description of the course and talk to the professor about the requirements. If you feel that you already know the course material, ask an advisor how to obtain either advanced credit or a waiver for that course.

Advanced placement is most often established by examination, though sometimes it is granted by simply asking the instructor for permission to enter a course. One standardized testing program that offers the chance to earn both college credit and advanced placement is the Advanced Placement Program administered by the College Board. Advanced Placement tests are offered in a variety of subjects, including languages, history, government, mathematics, computer science, and the other sciences. The examinations are based on specific advanced high school courses that are equivalent to first and second year courses offered in college.

Schools may also administer their own advanced placement exams. These exams may be used in determining if you have requisite skills to enter certain courses. Sometimes schools grant credit for their own examinations as well. The school's catalog should describe these examinations if they are available or required.

Company-sponsored Courses, Seminars, and Workshops

Major companies often have high-quality educational programs that are recognized as offering college-level training. In addition, companies often send employees to seminars and other skills-development courses that offer credible training. If you have been involved in such training programs, you may be eligible for college credit. As you continue to take such training in your company, be sure to get a record of your attendance and a formal description of the program, so it can be used to document your successful completion of the course.

Your college will be able to tell you the procedure for getting credit for recognized on-the-job and company-sponsored training programs. Be aware that a fee may be charged for the credits you are granted in this way.

The Prior Learning Program at Adelphi University

Adelphi University is a private university in Garden City, New York. Adelphi has developed a credible and creative program for assessing prior learning and granting college credit for documented experience. Adelphi's program is representative of similar programs at other universities. As stated in Adelphi's *Prior Learning Guidelines,* "The most essential thing to keep in mind about Prior Learning is that credit is not awarded for experiences (no matter how sophisticated) but for the students' ability to demonstrate . . . that they possess knowledge reflected in the coursework taught at Adelphi University." Using the Prior Learning program, Adelphi students have earned as many as one-quarter of the total credits required for a bachelor's degree.

The program works as follows: The student prepares an "Educational Resume." This document is a structured presentation of the student's experience and training. The Educational Resume contains the names, dates, and descriptions of each experience for which the student seeks credit. The resume also provides information on the documentation available to verify each experience.

The student meets with a counselor who reviews the resume and helps the student clarify any vague areas before forwarding it to the Prior Learning Office. The Prior Learning staff determines which experiences outlined can be considered college-level and set up an appointment for the student to meet with a faculty member who can evaluate the student's level of accomplishment. This faculty member decides on the maximum number of credits that a student can earn based on the prior learning experience and designs an assignment that will be used to evaluate the student's performance level. This assignment may be a written project, a portfolio, a performance, a working computer program, or something else that is appropriate to demonstrate proficiency in the subject area. The faculty member evaluates the project when it is completed and recommends the number of credits to be granted.

Credits received through prior learning at Adelphi are listed on the student's transcript like regular courses. This system makes it easier

> to transfer credits to another school or to make the transcript acceptable to graduate schools and employers.

Military Training Credit

If you were in the military you undoubtedly took training courses. While these course aren't from an accredited college or university, many schools will allow you to document your military training to gain life experience credits. The key to using military training, as with other life experience materials, is documentation. Recent surveys show that the recommendations equating military training courses with civilian academic courses are accepted by a large number of colleges. You must be able to get a letter describing the training as accurately as possible and also be able to prove that you completed the training successfully.

If you are still in the military, the DANTES programs are an invaluable vehicle for using your military training to further your education. DANTES, which stands for Defense Activity for Non-Traditional Educational Support, serves active duty and reserve personnel in all branches of the military. DANTES provides education information, manages independent contracts for educational services, and conducts developmental activities. The DANTES program also verifies that the quality of military training programs is acceptable to many colleges and universities. In cooperation with the American Council on Education (ACE), the Military Evaluations Program arranges for civilian educators to evaluate military training courses and service school courses. The results of the evaluations are published in the *Guide to the Evaluation of Educational Experiences in the Armed Services*, widely known as the ACE Guide.

Under DANTES's auspices several tools are available for gaining college credit for training received in the military. These include the Experiential Learning Assessment (ELA) process and examination programs. The ELA process, done in conjunction with a college, is a method by which a member of the services is helped to organize his or her learning experiences into a portfolio. This documented work in the portfolio can include exams and exercises done by the student for particular training courses, or it can be examples of work done for the military that was based on material learned through some form of training.

With all its examination, coursework, and planning options, DANTES can help military personnel get degrees faster and with less hassle. So, if you are still in the service and want to finish a college degree, or if you are thinking about finishing college when you retire or when you return to civilian life, be sure to take advantage of everything DANTES has to offer. The educational officer on your base can provide more information on the DANTES programs available to you.

Develop a Portfolio to Figure Out Where You Are

To establish what credit you may be entitled to and to quantify your own skill levels in general, we recommend that every adult student prepare a "working portfolio" that lists all the training and knowledge you have acquired. Even if you won't be using your past education to gain formal academic credit, it is a useful exercise to prepare a portfolio of past experience and training to clarify your current abilities and interests. This portfolio can also be used as a starting point when you make formal application to receive life-experience credits.

You should bring in your portfolio when you talk to the school counselor or admissions officer before you apply to a school. Go over each aspect of your experience, education, and training and have this person verify what items can potentially be used for credit at the school. Too many adult students come in unprepared when they talk with their counselors and as a result miss opportunities to gain credit for past experience. The first step in getting the credits you are due is *preparation*.

We have provided a worksheet to help you assemble your portfolio. At the very least your life experience and training portfolio should contain the following:

- Photocopies of transcripts from all schools attended. If you have taken college courses in the past, even if some were taken on a no-credit basis or at a local community college for recreational purposes, your first step in getting credits toward your degree is to make a list of the college courses you have already taken. List every school and every course—no matter how long ago the course was taken. If you don't have copies of your transcripts from the schools you have attended, you should get copies immediately. Then list the course names and the number of units you were granted for each course on a worksheet like the one we've provided in this chapter.

  If your college courses were taken within the last twenty years and were from an accredited school or a school with equivalent recognition, you should know that there is a school somewhere that will accept at least part of these past college units toward your degree. As mentioned previously, be aware also that there are schools that won't accept any past college work, or will accept only a limited number of units, or will accept only courses taken within the last ten or seven or some other arbitrary number of years. The catalog should tell you the school's policy regarding transfer credit from other schools. If it doesn't, ask a counselor or advisor.

  After listing your college courses, you may want to have the list reviewed unofficially by an admissions advisor to see approximately how many of the courses can be applied to your degree at that school. When you actually apply to the school, they will make an official determination about the courses they will accept and the courses they will replace in the degree program.

- A complete and up-to-date resume of all your past experience. This should be a detailed resume that fully describes your work responsibilities and accomplishments. Go back to the beginning of time—include your very first job. You will be surprised how many things you have actually done and learned in your life. This is not a resume for a job, so make it as long as required to document your accomplishments. Include volunteer work

Portfolio Worksheet (Part One)

Create a labeled folder to contain the records for each section.

☐ Transcripts from all colleges. List below.

School	Date Attended	Course	Units	Grade	Comments

Total Units ____ ____ GPA

☐ Company training. List everything.

Course or Subject	Date Attended	Proof or Documentation of Attendance	Comments

☐ Resume complete. This is not an employment resume, but a complete description of all past employment and activities, to include:

   ☐ Detailed description of all jobs since high school.
   ☐ Volunteer work with dates and description of duties.
   ☐ Special accomplishments, i.e., raising a family, remodeling a house, building a business, playing a musical instrument or other arts endeavors.
   ☐ Hobbies described in detail.

Portfolio Worksheet (Part Two)

❏ Military records: Service _____ Discharge date _____

Assignments	Dates	Rank	Responsibilities

❏ Credentials, certificates, and awards

Type	Date Issued	Agency Issuing	Comments

❏ Self-taught skills

Skill	How Used

❏ Books read recently

Title	Author

❏ Other special accomplishments

Date	Description

and work on committees as well as formal job experience. (Keep in mind that it's okay to list your first job with Dairy Queen because this resume will not be shown to anyone else.)

■ Photocopies of military records, if applicable. We discussed earlier the ways to get military credit.

■ Photocopies of training records from your past jobs. Most companies keep records of the formal courses, seminars, or other on-the-job training you completed while employed. If you don't have copies of these records, request them from the human resources department of your employers.

■ Copies of certificates and awards or receipts from any seminars or professional courses you have attended.

■ Lists of training and programs you can't document, but remember being involved in. List everything you can remember about the course, including a description, when it was taken, and what you learned. You may find that the school can advise you on ways to locate documentation for these courses.

■ Documentation of the skills you have taught yourself. Include photos and documentation of the work you have completed if possible. These skills may relate to maintaining the house or managing the household or may be hobbies or recreational activities. Remember—there are college courses in ceramics, golf, personal computer operations, swimming, sewing, gardening, and much more. There are even courses in cooking, jogging, and make-up application. Have you raised a child? If so, you probably have learned a lot about child psychology and family planning. Do you fix your own car? Then you know a lot about auto mechanics. If you had taken courses in these subjects, you would have earned college credit. If you have taught yourself these things on your own, your skill is just as valuable as that learned in a formal course—so put everything you have mastered on your list. You deserve the credit. And if you have any documentation to support your claims, be sure to include this as well. For example, include photos of the gazebo you built in the back yard or pictures of the wedding cakes you decorated for your friends. If you have invented recipes, include these—or if you wrote some poems, those should be included.

■ A list of all the books you can remember reading in the last five years and all the periodicals and newspapers you read regularly. Be honest and specific. If you actually *read* the newspaper every day, list it. But, if you only glance over the comics and the classified ads, it doesn't really count as reading. This list will serve three purposes: (1.) It will give an overview of your interests. (2.) It will indicate how much you like to read. If you are already an avid reader, college will be easier for you. If your list is very short, it will indicate that you may need to work on your reading skills. (3.) It may reveal subjects that you wouldn't have thought of otherwise that you may be ready to take an examination on in order to receive academic or advanced standing credit.

■ A list of any special accomplishments, such as publications, books, or awards.

Organize the portfolio by topic in a manila folder. If you have a lot of material in your portfolio, get one of those expanding folders with multiple sections and include a separate manila folder for each topic. Create a table of contents for the portfolio, using the worksheet we have provided in this chapter.

When you have finished assembling your portfolio, you will have a good idea of the types of courses you can document for experiential credit or ones you may feel comfortable trying to test out of. As you have new accomplishment and training experiences, add these to your portfolio. After you enroll in college, you should add a section for "Current College Records" to document your progress through school. Use these sections to keep records of application forms, grade reports, and registration materials. It makes college life easier if you keep these things in one place so you always know where they are when you need to talk with a counselor or make a decision about enrolling in a specific course.

By the way, there is no reason to stay in a college course if you already know most of the information being presented. At first this seems like it might be an easy way to get a degree—just take courses for things you already know. After all, some adults want the degree more than they want further education. Unfortunately, most adults who try this approach to college get bored and lose the motivation to finish. They start to feel they are wasting their time in college—and in some ways they are. Why spend time in classes if you aren't learning something? It is better to challenge yourself a little.

Even if your school doesn't offer academic credit for past life experience, make sure you get advanced placement in your courses. If a school doesn't have formal placement testing programs, it will often let you talk to a professor to be admitted to a course for which you don't have the "official" prerequisite. Do it—don't bore yourself into failure.

The PONSI Program

As you prepare your portfolio, you should be aware that the American Council on Education has developed a program called the Program on Noncollegiate Sponsored Instruction (PONSI), which recommends the following three-point strategy for gaining academic credit for things learned outside the traditional classroom:

1. Know what factors affect a college's decision to award credit. Every college has its own policies regarding credit for examinations, life experience, military training, and advanced standing. It is your responsibility to find out what these policies are before you can determine the amount of credit you will be able to apply toward your degree at various schools.
2. Find out which official at the school makes the decision to award credit for transfer courses and academic credit. Talk to this person. Some-

times this will be the admissions officers. Other times it will be the department chairperson or a dean. Sometimes a member of the faculty will be assigned to review your portfolio. The who and how of granting credit varies from college to college—so it behooves you to find out who will be making the decision and what he or she will be looking for.

3. Understand what your options are if your courses or credit requests are rejected. First, understand why the credit was rejected. If the courses are not appropriate for the degree, there isn't much you can do. But if the decision is arbitrary and capricious (and sometimes the decisions to accept one type of credit and not another seem that way) then you may want to appeal the decision—or you may want to look for another school that will accept your credits. ACE lists over 1,500 accredited colleges and universities that accept its PONSI recommendations. If you want more information about the recommended process for documenting academic credit, write to PONSI. We have included the address in the reference section of this book.

Once you complete your portfolio and have established the credit each school will grant you for life experience, past educational experiences, and advanced placement in required courses, you will be ready to develop a plan for the completion of your degree.

Adult College Students in Their Own Words
Diane Melling

I've always wanted to return to school to receive a four-year degree. I originally attended a two-year college and always regretted not heeding my parents' advice to finish my degree. After five years with one company, I was laid off and found that the two-year degree didn't qualify me for the positions I desired in other companies. I was forced to accept a clerical position just to get in the door of a larger company. It was a little humiliating at first, because I knew I could do more.

On the G.I. bill, my husband attended a traditional four-year college as a part-time student for more than ten years before he received his engineering degree; and he had already completed requirements for his two-year degree! When he started at 35, I didn't want to commit that many years to complete a bachelor's degree. Since I didn't have the job or make the money I wanted, I decided to take advantage of an educational reimbursement program through my job. The program was very enticing in that the company rebated 100% of the tuition and books at most of the local colleges and universities. I did some research and found an adult-oriented school to be a good choice for me. I was especially attracted to the classroom structure and amount of time required to complete the degree program.

Although I was apprehensive about returning to school, the problems encountered over the two and one-half year period were minimal. My company paid the tuition. Since my husband had just completed ten years of grueling schoolwork, he was really understanding about the reallocation of my time. I found that because I was in school for personal gratification this time, I was actually enjoying it. The faculty and my study group members were very supportive and were always willing to work with emergency situations that arose; i.e. having to travel for work, a death in the family, etc. The adult-oriented school really made a difference.

The only advice I can give to others who are considering returning to school is, "Go For It!" The time flew by, I met some really great contacts (both personally and professionally), I learned a great deal about many companies and their employees, and I qualify for better job opportunities both in and out of my current organization. The people around me admire my stamina in sticking with the program and recognize my dedication and desire to succeed.

Chapter Seven

How to Finance Your Degree without Robbing a Bank

Many potential adult students fear they will have to deplete their life savings just to get a degree. Fortunately, there are better ways to finance a college education as an adult, and this chapter describes the options available and provides guidelines for choosing the most beneficial financing situation for any family situation.

How Much Will Your College Education Cost?

Anything we write today about the costs of schools will be out of date tomorrow. The costs of a college are rapidly escalating. In 1988, the average traditional student (age 18–25, without a spouse or children to support) spent $57,000 to attend a private college for four years in the United States. This amount includes tuition, room and board (in a shared apartment or student housing), books, supplies, and basic transportation costs. It does not include automobile expenses or vacation costs. At public colleges, the average cost in 1988 for the same four-year degree was "only" around $33,000.

Though schools try to control costs, inflation remains a reality. Here is a projection of approximate costs for a traditional four-year degree in the future:

ESTIMATED COST OF A FOUR-YEAR DEGREE

YEAR	PRIVATE COLLEGE	PUBLIC COLLEGE
1994	$76,000	$47,000
1998	$88,000	$53,000
2003	$117,000	$69,000

Traditional students who enter college during the twenty-first century (only a few years from now) can expect to spend over $100,000 in pursuit of a degree in an average private college. If you now have young children whom you want to send to college directly out of high school, this is a sobering thought. And if you haven't started saving for your children's education, now would be a good time to start.

But this book is *not* about *traditional* students; it is a book about *adults* in college. The costs of going to college as an adult are different in scope and impact than they are for younger students. Most adults do not move from their homes to share an inexpensive, run-down apartment within walking distance of the college campus. Most adults have pre-existing family and financial obligations that are difficult to curtail. As an adult you already have fixed expenses for the mortgage or rent, insurance, child care, and the other necessities of everyday life. College simply becomes an additional item in your list of life expenses.

The largest additional cost in your college education as an adult will be the tuition and fees required by the school you attend. Traditional private universities are usually the most expensive schools. In 1992, just the tuition for a full-time student at Harvard, Stanford, or the University of Southern California was about $15,000 a year. Some private schools, whether traditional or alternative, may charge as little as $5000 a year in tuition, but you won't find many accredited private schools that charge less than that for a full-time program of study.

State-operated universities typically cost less than private schools, *if* you are a resident of the state. For example, full-time tuition for residents at Arizona State University was $1600. However, the tuition for a non-resident was almost $6900—almost as much as a private school.

Community colleges are a relative bargain if you are a resident of the county, state, or district that supports the college. Tuition for a full-time student at a typical community college is only $500 to $850 per year for residents. And if you attend part time, you can attend for as little as $30 a course. For college credits, that's almost free. (Of course, you pay taxes to support these institutions—so you pay for them whether you take advantage of them or not.)

The length of your school's program also affects your costs. If you have four years of study ahead of you in a traditional school, the total cost for your degree will be significant, especially if you attend a private school. This is where alternative schools and non-traditional programs become cost-effective. If you can finish a four-year degree program in only three years in an accelerated program, you will have reduced your expenses by over 25 percent. Thus, the tuition in a non-traditional school may seem high at $7000 a year, but compared to the cost of earning the same degree in traditional private universities that take twice as long, the non-traditional college can be a relative bargain. And the private, non-traditional degree may not cost any more than a traditional degree earned in a state university when all the costs for traveling, parking, and fees are calculated.

The location of the school obviously affects your costs as well. In most cases adults do not choose to move to another city or state in order to attend school. However, in a few special circumstances adult students do decide it is worthwhile to move in order to attend a specific college or university. (And if you have a family, these expenses can be significant.) If you are one of these special cases, be sure to calculate any moving and relocation expenses associated with your choice of college. If you will need to commute a fair distance to attend school, say thirty miles or more, those costs should also be calculated in your college expenses.

The cost of your complete college program also increases proportionately with the length of time you take to complete the program. In private universities, you often pay for courses by the unit, so this doesn't increase the cost of the program significantly—but you will have added expenses for fees, etc. that wouldn't be incurred if you proceeded through the program efficiently. In non-traditional schools, you may pay a flat fee per semester, regardless of the number of units you actually earn toward your degree. Thus, if you don't make the expected progress in your program, it will cost you—in both time and money.

Other costs that you will need to plan for include books (you will probably be shocked by current textbook prices, which can be as much as $75 or more for a single book), supplies, and fees for special services, such as online bibliographic searches, telephone charges if you are enrolled in a distance-education program, computer lab fees, and other miscellany.

Complete the Worksheet to Determine Your Total College Costs

Based on these general ideas, you can determine the overall cost of your planned college education by completing the *College Financial Planning Worksheet* we have included in this chapter.

To complete the worksheet, you will need to start with the college catalog again. First, determine how long it will take you to complete your program of study (you can do this after completing the work in Chapter Four and Chapter Eight.) Note the cost of tuition and fees per year for each year you will attend school to complete your program. Then fill in the appropriate blanks on the worksheet. (Add about five percent a year for tuition and fee inflation for each year after the first.)

Now determine the cost of books. In a traditional college, the average cost for books is about $75 per course. Multiply the number of courses you will take each year by $75. If you are in a scientific discipline the texts could cost more. If you major in some liberal arts fields, such as English, the costs could be less. But as an average in 1992, this is about right. Again, add about five percent a year for inflation in subsequent years.

Supplies vary by your major. At a minimum, you should expect to spend $250 a year on paper and general supplies. If you will be attending labs or taking art courses, the supplies could cost a great deal more. If you list what you can think of, total it, and then add 25 percent to cover things you forget, you'll probably have a reasonable estimate of what to expect.

If your college program involves a significant amount of writing (and almost every program except art does) then we suggest you get your own personal computer. Of course, if you decide to enroll in an online program, you will have no choice but to get one. A basic system with a slow but acceptable printer can be purchased for under $750. Of course, you can spend as much as $3500 or more for a state-of-the-art setup. Get something basic in the first year if you don't have a system already. The cost of a computer will be either a monthly credit card expense or a one-time expense, if you have the cash on hand to buy a system outright. And be sure to look into the college-student discount programs offered by many computer companies, including Apple and IBM. The college bookstore can usually provide information on these discount programs.

When you have completed the worksheet and totalled the columns, you will have an idea about the total cost of your planned education program, broken down

College Financial Planning Worksheet

School Costs (list annual costs)

Check if Applicable	Year One	Year Two	Year Three	Year Four
☐ Tuition				
☐ Fees				
☐ Textbooks				
☐ Supplies				
☐ Commuting Costs				
☐ Computer/Printer				
☐ Office/Study Area				
☐ Day Care				
☐ Health Insurance				
☐ Examination Fees				
☐ Other				
Total Annual Costs				
− Personal Contribution				
= Amount Required				

Sources of Funding

	Year One	Year Two	Year Three	Year Four
☐ Employer Reimbursement				
☐ Financial Aid				
Source _____				
_____				
_____				
☐ Scholarships				
☐ Loans				
Source _____				
_____				
_____				
☐ Fellowship				
☐ Other				
Source _____				
_____				
_____				

by year and category. After the shock of the total subsides, the first thing you'll probably ask is: Is the college degree worth the expense? Recall that we discussed the value of a degree in Chapter One. In terms of higher salary, increased likelihood of getting better jobs, and personal satisfaction, the value of a college education is well demonstrated. The data available in 1988 show that the average worker with a bachelor's degree was earning a whopping 75 percent more than an average high school graduate. With this kind of potential, the expenses of your degree will soon be compensated for in money, if not prestige.

And if you do your financial planning properly, your lifestyle shouldn't have to change too much. (Unless, of course, you decide to go to one of the most expensive private institutions. And even then, you can probably get loans that will take the bite out of the tuition—as long as your credit rating is acceptable.)

Where Will the Money Come From?

As an adult, you have a significant number of options available to finance your college program. Many adults assume that they aren't eligible for the financial aid, scholarships, and grants available to younger students. Years ago that was true, but today there are very few restrictions on financial aid that are related to age. In fact, over 60 percent of the students in college today receive some kind of financial aid. And, since more than half the students in college today are over 25, there must be a significant number of adult students receiving financial aid of some kind to further their education. In the rest of this chapter we will describe the general sources for financial aid and offer suggestions for finding information on specific financial support

Start with Your Own Finances

The amount of money and aid you require obviously depends on how much you will be able to contribute from your own savings and income. To determine the amount you can reasonably contribute from your own savings and income, ask yourself the following questions:

1. How much of my regular savings am I willing to invest in my college education? If you don't have any savings, the answer is obvious. But, if you have been saving for retirement or other purposes or if you have a regular savings program, there may be some money that can be used from this nest egg to help you reach your educational goals. Promise yourself to put the savings back after you finish your degree, however—and make sure you discuss the use of the savings with other members of the family.

2. Is there any discretionary money that I spend now that would be better spent on my college education? To determine this, list your monthly expenses and the money you spend on discretionary activities such as vacations, new clothes, and entertainment. Could you stay at a less ex-

pensive hotel next year to save a few dollars toward your schooling? How about one less new outfit now and then? Don't bankrupt yourself. And don't eliminate all of your leisure activities or family entertainment events. We recommend that you try to maintain as much of your normal lifestyle as possible when you start school, because that way the adjustment will be easier on you and your family. Still, there are always a few places you can save money—and you should consider these saved funds as a source of your college financing.

On the worksheet, list the amount you will be able to provide each year on your own. Subtract this from the total cost of school. That is how much money you will need to find from other sources.

Visit the Human Resources Department to See What Your Company Will Pay

If you work for a large company, your first stop should be the human resources department to determine if your company has an educational support plan. If it does, be advised that the plans are diverse and sometimes complicated. Here are some of the questions to ask about the plan at your company:

- Will the company reimburse me for any program or only programs approved by the company as related to my job?
- How much will the company pay? What are the limits?
- Will my grades affect the level of reimbursement?
- Does the program cover books and supplies or only tuition? Are fees included, or commuting costs?
- Will the company pay for programs at any school or must the school be approved by the company in advance?
- Can the money be paid in advance or is it only reimbursed after satisfactory completion of the course?
- How much advance notice must I give the company before I enroll in a program of study?
- How often must my program of study be approved, and by whom?

Get all this information in writing—and before you start school, have the firm's administrator approve your program of study for reimbursement. We've seen many adult students get stuck with their college costs because they didn't ask the right questions or get their program approved in advance. Don't let this happen to you.

Look into Financial Aid Programs and Loans

After determining your own contribution and the contribution of your company, you'll have a good idea of how much money you need to come up with from other sources. The sources to consider for financing the rest of your college costs include those we describe in the next few pages.

Federal and State Student Aid Programs

More than 8,000 schools take part in the U.S. Department of Education's financial aid programs. These programs require you to fill out an Application for Federal Student Aid. It takes four to six weeks to process the application. Be sure it is accurate and complete. A mistake will cost you another six weeks. In addition, most states offer additional grant and loan programs to augment the federal programs. The Office of Financial Aid at your college will be able to tell you the specific requirements for applying for the various state and federal programs.

Most state and federal grants are given to students with demonstrated financial need. (Unless you are applying for a research grant in a specific school or department—we'll discuss those grants later.) There is a very specific formula used to determine this need based on "average college expenses" and the specific costs attributed to the school you choose to attend. There are also student loans supported by government subsidies and guarantees. For adults who are not working, there are also "work-study" programs that provide flexible jobs on campus. Mind you, these jobs don't usually pay very much—but if you aren't working elsewhere and need the money, they can be a good way to make a few extra dollars and meet people on campus at the same time. Remember—the federal and state programs may have restrictions based on financial need or attendance criteria, but almost none of the programs have age limits.

In most instances, you will be offered a financial aid package that includes a combination of subsidies to meet your college expenses. If you meet the financial need requirements, this will typically include a grant combined with a loan and perhaps additional state support. Though many working adults do not qualify for the need-based programs because of their full-time income, there are still federal and state-sponsored loan programs that do not depend on need. These are offered in conjunction with banks.

Some of these loans are based on financial need; others are based only on your good credit. The advantage of these federally and state guaranteed loans is that you don't have to pay back most college loans until after you quit school—and the interest rates on the loans are low.

To get current information on federal and state financial aid programs in your state, call or write your state department of education to get a current listing of the programs and the application requirements.

Consider Applying for a Scholarship

If federal or state aid doesn't appeal to you or is not adequate to meet your needs, scholarships are a definite possibility. Every year thousands of scholarships are not taken advantage of, simply because no one applies for them. Scholarships don't always require good grades or high test scores either, you may just need to meet a specific criterion specified for that scholarship. Of course, there are also scholarship programs offered by schools, but these are very competitive. If you qualify, definitely apply—but don't count on school scholarships to meet your financial obligations. We have recommended some books on scholarship sources.

Almost every organization offers scholarships or grants of some kind to members who want to further their education. Check them out. After all, all they can say is "no."

If You Are a Graduate Student, Explore Research and Teaching Opportunities

Almost every graduate school and graduate department has some type of research grant or teaching assistantship program. These programs are diverse, and some are competitive—but they are worth looking into. Some programs pay your tuition, in addition to providing a small salary for work that is relevant to your major. If you don't have to work full time in order to go to school, and if you want to pursue an academic career after graduation, the teaching assistantship or research assistantship will be a great addition to your resume.

Spend Some Time to Determine the Best Options for Financing College

We have covered the major sources of money for any adult who wants to go to college. But there are more options than these. There is no way we could offer a complete listing of financial sources in a book of this scope. Besides, there are so many guidebooks and resource compendiums available on getting money for college, it would only be redundant to duplicate that information here. We suggest you start your search for financial information in a bookstore or library. In the reference section of this book we have recommended some publications on financial support and scholarships to get you started.

In addition, there are two sources of financial aid information that you should contact before you apply to any school:

- *The Financial Aid Office on Campus.* The financial aid counselors can provide a complete list of federal, state, scholarship, grant, and other aid offered by the school. Even non-traditional schools have financial aid advisors. These people will also be able to provide the (many) application forms required for federal and state student assistance programs.
- *The Department of Higher Education in Your State.* The state education departments (addresses provided in the reference section of this book) provide application forms and information on a wide range of financial support programs.

We should also let you know that in order to apply for any kind of loan, grant, or aid you will most likely need the following information:

- Your social security number (a universal requirement for almost everything).
- Copies of your last two income tax returns.
- List of *all* your financial obligations, including existing loans and credit

cards with account numbers, alimony payments, child care costs, etc.
- Verification of employment and income for you and your spouse (if you have one).
- Verification of citizenship, alien registration card, or a visa that entitles you to remain in the United States.

In addition, you may need

- Transcripts of college work (especially for scholarships).
- Official test scores, usually SAT, ACT, GRE, or other relevant exams.
- Letters of recommendation.

And If You Still Can't Find Enough Money . . .

If you exhaust all the resources we have listed and still don't come up with enough money (we don't believe it's possible, but it might happen), you still have some options:

- If you can't qualify for a student loan or a personal loan, consider a home equity loan. If you've owned your home for a while, the equity you've built up in your home could qualify you for more than enough money to get through school. The interest is usually lower on a home equity loan than on a personal loan, as well.
- If you absolutely refuse to borrow money for your education, start a savings program and wait a while to start school. We don't recommend this option, but for some careful people, it works out well in the long run.
- To make a few extra dollars, sell things that you don't need. It's amazing how much money people can make by selling that extra VCR or the toys the kids don't play with anymore. Have a garage sale or advertise specific items in the classified ads of your local newspaper. Try it—it's worked for us many times. We made over $900 in one garage sale—and all we sold were old clothes, used records, and well-read books. One garage sale a year could pay for your books and fees at a community college.

One final recommendation about financing your education: Make sure you are comfortable with your financial program. If you are stressed by your finances, it will make school all the more difficult for you and your loved ones (who must put up with your anxieties and grumbling). And by all means, don't bury yourself in debt if you aren't sure about your college program. Choose a less expensive school or try things out for a while before you go into debt for a program. We believe most accredited college programs are ultimately worth the expense—and thousands of people will verify this in their testimonials about the value of their education—but you need to feel comfortable that the finances are workable to be able to succeed in college. Most important, you need to believe the money is there for you and be willing to search it out. Take some time to find it. Your reward will be the education, prestige, and fulfillment you deserve.

Adult College Students in Their Own Words
Michelle and Michael Sbraga, as told by Michelle

Either Michael or I have been going to school at night since 1970. At first we took night classes at a community college and at Arizona State University, which is right down the street from us. Going to school at night at a traditional school was both rewarding and frustrating.

Ultimately, however, both of us found going to night school at a regular college boring. Each course dragged on too long. Fifteen weeks of the same course. And the students were very young, and there wasn't much interaction between students.

If not for the accelerated program at the University of Phoenix, both of us would still face many more years of schooling to finish our degrees. At one point our goal was to finish college before retirement; now we actually have a chance to put to use the knowledge we have acquired.

I went to school because I realized that to get ahead, one needs at least a bachelor's degree in today's business climate. It was also a personal goal of mine.

There is a rewarding feeling of accomplishment at *finally* being able to graduate, but it is very frustrating to continually have to schedule your time around going to school. Michael went on to school because his associate degree in architecture wasn't enough, and for him to keep his job or get another job, a bachelor's degree was necessary.

Both of us got more out of the University of Phoenix than we originally anticipated. The courses were accelerated, five weeks long, and that really keeps your adrenaline pumping. Because the students work, they have a lot of knowledge and information to contribute. There is a lot of interaction between the students, and the group concept offers ways for the students to develop teamwork.

There wasn't anything about the University of Phoenix that we really didn't like. Since Michael did go to Temple University for his associate degree and to ASU for several years, he felt that a campus feeling was missing.

Our advice to students is to get that degree. Even though only 15 percent of the jobs today need a degree, many employers today are using the degree as a part of the weeding-out process. Because of the number of people who have bachelor's degrees today, a master's degree is really necessary for a high-paying job.

Chapter Eight

Getting Started: The Plans, the People, and the Pleasures of the First Days in College

Well, you're finally ready to get going on your degree. You've selected a school and major, figured out how to finance your education, tabulated the credits that will apply to your degree, applied to the school, and been accepted. You've jumped through schedule hoops, financing hoops, personal hoops, and bureaucratic hoops just to get this far. You are finally ready to hit the books.

Not so fast. There are still some things you need to consider. You can't just walk into the school and take any course you want. You have to plan a course of study, register for the courses, and meet a variety of new people you probably haven't even considered yet. Even in non-traditional and adult-oriented schools there are a number of administrative and planning activities that must take place before you can start the learning part of your college program.

Plan Your Program to Reach Your College Goals

The first thing you should do after you have been accepted at school is sit down and figure out a program of study from start to finish. Sure, your plans may change if you have two or three years left in your program—but it is a good idea to make a plan. For each calendar period (this will vary from school to school, remember—semester, month, trimester, quarter, or whatever), lay out exactly what courses you will take and what other requirements toward your degree you plan to complete, such as exams, papers, petition to graduate, and/or thesis. Lay out the plan course by course and objective by objective. We have provided a worksheet to help you do this. (By the way, you can't do this until you know exactly how many credits will be granted toward your degree, based on the information we provided in Chapter Six.) In most schools a counselor or advisor will help you do this. Use this person's help. And get the plan approved if possible. Sometimes you will be required to do so; other times it is voluntary.

The Learning Contract in a Nontraditional School—Your Study Plan

Almost all non-traditional schools require students to complete some sort of learning contract. The learning contract may be as simple as a plan of activities like

College Program Planning Worksheet

Use one copy of worksheet for each six-month period of the program.

Year _____ Units of Credit	Month Course/ Activity	Month Course/ Activity	Month Course/ Activity	Month Course/ Activity	Month Course/ Activity	Month Course Activity
_____	_____	_____	_____	_____	_____	_____
_____	_____	_____	_____	_____	_____	_____
_____	_____	_____	_____	_____	_____	_____
_____	_____	_____	_____	_____	_____	_____
_____	_____	_____	_____	_____	_____	_____
_____	_____	_____	_____	_____	_____	_____
_____	_____	_____	_____	_____	_____	_____
_____	_____	_____	_____	_____	_____	_____
_____	_____	_____	_____	_____	_____	_____
_____	_____	_____	_____	_____	_____	_____

Other objectives for this period:

_____

_____

_____

_____

Notes:

_____

_____

_____

_____

Approved by: _____

Title: _____

Date: _____

the one we just described. However, most learning contracts will have the following additional components:

- Description of the specific learning and life objectives you intend to achieve
- The specific ways you will meet each of the objectives you have listed.
- The resources, including libraries, courses, research, books and other publications, written projects, etc., that you will use and have available to complete your individual course of study
- The credits you will be granted for achieving each of the objectives in your program
- The evidence you will use to prove your completion of the objective. This may include faculty reviews, presentations to a group of other students, an examination, or other recognized evidence that you have finished the work you set out to do.
- The way your achievement of the objectives will be validated. This is the way your work will be "graded," even though traditional grades may not be given in some non-traditional settings.

Learning contracts may be required for specific courses or for an entire course of study toward a degree, depending on the school. Restrictions on the content and format of the learning contract are specific to the school. In addition, the learning contract must always be approved by faculty members or a committee of administrators and faculty. Occasionally students in the same program have input into the format and approval of your program. The non-traditional institutions provide detailed instructions on the format and requirements for their learning contracts.

Registering for Classes in a Traditional School

After you have an approved course of study, you can enroll in your first courses. Probably the single most difficult activity of going back to school is registering for classes for the first time. In some adult programs, classes are selected automatically for you. In distance-education programs, you choose your classes by mail or on line using a computer. If this is the case, great. The process is relatively simple—just fill in a form and pay the fees and you are ready to start.

But, if you are attending traditional college or university classes on campus you will have to go through a procedure that will be something between partially to completely frustrating. While the more "humane" colleges and universities allow you to choose your classes from the class schedule and register by mail or by computer, new students or those who are unable to get into the right classes by mail often must do it in person. Unfortunately, where at some colleges this process moves like clockwork with an assigned registration time being given to each student to keep the lines short, most of the schools we have attended or taught at make the process haphazard and the lines long. In most cases, the bigger the school (based on number of students) the more sloppily the procedure is handled.

What makes registration at a traditional school particularly difficult the first time you go through it is that at many colleges, registration requires several procedures and each procedure takes place in a different building (often at opposite ends of a sprawling campus). As a new student you won't know which building to start with. Getting in the wrong line can waste a full hour or more.

Make Registration Easy on Yourself

"Forewarned is forearmed" is especially true of making it successfully over the hurdles of the registration process. If you must register in person, make it easy on yourself by doing the following:

Before Registration
- Read the class scheduling information carefully to locate any "gotchas" it may contain.
- Get recommendations from other students on which teachers are best. Many schools have a formal or informal guidebook, written by students, that rates the faculty. Find out if such a book exists and buy it if it does. Bone up on who's who in the faculty. Keep in mind, however, that if the guidebook is old it may be useless (check the copyright date at the front of the book). A book for a university we attended listed a professor as Teacher of the Year because of his wonderful attitude towards his students. Upon enrolling in his class, we found out that the "Teacher of the Year" had become an impatient, gruff alcoholic, and the guidebook was out of date.
- List the classes you want to attend and list two alternate choices for each one in case the classes are full (common at many schools).
- Pack a briefcase, backpack, or purse large enough to hold your class schedule, notes, extra pens and pencils, and your identification and means of payment. Also bring change for refreshments and a paperback book or small cassette player for entertainment in case you have a long wait. Make sure you have a map of the campus labeled with all building names.

On Registration Day
- Wear clothes suitable for the weather and comfortable shoes that you won't mind standing around in. Plan on being at the college for most of the day, although hopefully the process won't take that long. If you will be a night student, consider taking a day off from work instead of registering at night. At some schools, registering in the evening is the busiest time with the longest lines. A few schools offer Saturday registration for working students. This is usually as much of a zoo as is night registration.
- Make sure that you bring everything required for registering. At some schools, you must bring your admission papers, particularly if you were admitted close to registration time. If you are simultaneously applying and enrolling in a program at a community college and are not an American

citizen (or a Canadian citizen in Canada), bring proof of lawful admission to the country, such as an Alien Registration Card. You may also need proof of residency; check with the college for details.

- Arrive early, possibly even before the registration facilities open. Keep in mind that at most schools, traffic is heavily congested and parking may be extremely difficult during registration time. Or solve this problem by parking your car close to school and taking a taxi to campus to register because the cab can place you right in front of the building where registration takes place and eliminate the parking hassle.
- Be patient, relax as much as possible, and chat with your linemates if they appear friendly. Registering with a friend is more fun than going by yourself, although initially you may know no one else at that college. Standing in line and talking to people is a great way to make friends for next semester's registration ordeal.
- If the process turns out to be long and frustrating, don't get angry or panicky, jump in your car, and give up. Instead, take stock of how you feel. You could be suffering from low blood sugar caused by a quick breakfast and no lunch. Take a break and get something to eat.

After Registration

- Go home and put your feet up—you deserve a rest.
- Once you are rested, check the list of classes you were able to enroll in against the list of desired or planned classes you made before registration. If you were forced to substitute classes, make sure that the substitutes can be fully applied toward your degree and that you change your degree plan accordingly. You will also need to make sure that the classes do not conflict with other classes or your work schedule. We've seen many schools where the computer will let people schedule themselves to be two places at the same time—computers may be able to do this, but people can't (yet).

What If I Can't Get the Right Courses?

Even after all your time waiting in lines and filling out forms, in a traditional school there is often no guarantee you will be able to register for the courses you need in a particular semester or quarter. This is not only frustrating, but can wreck havoc with a well-planned educational program for an adult who wants to finish a degree within a reasonable time. If you are unable to get the classes you need because they are full, at most schools you can attend the first class and talk the instructor into letting you add the class. Unless the class is enormously popular (or a requirement), some students register for classes and do not bother to show up or drop out after the first week or two. This process usually opens up space for people like you—who are serious about taking the course.

Be Careful of Enrolling in "Fun" Classes

Some people register in some "fun" courses during their first semester just to get started. Though this isn't a bad idea, you should know that some of the easiest-sounding courses turn out to be toughest and most time-consuming. These "easy" classes may seem innocent in the catalog because they are worth only one unit. Beware! These classes may require far more time and commitment on your part than most regular classes. This time commitment will seriously infringe on your other college activities. For example, a one-unit Theater Practicum sounds like fun in the catalog, "Performance and production assignments in theater. Production or acting experience recommended but not required. May be repeated for credit." While this sounds like an easy class, you will spend most of your semester hooking up lights and creating props and then working in the lighting booth every night the play is performed.

Once you get through the registration process the first time, you'll be able to plan better for the next one. Hopefully, as a continuing student, you will be able to register by mail for the next semester.

Between Registration and Your First Class

Develop a Weekly Schedule

One of the most important things you should do after registering for your courses is to complete a detailed weekly schedule of your activities. This will become a master schedule that you can then modify each week to include unschedulable events.

The weekly master schedule should include your work, school, leisure, and family activities. Make sure you schedule at least one time each day to do something with your family—besides eat dinner. And you need one time each week that you do something special with your family, such as see a movie, go for a walk, play baseball, or whatever is appropriate.

We have provided a worksheet in this chapter to help you develop an appropriate schedule. Don't forget that you need to schedule regular studying time. Each week you should adapt the master schedule to accommodate special priorities and events. It is very important that you develop your schedule on a weekly basis. People who schedule their activities on a daily basis will miss the overview required to incorporate other priorities like family, leisure, and life in general. There is more to life than college.

After completing your schedule, there are some other things you should do before classes start. Depending on the kind of school you are attending, you may want to buy your books early because the bookstores at most colleges are jammed once registration starts and during the first week of school. If you were able to register early, this won't be a problem. But if you must go through registration late, buying books early is risky because you may not get the classes you selected. That means a return to the bookstore for a refund or exchange.

At many adult-oriented or alternative schools, a binder of information that includes the outlines of the course, specific assignments, and the textbooks will be

Weekly Life Schedule for Adult College Students

Week of _____ to _____

Time	Mon	Tues	Weds	Thurs	Fri	Sat	Sun
6:30 a.m.							
7:00 a.m.							
7:30 a.m.							
8:00 a.m.							
8:30 a.m.							
9:00 a.m.							
9:30 a.m.							
10:00 a.m.							
10:30 a.m.							
11:00 a.m.							
11:30 a.m.							
12:00 p.m.							
12:30 p.m.							
1:00 p.m.							
1:30 p.m.							
2:00 p.m.							
2:30 p.m.							
3:00 p.m.							
3:30 p.m.							
4:00 p.m.							
4:30 p.m.							
5:00 p.m.							
5:30 p.m.							
6:00 p.m.							
6:30 p.m.							
7:00 p.m.							
7:30 p.m.							
8:00 p.m.							
8:30 p.m.							
9:00 p.m.							
9:30 p.m.							
10:00 p.m.							

Specific goals this week: _____

_____

The following have been scheduled: Total time scheduled:

☐ Family time   _____
☐ Personal time   _____
☐ Study time   _____
☐ Research & exploration time   _____
☐ Commuting time   _____
☐ Courses   _____
☐ Work   _____
☐ Open time   _____

provided to you by the school after you register.

If you buy books from a bookstore and discover a book is not correct or not really required, always return the unneeded books to the bookstore immediately! Most college bookstores limit the return period to discourage students from buying books, photocopying them, and then returning them for a full refund. If you don't return the books quickly, you will need to wait for the book buy-back at the end of the semester and will settle for pennies on the dollar—if the bookstore is buying the book back at all. New editions of textbooks supplant existing ones regularly, making your copy worthless to the bookstore.

Your First Day at College

Unless you are enrolled in a distance-education program, your first day back at school will be a little disorienting at first. (Distance education may be disorienting as well, but for reasons other than the ones we'll be discussing now.) As we suggested for registration time, is it also important to get to school early because traffic and parking may be a problem, especially at a large school. During the first couple of days almost every student is on campus at the same time, shuffling class schedules and being hassled with paperwork. We've experienced freeway backups in San Jose and Los Angeles the first day of classes at major universities that affected traffic as far as fifteen miles from the schools.

To make things as easy on yourself as possible, use your map of the campus to identify where each class is located. If you're going only part time, this won't be much of a problem. But if you are going full time at a traditional school, you'll probably be taking more than one class a day. Target the first class of the day so that as you look for parking, or when you arrive at school, you will know which direction to head in as soon as you arrive. If you arrive early enough, take time to visit the student center, buy yourself a cup of coffee, and look around a bit at the facilities. You may also want to check out the college's library—a place where you are likely to spend a fair amount of time researching and writing papers. Especially note the library's hours. Some college libraries are very accommodating, remaining open seven days a week with extended hours. At other schools, especially small ones, the library may have unusual or inconvenient hours.

On the first day or two of school, you will meet your instructors for the first time. Usually the first class of a semester is short, with the instructor introducing himself or herself and handing out a class syllabus explaining what will be required from you to successfully complete the class. The class is then dismissed about half an hour or 45 minutes into it. The exception to this scenario is adult programs that meet only once a week for a few weeks. In these programs, because class time is limited, the first night is used as a regular class meeting with the instructor delivering a lecture as well as introducing himself or herself to the class.

The first meeting of each course you have enrolled in is an excellent time to size up the instructor and change classes if you do not like what you see or hear. While some instructors appear their most threatening in the first meeting by demanding large chunks of your time or explaining how almost no one passes the class with a grade better than *C*, most of this turns into hot air as the course progresses. Some instructors make these kinds of threats early in the class simply because they want anyone that's only half committed to the program to pack their bags. Few teachers like working with students who participate in their class half-heartedly.

Getting into "Student" Mode

To get through college as an adult, you must be able to get into "student" mode. This is a new role for you, so it will take some adjustment, but it is not complicated for most people. Being a student involves learning to ask questions and do homework assignments that at the outset, may seem trivial or boring. For a senior manager in a company used to giving orders all day, this transition may be somewhat more difficult.

To get into student mode:

■ If your college has an interesting or historically important campus, walk around it to get a feel for the place, the students, and the faculty. A walk around campus is a good way to separate the thoughts of a day job from the appropriate attitude for attending night classes.

■ Learn to listen carefully before challenging the instructor.

■ Ask questions in class, but do not dominate the class meeting as you might do a meeting at your job.

■ Do the paperwork required by the school without complaining about it. In most instances, it takes less effort to handle the paperwork then it does to complain or fight the unyielding process.

■ Attempt to use what you are learning at school to better understand and accomplish work at your job. This kind of adaptive thinking improves both your work at work and your performance at school.

■ Do the reverse of the last point. Attempt to apply what you have learned at work or in life to your assignments at school. This will help you finish assignments faster and manage the entire school process more efficiently.

What If I Feel Overwhelmed the First Week of School?

If you feel overwhelmed because the mix of family, work, and school seems more than you can handle, sit down and go over your schedule objectively to see if the problem really exists or if the sudden plunge into academe is really manageable but uncomfortably different from your usual life routine. To understand this better, list your work, school, homework, and family hours for the next couple of weeks to see whether there really is a problem. Make sure you include time for commuting to school and any time required for activities such as grocery shopping and taking kids to daycare.

If you list the hours and find that the only way you can juggle the schedule is to cut back on family hours or reduce sleeping time, then you may need to drop a class or two. If, however, there are enough hours for everything, stick with it for another week and repeat this exercise. By the end of the second or third week of school, you will find yourself suddenly becoming confident in your abilities to manage school, work, and home life. After this period, class and college will begin to become a familiar routine, just like going to work.

Meet the New People at School

At almost every college, you will meet several groups of people much different from your coworkers. While you may have met all of these kinds of people before if you attended college just out of high school, as a mature student you may look at them much differently now than you did fifteen or twenty years ago. Depending on how old you are, many of these people will be younger than you, and the freshmen students in a traditional school may look like children, because many of them are still as young as seventeen.

Younger Students

A large number of students at traditional colleges and universities range in age from a very young seventeen to the mid-twenties. You may have children the same age as these youngsters. You may find the antics of the youngest students extremely juvenile and their conversations often concerned with dating and the opposite sex. This group may ignore you for the most part unless they need your help with a problem or view you as a resource for helping them skate through missed class sessions or repair botched homework assignments. Many of these students are just finding their feet in life after leaving home to attend college in a distant city. Those you get to know will ask your advice on subjects that they would normally go to their parents with. This can be a satisfying relationship for many adult students, so don't ignore the younger students. Besides, some of them have the "inside scoop" on how to survive on campus.

Fortunately, most of the younger students are quite mature and serious about college. This second group may be quite engaging to talk with. For them, you and your life experience will be an inspiration, particularly if you hold a day job that they are aspiring to.

Other Older Students

As explained earlier in this book, many of the students attending college are over thirty years of age. They, like you, have much different reasons for attending college than younger students do. Where the twenty-year-olds are talking about who is sleeping with whom, the adult students talk about work, family, and getting an education—quite possibly the same topics you like to discuss! When you are just starting school, look for students of your age who have already been attending college for a while. They can be an invaluable resource when you are choosing classes and learning the mechanics of making it through school as a mature student.

Faculty

Depending on the kind of college you are attending, the faculty may be professional instructors who love to teach, or they may be primarily concerned with research and teach only because it's part of the requirement to keep a job at the university. You may find it difficult to work with an instructor younger than yourself, much the way some people are uncomfortable working for a younger boss. For the most part, the difference in age doesn't matter, although some of the older faculty may be easier for you to relate to. It works the other way as well. Some of the younger teachers work hard to be good teachers, where some of the older ones may be burned out and tired of teaching the same classes over and over.

Be particularly careful of taking a low-numbered general education class such as English 1A or History 1A from an older instructor. In most departments, the youngest and least experienced instructors are given these classes while the older and more experienced instructors take on the more interesting upper division and graduate classes, which are more of a challenge. An older instructor teaching an entry-level lower division class may not be doing it because he or she likes to. Such a person may turn into a difficult or uninteresting instructor. (This isn't always true—but find out anyway.)

As you work with your instructors, you may find one or two you particularly like. They may like you and your work as well, and will help you get through school by providing a friendly ear when you run into obstacles at the college. At many schools, an advisor is assigned to help you choose the right classes; if it's possible, you may want to have one of these "friends" selected to be your advisor. Because they know more about you and your interests than an advisor selected by the college (or its computer), such people work harder at matching you up to the right faculty and elective classes than someone who hardly remembers you between advising sessions.

Administrators

There are a variety of administrators in all colleges. Often these people are academics who worked their way up over a period of years from assistant professor to the high rank of dean. In most universities there are many deans responsible for combinations of related departments, called "schools". For example, a single dean may oversee all of the humanities departments, called the School of Humanities. The department chairpeople, who also have administrative responsibilities, report to the dean. The chairperson may teach in some departments, or in an unusually large department, this person may do nothing but administer the department's day-to-day operations. In some colleges, the department chairperson may be chosen from the faculty and put in the position for only a year or two and then replaced with another faculty member. Deans almost never teach—they plan, budget, and manage (if they're good). Deans may change jobs, but they rarely go back to being professors. A dean who continues up the academic ranks can eventually be promoted to Provost, Vice President, or even the President of the university.

There are also a number of administrators of greater and lesser rank working in departments that are behind the scenes. These "invisible" people run departments such as Admissions and Records, the Registrar's Office, and Operations. The people who run these departments may be called deans, directors, or vice presidents or given other titles.

If you ever have a serious complaint that can't be resolved at the department chairperson level, then an appointment with the dean or director who oversees that department or functional area is your next option. In most cases this is the only time you will meet a senior administrator in person.

Counselors

All colleges have counselors or advisors who help you choose your classes unless the curriculum is rigidly predefined (rare). Some schools also have vocational or career guidance counselors who help you choose a line of work to pursue after college. A large university may even have mental health counselors to help students with emotional or psychological problems.

Since you may rarely see your counselor, often only at the beginning of a semester or academic year, you want to make the most of such meetings, and it helps if your counselor is both highly knowledgeable about the school and someone that you can talk with comfortably. If you are assigned a counselor who appears unknowledgeable or indifferent to your needs, try to change counselors. Most colleges have a mechanism that allows you to switch counselors if necessary.

After a counselor lays out a program, check it carefully against the requirements for your degree in the college catalog. Mistakes are common and as an adult learner who must get your degree as quickly as possible, you can't afford to take classes you don't need. At some colleges, the advisors are completely unaccountable for making mistakes. If they put you into the wrong classes, it's your problem, not theirs. You still need to make up the missing classes and pay the tuition to get your degree.

Others

Many other people are associated with a college. These include library personnel, engineers, employees who oversee the campus physical plant and grounds, and people who operate the bookstore and food concessions. Some of these people have degrees, especially the library personnel and people running facilities such as the student medical center. These degreed people are called Academic Professionals because they have degrees similar to those of the faculty and fulfill educational functions at the university even though they do not teach. In most schools, Academic Professionals have ranks just like the faculty.

You now have a snapshot of the people you will meet in your first few days at school and have been introduced to the processes you will encounter when you begin your college program. While at a few adult or distance-oriented colleges, many of the people and mechanics explained in this chapter will be less visible, if you attend a program in almost any community college, public college, or university, most of the people and procedures are standard. They may simply vary in size, complexity, and effectiveness.

How to Get through Your Program

After getting through the first few weeks of your program, you'll be on your way, and if you stick to the plan, you'll reach your college goals.

If it's really that easy, why do some adult college students quit before they finish? After putting all the effort into the beginning of a program, it's a shame to leave school before the degree is earned. It's simply a waste of time, energy, and money to drop out of school when you're only half done, unless there is a very good reason to do so.

When adults leave a college program unfinished, they can feel debased and humiliated because of their perceived failure to live up to their own expectations. But this never needs to happen if you are prepared in advance. All that is required for anyone to finish college is a realistic plan, a rational approach, some motivational skills, and a support system. We've already provided some guidelines for putting these components together so you can get the education and degree you need and want. In addition, you may find that this general advice, gleaned from our own students, makes it easier to get through your program:

Advice for Any Adult Student:

- Ask questions in class. No one will think you are stupid. For every question you have, there are ten other people in the class who wanted to know the answer too, but were afraid to ask.
- Get involved in class discussions. Be visible. This is very important in traditional schools with large classes. Research has shown that students who are recognized by an instructor consistently do better on exams and papers than students who are viewed as strangers.
- Don't make cramming your usual way to study for exams. Cram only when absolutely necessary. Cramming is stressful and not always efficient. And material memorized this way for a test or exam is largely forgotten within as little as 48 hours. That means that you won't have it available for later tests and for use in life after college.
- Find and read the professor's publications, if he or she has any.
- Talk personally with your professors, but don't waste their time with too many annoying after-class questions. Remember that these people may be as busy as you are.
- Find out which professors are most respected by reading *Who's Who* and other academic indices and by asking others in the school and the department.
- Visit professors during office hours to discuss a subject that interests you and get to know the person who teaches it.
- Find out which research or special projects are going on and join in on any basis, from volunteer to paid professional.

- Become acquainted with your advisors and the staff for financial aid, grants, and support programs.
- Get to know the department staff of your declared major or one in which you have a budding interest. Every dean, for example, has a counselor, secretary, and assistant. Introduce yourself, ask questions, and read bulletin boards for events.
- Meet the dean of your school informally through social means and formally by attending open meetings and lectures. Deans are very powerful people and can come in handy if you need a waiver or a special approval.

Advice for Adult Graduate Students:
- Establish close relationships with professors and teaching assistants who may be advocates for you later.
- Ask to attend meetings or conventions with professors, at first on an observation basis, then with some duties.
- Get the reading list for comprehensive examinations (if required) before you enroll in the program. And start reading the material before you apply to the program. If you can't handle the reading list, you won't be able to stand the program.

Advice for Completing Research Papers and Term Projects:
- Try not to procrastinate. Start assignments early, especially research papers. If possible, meet with the professor or teaching assistant to discuss the structure and concept of your work before you turn it in.
- Find people in your company or in your chosen field who will be willing to act as advisors or provide you with case materials from their experience for your projects. This will give your work a real-world perspective and may have practical benefits in getting your abilities noticed in the outside world.
- Compare your papers with those of other students. Form a study group. Learn how to express ideas successfully.
- Write your papers for the additional purpose of trying to publish them in a campus newspaper or magazine or in a professional journal or popular publication. This is very important if you want to pursue an academic- or research-oriented career after graduation.
- Build on your projects and papers as you go through your course of study. Allow each research assignment to serve as part of a whole concept that could be expanded into a thesis or dissertation. (This is especially important for graduate students.)

Advice on Outside Activities:
- Find out the array of activities that are geared toward adults (there will be some on almost any campus, and some that are available to adult and younger students, such as theater, debate clubs, business forums, etc.) from the student organization office, other students, or professors. Deter-

mine which skills are required for activities that interest you, and get involved with at least one activity for each school calendar period.

■ After you get involved, observe the style of the club members and try to assimilate it before suggesting something new.

■ Don't isolate yourself because you are going to school. Develop your business, arts, and service contacts outside the campus.

Advice about Using Career Counseling Services:

■ If you are interested in career development, go to the career counseling center early and discover what it offers. These centers are not only for younger students, so take advantage of the services.

■ Take workshops and seminars to make professional contacts with people in your field of interest who are not involved in school. These people can give you more real-life perspective on your education and the skills required to succeed in your new career.

■ Start a placement file with letters of recommendation from professors whose courses you have recently taken and excelled in. It helps if you draft a letter for them, even if it is difficult for you to say glowing things about yourself. A career counselor will show you samples of appropriate letters for your file.

■ When you get close to graduating, sign up for mock interview sessions. Practice and then tape yourself. Ask others to coach you on improving your presentation. This opportunity is as useful for experienced executives as it is for traditional college students.

■ Be sure to contact graduates of the school (alumni) who work in your field of interest. This is called "networking," and it is an incredibly important and powerful tool for putting your degree to work after you graduate.

Develop Your Support System

Though your education is a personal quest, it does not have to be a solitary activity. One of the most frequently cited reasons for dropping out of college is the lack of support of other people. So that this doesn't happen to you, it is important that you start the development of your support system in college from day one.

No matter how independent and self-motivated you are, there will be times when you need other people to help you get through. These people can provide advice, counseling, or just plain moral support. The school personnel, faculty, students, and advisors we discussed earlier in this chapter are all part of the important support system you require and should develop to get through school. The other important people in your support system are your family and friends. If you keep them involved and informed of your school activities, it will be easier for them to support you—and we can't overemphasize the importance of family support for an adult student in college.

Develop a Study Group

One additional support mechanism that is consistently useful to adult students is the *study group*. (Study groups are also called learning teams, support networks, etc.) Many non-traditional and adult-oriented schools require students to form study groups or teams as part of the school's prescribed educational program. If you are not attending one of these schools, we still recommend that you develop a private study group with other adult students. Just ask people you meet—many will be happy to have a new friend and share the experience of school with someone with a similar background.

The trick to making study groups work is to meet regularly. The closer the relationships are in the group, the more support the group will provide when individual students need it. The study group can also reduce studying time by taking advantage of collective insight and wisdom to complete course assignments and is a great source of understanding and sympathy when your family and friends just don't seem to relate to your school priorities or interests.

Consider Getting a Mentor

In addition to a study group, you may want to consider getting a mentor to help you through school. As you've undoubtedly discovered already, many times it is not *what* you know but *whom* you know that counts. This is true in college as well as in your career. As someone new to college, you will need to learn the unwritten rules and "insider" behavior necessary to make your college work easier and more profitable. One good way to get the inside scoop on things is to search out a mentor for yourself. Mentors can save you time and energy, two things that are precious and limited in your life as an adult college student.

The ideal mentor for adults in college is one of the following:

- A well-regarded graduate of the same school who is about your age and who majored in the same area.
- A faculty member or other school advisor who is willing to take you under his or her wing.

A mentor should also have significant achievements in areas of interest to you and in school-related accomplishments that can serve as models for your own endeavors. Mentoring relationships can be either casual or formal. Casual mentoring relationships involve getting together over coffee or lunch and having discussions about your questions, problems, and concerns. Formal relationships may involve a regularly scheduled meeting, say once a month. Besides meetings and discussions, your mentor may get you involved in organizations, seminars, and other activities that will expand your network of contacts.

Mentoring relationships don't just happen. You need to pursue them. If you want to take advantage of a mentoring relationship, we suggest you search out an appropriate person. Try to get work as a research assistant if you have the time to meet potential mentors on the faculty or staff. If you aren't able to spend much time on campus, take the initiative and schedule some meetings with faculty and advisors. Ask these people for help. Invite the ones you like to lunch. Eventually you will find a friend and a mentor, if you keep looking. When you meet someone you feel has the right "chemistry" and the right background, ask him or her to be your mentor.

Ultimately, the mentor relationship is a special kind of friendship. You must like the person and the person must like you for the mentor–protégé relationship to be of value. A mentor should believe in your abilities. A mentor should always have your best interests at heart. Like any friendship, the mentorship relationship requires ongoing commitment from you and your mentor. The benefit of this commitment can be a lifelong supportive relationship for both of you.

One bit of advice for adults who want to finish college: Never lose sight of those around you who have feelings for you. Embarking on an intensive program, especially if you are also working, can leave many burn marks if you don't pay attention to your family as well as your studies. It's possible to work full time, go to school, and be with your family—but you need to manage your time effectively to make things work. Also, keep things in perspective—there *is* life after college.

At this point, you have enough information to put a program of study together and get started. Now finishing school is only a matter of getting your academic skills in shape and working through the course assignments. We'll give you some advice for getting those study skills developed in the next chapter.

Adult College Students in Their Own Words
Sal LaDuca

I have weathered several setbacks, recouped, and been set back again—you might call it a recurring saga—and now I finally have my degree—thanks to the flexibility of the Online Program at the University of Phoenix.

I came to this country when I was thirteen. I was immediately kept back two grades in school due to the language gap. A girl my age was assigned to assist me with the English language. I was embarrassed to ask the girl for help, but within three months I spoke fluent English. I mastered the language, lost my accent, and excelled in college entrance tests.

After high school, I went to the University of Pittsburgh at Bradford. The Bradford campus is small and provincial. I did quite well the first year, but was spending most of my time studying. The second year I began participating in extracurricular activities. Then there arrived women, wine, and song. My grades began to slump. Vietnam was just over the horizon, and I was contemplating getting drafted and shot. I dropped out. College setback number one.

I sought work, found some, got hit by a recession, and lost my job in a strike. I thought I'd give the military a try to acquire some hard skills—hoping I wouldn't see action in Vietnam. I joined the Navy, as a Reactor Operator/Electronic Technician. From the quiet Pennsylvania surroundings I was catapulted to Illinois, Florida, and then New York for training. I got assigned to a ship that was not fully built. While at the boat works I took some courses at a local college and completed an associate degree in liberal arts. (My previous major was physics.) The Navy had other collegiate programs. My favorite, NESEP (Navy Enlisted Scientific Education Program), would allow me to complete my bachelor's degree and return as an officer. I was told that the program had run out of money about four months before I applied, I replied that I needed only two years to finish my degree, but it didn't matter. College setback number two.

I completed my Navy contract and was offered a job with Jersey Central Power and Light. They too had an academic development program that provided career opportunities. When I asked about the career opportunities, I was asked if I had a degree. When I said I had an A.A., they said to get the bachelor's. Though I took some courses in computer programming at a community college, these didn't count toward my bachelor's degree.

I changed jobs within the same company and began working different shifts. My job situation became burdensome, and I sought a way out. Concurrently I was looking at what I could possibly do to get a degree to open a few more doors. My wife and other relatives suggested finishing school—somehow. I bought a computer and a modem. After having the modem sit for eleven months and gather cobwebs, I borrowed a friend's software and was able to activate the modem. The first thing I tried was CompuServe. CompuServe publishes a monthly magazine, and it was there that I saw a peculiar ad about online college degrees offered by the University of Phoenix. I thought, "How is this possible?" I sent a query to UOP in February, 1990. In April I was enrolled, and my company gladly paid the bill for tuition. I graduated in May of 1992 at the age of 38 with a fully accredited bachelor's degree in business. And now I am considering getting a master's degree as well—I think.

Chapter Nine

Rebuilding Your Study Skills

Like most adults returning to school, you have probably been away from the demands of reading, formal writing, and other requirements of higher education for many years.

Some adult students never had great study habits to begin with. Adults relate to information in different ways and have different retention patterns than do younger learners. This means that new study skills must be adopted to meet the academic requirements of modern college programs. Whether or not you were a good student before, study habits must be relearned and reformulated to meet the challenges of attending college in mid-life. This chapter offers advice and techniques to help you meet the challenge.

Remember, there are really only six things which all good students are able to do, regardless of their particular aptitude in specific areas:

1. Manage their time.
2. Prioritize what needs to be done.
3. Take adequate notes.
4. Study and retain information.
5. Read and write.
6. Take tests effectively.

Anyone can learn to do these six things—it's just a matter of putting your mind to it. The first step in rebuilding your study skills is to establish your current strengths and weaknesses. To do this, complete the Study Skills Worksheet we have provided in this chapter. The worksheet will identify your weaknesses and your fears about studying. Once you know where you stand, don't wait until you begin college to start improving your study skills; start today.

The First Study Skill Is Time Management

We suggested, in Chapter Eight, that you create a schedule of your time. Every hour and virtually every minute of your life must be scheduled and organized if you are to get everything done. In addition to developing a comprehensive weekly schedule, here are some other suggestions to maximize your study time:

Study Skills Worksheet

Skills In each box, rate your ability in each skill area on a scale of 1 to 5. 1 = weak, 5 = very strong.	Plan for Improvement
☐ Reading skills	_____
☐ Vocabulary	_____
☐ Writing skills	_____
☐ Math skills	_____
☐ Note-taking skills	_____
☐ Listening skills	_____
☐ Time management skills	_____
☐ Library/research skills	_____
☐ Test-taking skills	_____
☐ Memory	_____

My biggest fear about studying is:

_____

_____

_____

My most important studying strength is:

_____

_____

_____

My greatest weakness in studying is:

_____

_____

_____

_____

■ Determine your most effective study time and schedule your schoolwork accordingly. Studying depends on your concentration. To concentrate you need to be mentally alert and energetic. Adults have different clocks— some of us are early birds, some of us are night owls. There's no sense scheduling your study time late at night if you just fall asleep in your chair. Recognize the times when your mental energy is at its peak. Schedule your studying time (as much as possible) during these optimum times. You should then schedule leisure, family, and other activities around the study times.

■ Use *half* your lunch hour as reading time at work. Don't use the entire lunch hour, however. You still need a break and time to talk with other people. Besides, its not good for your digestion to work and eat at the same time. Eating time is for eating. Study time should be separate.

■ Read your notes into a tape recorder. Then, listen to them in the car while you are commuting to and from work. It's a great way to reinforce material before exams.

■ If you commute to work by bus or other public transportation, use the commuting time as study time.

■ Have a family get together each week in which you explain five interesting things you learned that week. This helps reinforce the material you studied and also gets your family involved in your education.

You Can't Finish College If You Can't Read

> Reading makes a full man, meditation a profound man, discourse a clear man.
>
> —*Benjamin Franklin*

There is no way out of it—you need to be able to read to finish college. You need to read a lot. If you are already an avid reader, this shouldn't be a problem. But if you have become a television couch potato over the last few years, whose only contact with the literary world is the listings in *TV Guide*, then you need to start a reading program immediately to build your skills.

If you are a good but slow reader, we have heard many students say they benefit from taking a speed reading course or getting a book on speed reading and implementing its recommendations.

Vocabulary development books are a good idea as well if you haven't been reading much lately. Some books we recommend on developing your reading skills are listed in the reference section of this book. Most schools provide basic skills courses to develop your reading skills as well. Take advantage of them if you need to.

After Reading Comes Writing

You will definitely be required to write in order to finish college. If you write for a living, you can probably skip this section. Some adults write in their work or for pleasure, but most people don't. In fact, writing is one skill learned in school that most adults fail to develop during their working lives. It may have been years since you wrote a formal paper. (Maybe you have *never* written one.) Even if you write business letters and simple correspondence at your job, you probably don't write research papers or essays. The bad news is that your writing skills are probably worse now than they were when you left school years ago. The good news is that your poor writing skills are not an obstacle to finishing college because there are so many books, classes, and writing development programs to get your skills back in shape.

You should know that almost every college has a remedial writing program or a reentry writing program for returning adult students. These courses are always full of people. This indicates two things: (1.) The average writing skills of Americans today are not adequate to begin college. (2.) You will not be the only person in school who has writing deficiencies. If you're willing to ask for help with your writing, it will be there.

Improve Your Memory with Smart Studying Techniques

First, as mentioned earlier in this book, forget the myth that your memory and intelligence deteriorate as you get older. You're just out of practice. Unless you've had a debilitating illness or an accident that has affected your neurological system, you have plenty of mental capacity to do what you need to do to get through college. (And, if you have had an illness, there are special services for handicapped adults to help them through college—so don't despair. Just contact the disabled student's office and find out what tutoring and support services are available for you.)

We suggest that you start a mental exercise program as soon as possible— even before you start school. If you don't read, start reading. If you don't go to the library, make some weekend trips and find out what's happening there. Watch the educational channel instead of sitcoms on TV. Get some books on speed reading, study skills, and memory improvement, and implement the exercises, and practice the techniques.

Once you make mental exercises part of your regular regimen, there are some other ways that you should know about to maximize your retention of information. First, it is important to know that information is stored in different ways depending on how you acquire it. Information from written material is stored in one part of the brain, information obtained by ear in another, and non-written visual information in yet another. Though this is a gross oversimplification of the overall psychological and neurological processes, it gets to the heart of the memorization and studying issue. Simply put, the more ways you record the same information in your brain, the easier it will be to retain and recall when you need it. We suggest the following studying method, based on this principle, for maximum retention when you are studying written material:

1. Get an overview of the material you are studying by reviewing the outline and summaries in the text or in your notes. This prepares a mental picture of the material or a framework for you to hang specific information on. Your lecture notes as well as the textbook can be used for getting this overview.

2. Ask yourself some questions about the material you are studying. What fascinates you? What do you want to know? What confuses you? What things were left unanswered in class? Make a list if possible of all the questions that come to mind *before* you start your formal reading. If you have questions in your mind, you will automatically search out the answers as you study. Thus, you brain looks for answers and stores them for future reference. This is something we call the "eureka" effect—when you find the answer (eureka), your brain gets excited and records it.

3. Take written notes on key concepts, terms, and references immediately after reading the material. Some people also like to underline with a highlighting marker as they read, but we recommend that you read the material first without highlighting it. Then, if you want to highlight important concepts for future reference, do so as a separate activity. If you highlight as you read, you lose the overall flow and presentation of the material. When you write the information (and highlight it) you are using a physical activity to record the information in your brain, and this again reinforces what you have read.

4. Read your notes out loud. Some of our students also read their notes into a tape recorder so they can play the information back and listen to the notes later.

5. Review the material and test yourself. Try to figure out what an instructor would ask about the material, or make a list of the things you want to retain for the future and then try to recall them the next day on your own, without the notes.

If you follow these five steps religiously, you will find that your memory gets into shape in almost no time. It's like any exercise—the more you do it, the easier it gets.

Improve Your Listening Skills, Too

Good studying also involves good listening skills. It is through listening that you are able to take good notes—and your class notes (if you are taking traditional courses or even telecourses) are the key to doing well in college. There are two ways to take notes. The way you choose will depend on your time and your ability:

1. The Traditional Way.

This involves taking notes as you listen to the lecture. The trick here is to develop a personal shorthand that is legible. Also, learn to take down key points first and then add the details as you are able. We suggest you rewrite the notes as soon after class as possible, to add the details you were unable to jot down during the lecture.

2. The Smart Student Technique.

Record the lecture. There are some great miniature tape recorders and dictating machines that are silent and unobtrusive for under $40. They are available at most discount houses and business supply stores. The only trick to recording a lecture is to get permission in advance. Almost every professor will let you do this, though some will make you promise to erase the tapes after the course. (If the instructor is unreasonable, inform him or her that you have arthritis in your hands that prohibits you from taking notes. Since most adults have some arthritis, it's only a little stretch of the truth.) Always sit in front of the class if you plan to record the session, and put the recorder on top of a purse or notebook to reduce the vibrations that can make the tape unclear. The recorder can free your attention from taking detailed notes during the lecture, so you can really absorb what is being said. We suggest that you still take notes on any information on the board or presented in visual formats that cannot be recorded. When you get home, listen to the lecture again and take notes as you listen. This will reinforce what you have heard—and you won't miss any key points, because you can just rewind the tape and listen again.

We recommend the recording technique whenever possible. The only downside is that it takes a bit longer. But because it uses the multiple-input rule we spoke about before, you will retain more from the lectures. Remember, the more ways you record the information, the easier it is for your brain to recall it. Of course, you will need to practice listening for this method to work. If you just fall asleep during the recording session, you haven't gained anything in the process.

Developing good listening skills involves the following:

- Being mentally awake and prepared to listen.
- Being in tune with the topic when you are listening. If you are thinking about something else you are not listening.
- Asking questions when you don't understand something the speaker has said.
- Becoming aware of your own "filters," processes that cause information to be modified in your brain as it is stored. Filters include biases, past experience, and attitudes that color what you hear. Past experience and existing knowledge always affect and color what we learn. In listening this is especially true. We "hear" what is simple to understand. We filter out the details and the complexities. We misinterpret what a person says because we have a bias or other wrong information stored in our brain already. We let other people's comments affect our interpretations of material. Be aware of these problems and try to remain objective as you listen. Listening skills are more difficult to teach and learn because of these internal filters—it will take practice to overcome them.

Use the Library and Online Bibliographic Search Services

If you haven't visited a major research library lately, you'll be surprised to know that libraries don't contain just books anymore—they contain computerized databases, microfiche records, journals, dissertations, videotapes, interactive courses in various formats, recordings, and much more. Because of the information and resources contained within, the library should be your favorite place to visit when you attend college. Effective use of the library can markedly affect your performance in school. If you are not aware of the many and wondrous things in your university library, ask the librarian about scheduling a tour of the facilities.

For some reason adult students often feel they are wasting the librarian's time when they ask for help. They mistakenly think they should be "old enough to use a library." As a result of this misguided thinking, librarians are often the most underutilized professionals on campus. Modern research libraries are vast and complicated. Librarians need master's degrees in library science because it takes a long time to master the intricacies of modern information storage and retrieval. There's more to using a library than learning how to use the card catalog. Librarians have a wealth of knowledge about resources and reference materials that is not available from any other source. Meet the librarians and ask them to help—they are there to make your time in the library more effective. In addition, every traditional school with a library has a library orientation program—take advantage of it. If you will be using a local library for research, meet the librarians there as well. They have the same advanced degrees in library science as the professionals who oversee the university libraries. They would much rather use their knowledge to help you locate information than collect fines for overdue books.

Besides using the library, you should learn to use one of the online bibliographic search facilities. These computer-based services can save days in accessing information on topics of all kinds. These services are available from the school libraries as well as through information services like CompuServe. The librarian will be glad to give you information on the services available through the school.

Learn to Take Tests and Reduce Text Anxiety

Failure is success if we learn from it.

—Malcolm Forbes

It's the tests more than anything else that put fear into adult students returning to college after many years away from school. Some courses and programs have more "traditional" tests than others. Traditional tests are those timed multiple choice and essay tests done in a tense classroom with the instructor lording over the front of the room. Fortunately, some of the more progressive schools have determined that there are other ways to evaluate a student's mastery of college material.

But, even in the most progressive program, you will have to take a test eventually. Most adults have not had to take tests in years. And test taking is definitely a skill that requires practice. To get over your test anxiety, we recommend the following:

1. Adequate preparation for a test is always your first defense.
2. Practice taking written exams by writing the questions and answering them on your own. When you actually take a written examination, remember to do the following:
   - Compose each answer as an entire essay, with a defined beginning, middle, and end. Bring in related subjects and expand when clearly called for, not simply as filler.
   - Approach your professor early with questions when topics have been given or alluded to. Show an outline of your answer to determine whether the substance and style are appropriate.
   - Learn to think about what the facts mean instead of merely reciting them by rote. Learn what recognized theorists believe and state whether you agree or disagree.
   - Discuss your exam afterward with your professor to find out how you can improve your answering style or where you went wrong. Don't worry about changing your grade; concentrate on learning.
   - During the meetings with the instructors, take notes about your exams; it's easy to forget what is difficult to hear.
3. When taking objective tests (tests with multiple choice or fill-in-the-blank formats), remember to do the following:
   - Read books on the psychology of multiple-choice tests and learn how to distinguish the patterns.
   - Find old exams on file in the departments, if possible, and study the questions and answers. Ask for help if necessary.

And always, *always* remember—cramming is not a substitute for planned studying, but it is sometimes better than nothing.

Establish a Private Study Area in Your Home

Your study area is almost as important as your study skills. You need a place that will be acknowledged by the rest of the family as your private study place. When you are in this room or place, family members automatically know it is your study time and refrain from interrupting your work.

Your study space should be as spacious as possible. It should include a desk or writing area and a sitting area with a comfortable chair for reading. In addition, there should be a bookcase or shelves for storing your texts and other materials. It should also be well lit and as quiet as possible.

If you don't have enough space in your home to dedicate an entire room to your study area (and few adults with families have this luxury,) then you must be creative in designing your study space. We have seen excellent study areas made from closets, attics, cellars, and garages. A room can be partitioned temporarily with a screen. People have even built tree houses or purchased portable storage sheds to use as their study rooms. What the study area is made from doesn't really matter—the most important thing is that it is your own private space.

We also recommend your study area be equipped with the following:

- A personal computer and a printer, or if you still don't believe in the advantages of the computer, a self-correcting electronic typewriter.
- Bookshelves.
- A small filing cabinet (surprisingly inexpensive at local office supply stores).
- Lots of pens and pencils.
- Multiple lamps for reading.
- A big wastebasket.
- Manila folders and lots of paper.
- A comprehensive dictionary (spend some money and get a good one), a thesaurus (either a computerized or a traditional printed one), and a writing guide such as the *Chicago Manual of Style*, *Words into Print*, or the *MLA Guide to Research Papers,* or some similar reference about editing your writing and formatting papers.

You should make sure that everyone in the family knows that your study area is not to be touched and nothing is to be borrowed from your study area until *after* you finish college. It's extremely frustrating to settle into your study room for the night and find all your pens missing and your papers rearranged. You end up wasting precious time looking for things instead of getting your reading and assignments done.

Eventually, you will learn to study anywhere whenever you have a few minutes to read or jot down notes. But, it is still important to have a "home base" for studying that you can call your own.

As you continue to study and start reaping the benefits of your new knowledge, it will become easier to find the time to get your college assignments done. But, even with the best laid plans and most highly developed study strategies, problems and frustrations will inevitably arise in your pursuit of a college degree. In the next chapter, we deal with some of these frustrations and obstacles and suggest ways that will help keep you on track toward meeting your lifelong learning goals.

Chapter Ten

Dealing with the Problems Everyone Encounters

We have worked with many hundreds of adult college students over the last fifteen years and recently interviewed hundreds more in preparing this book. Most of the students we have worked with admit that they had at least some problems and setbacks getting through college. They consistently comment that in retrospect it would have been easier if someone had warned them that their problems were normal and expected. One reason we wrote this book is that we strongly believe problems anticipated are problems avoided.

Going back to college as an adult inevitably brings changes in a person's lifestyle, schedules, and social interactions. This chapter provides an overview of the changes that can be expected and ways to deal with the expected and the unexpected challenges that every mid-career student encounters in the process of obtaining a degree.

The Changes You Should Consider Normal

Going to college will irreversibly change your life. It will take up a considerable part of your time, and some classes will get you excited about learning and more in touch with the world around you. You initially may find it difficult to keep your mind on your job and your family because of the enthusiasm you feel for your classes and the challenge of putting your mind to work learning and integrating knowledge. You may even find it difficult to sleep when a particularly intriguing project is underway.

Other changes may occur as well. You may find that as you progress in your classes, you become less interested in your coworkers and some of your less educated friends because you are beginning to explore a world that they don't really know exists. You also may find yourself having more interesting conversations with your children who are also attending school. Depending on the classes you are taking, you may have much more to share with your kids, who may be studying the same subjects. This kind of dialog is useful because it helps you frame your thinking to better understand the information, and your children may get a deeper understanding of the topic than they would at school. You may also find their point of view on a topic an interesting twist to the way you had been looking at it.

As an adult in college you can also expect people to change their attitudes toward you. As a student, you assume a new role and a new prestige. People, espe-cially other adults who have been thinking about college themselves, will be curi-ous about your program, the amount of work you have to do, and your motivations for returning to school. Most people are just curious, but many are also asking themselves at the same time whether college is something they should pursue. Most of them will treat you with respect and admiration for returning to college, though you may find a few skeptics and jealous individuals who attempt to trivial-ize your efforts. Ignore the negative and instead revel in the positive reinforcement you get from most of the people you'll meet.

You will meet a new group of people who have a different attitude: college employees. From the professors to the administrators to the janitors, you will be treated as a student, regardless of your age. For the most part being treated as a stu-dent is pleasant; your professors will enlighten you with their enthusiasm for their subject matter while challenging you to learn and prosper from the experience. Other college and university personnel enjoy watching the students and their ac-tivities and are quite friendly, accommodating, and helpful. Unfortunately, a small percentage of college staffs are less friendly. To some professors and the more bu-reaucratic members of the school's administration, you may seem unimportant, more like a number to be processed than a student. Avoid such professors wherever possible by changing to another class or class section and ignore the unfriendly at-titude of some administrators and have as little contact with them as possible.

You will also have much less free time than you may be accustomed to. This isn't much of a problem once you adjust to it, but you may miss your favorite TV shows when you are attending class or working on projects. You will also have less time for your family, and you must be careful to set aside time for them. For many students, using a calendar or organizer with days broken down into hours is a good way to manage time and make sure that home, work, school, and family get the at-tention they all deserve. This is explained in the next section.

You Will Need to Keep Family and Work in Proper Perspective

Because school is important to adults, once they make the commitment to finish, it's easy for the college program to become a person's first and only priority in life. As important as college is, it should only be one priority among many. It's important to keep this perspective. We've seen too many students get into family or employment trouble because they lost perspective about their other priorities. Planning is your first defense so this doesn't happen.

You also need to plan a schedule that makes the best use of your time so that classwork is evenly distributed across the time you will attend college. Otherwise, an unusually heavy schedule during one semester or year may interfere with your family and employment commitments. Remember, you need the support and un-derstanding of your family and friends to help you get through your program, so make them part of the plan.

Dealing with Family Obligations

When setting up your program, you must first get a commitment from your family that they "buy in" to your education program. To make them aware of the level of commitment, carefully outline the course work you will be engaged in, estimate the time requirements, and ensure that your family understands that during these times, you will be unavailable for family matters except those of great urgency.

Explain that when you are home studying or working on projects you can't be interrupted and that noise is detrimental to completing your work. Let each family member know that you are not ignoring him or her, but instead doing something good for the entire family even though it will mean slightly less contact with them until you complete your studies. Tell them you're counting on their emotional support to help you make it through your program.

To further keep family members informed of your activities, buy a large wall calendar and hang it prominently in a part of the house where your family frequently congregates, such as the kitchen or family room. Mark estimates of time that will be required for school each day of each month and mark your free time to be with family and friends, so that family members will get a better idea of your time commitments. Do this at the start of each month rather than for an entire semester so that the times and dates more accurately reflect your professors' class agendas. Make sure to mark extra study time for weeks with exams. As for external family members (ones not living with you), make sure that the entire family knows that you are busy with college, but set aside time for these people as well. If you keep in contact with these family members, they won't feel abandoned. By keeping your calendar with scheduled time-off periods, you can take the time off without feeling guilty or worrying that you are neglecting a school project. After the first couple of months, you will get better and better at creating schedules that accurately reflect your time requirements.

Dealing with Employment Obligations

Because your job is important to your continued welfare, you must take extra care that the boss doesn't perceive you as letting work slip for school. The best way to do this is to discuss your program and objectives with your boss before starting out on your program. (But do not tell the boss that your objective is a better job somewhere else!) This should probably take place in two meetings. The first meeting should take place before you are firm on a program to let your boss know that you plan to go back to school. Then a second meeting should take place to provide your boss with more information on your program and how much of your time will be required during a typical week. Either or both of these meetings can be used to discuss financial support from your company, as explained in Chapter Seven.

If you can attend classes during work hours, use a calendar or message board at the office to let your boss and coworkers know where you are. If you communicate your activities, no one can say that you were sneaking off to school during time you pretended to be working.

Perhaps the most important idea to keep in mind is that there are many scheduling options. If you plan your schedule intelligently, you need not be overwhelmed by several assignments coming due at the same time. Many counselors stress that proper scheduling can be a critical factor in the success or failure of a student. The flexibility of scheduling helps not only in coordinating courses with each other, but also in coordinating classwork with the demands of the "real world." It is possible to schedule lighter loads for your busier seasons and heavier loads for when you have more time to devote to your studies.

The Bureaucracy Will Drive You Crazy from Application to Graduation

In addition to the problems we've just covered, there is one pervasive problem we hear adult students talk about more than any other—the bureaucracy of the school. Each college, university, or degree program, even the smallest, most humanistic one, have a bureaucracy that will at one time or another seem difficult to access or tedious to work with. While some schools have less bureaucracy (forms and procedures) than others, there isn't a college student we have spoken to, adult or otherwise, who hasn't expressed some anxiety and frustration with the system for one reason or another.

One way of dealing with and getting through the bureaucracy is to anticipate that there will be some. You can also expect to complete a lot of forms before you get your degree. There are forms for applications, forms for graduation, financial aid forms, schedule forms, enrollment forms, and planning forms. Resisting them and dreading them won't help. Just grin and bear it. It's part of the program. Some of the forms are useful. Many are redundant. Of course, it is reasonable to provide constructive criticism, along with suggestions for improving the forms or procedures, to the school administration. Your feedback will not likely help you, however—it will benefit only those who come after you. Remember what we've said before—part of getting through college is learning to jump through the hoops. Bureaucracy is just another hoop.

Of course, your best defense against the negative aspects of bureaucracy is your own planning and research about the system, requirements, and procedures at the school of your choice. Here are the steps we recommend for minimizing bureaucratic problems while going to college:

1. Read everything your school sends you as soon as possible. Read it carefully, and understand your obligations. Nothing that is printed in your school catalog or schedule should ever be a surprise to you. *Read it all.*
2. Ask questions about anything you don't understand before you complete any form. If you get an unreasonable response, ask someone else and verify the response with someone of authority. Yes, this is frustrating—but we guarantee that there are some employees at every school who give arbitrary and uninformed responses just because they don't want to take the time to find out the accurate information. At other

times, the program may have changed and employees of the school are simply unaware of the new requirements, guidelines, or procedures. We haven't found a school (or business, or family) with a perfect communication system yet; we don't expect you will either. (If you do, let us know. It will make a great book.)

3. Know the deadlines, and always get the forms in early. We've said this before, but it deserves repeating. If you wait until the last minute, you are asking for problems.

4. The minute something is wrong in your records, find out how you can correct the information, and make sure the process is initiated immediately. Don't wait until the week before you plan to graduate to verify that grades have been changed or to add a course that was missing from your grade report. Verify grade changes and course records each semester. If something isn't right, get it fixed while you can still remember the instructor's name and have the finished assignments to prove you completed the course.

5. Always get approvals, in writing, to change programs, substitute courses, take a leave of absence, or transfer credit—and always get the approvals from someone in the department who actually has the authority to give them. Department secretaries do not have authority to issue changes or grades or make recommendations about courses. Deans, department chairpeople, and other senior administrators usually do. In some schools faculty are authorized to approve program changes, but in some schools they are not. Find out before you act on their recommendations.

6. Don't just take anybody's word that one course is the same as another. Sunny once had a student who was told by a faculty member, "I don't see any reason why International Marketing shouldn't meet your core marketing requirement." Of course, the faculty member also taught International Marketing. The student took the course and received an A. When this same student thought he had completed all the courses for graduation, he found that International Marketing did not substitute for the core marketing course required for the M.B.A. degree. He was frustrated and upset, but he still had to take an additional course before he could graduate. The moral: Just because someone says something to you doesn't mean it's so. And if another student tells you she did it, that's fine. But don't think that means it will fly for you unless you get it approved. The school's catalog is your first source of information. If the course you want to take is not specified in the school or program catalog as an approved option, get your program changes approved in writing by someone of authority before you take the course and a chance.

7. Be patient and understanding with the administration and support staff, and they will be more patient and understanding of you. Remember, you are not the only student in the school. Though you deserve to be

treated with respect and dignity, so do the people who are just trying to do their jobs in the administration offices. A kind word or a thank you goes a long way with these folks. The office staff probably dreads the forms and procedures more than you do, but in order to keep records, schedule classes, and get grades out, forms and records are a necessity at any school. On a positive note, each form completed correctly puts you that much closer to your college degree.

8. Be thorough and neat. We don't want to insult your intelligence by saying this, but you won't believe some of the coffee-stained, smudged, illegible junk we have seen otherwise intelligent adults submit for their permanent files. Usually the unreadable messes are turned in with sincere excuses like, "The kid got sick," or "I had to write it at lunch hour," or "My hard disk crashed last night and I had to write it out by hand," or something else predictable. Forget the excuses—the faculty and administrators have heard them all before. Things will go smoother with the entire college process if you make your forms readable, timely, and complete. Type them if your handwriting is of questionable legibility. If you absolutely refuse to learn to type at this point in your life, look at the services bulletin board at any community college or in the college newspaper and you'll find someone who will be glad to type from your scribbles for a dollar or two a page.

Other Things to Expect

You could have probably guessed that people experience problems with the choice of schools, the application process, finances, scheduling, and study skills. You probably also knew to expect changes in your relationships and your lifestyle. We have covered ways to deal with these expected aspects of getting through your college program in this and other chapters. However, there is a long list of other problems that were repeatedly mentioned by the many adult students we spoke to. The following is a collection of these frequently mentioned problems and ways to work around them to help you deal with the expected, but less obvious problems that you will undoubtedly encounter on your trip through college. The list is not in any particular order. Here goes:

In spite of careful planning, college can sometimes make unreasonable and unexpected demands on your time.

We have provided some scheduling tips and methods in the book to help you anticipate these demands, but even with planning and foresight, you can expect to be occasionally overloaded. When this happens, you need to cross some of your priorities off the list or adjust your deadlines. If you still can't fit everything in, then you may want to consider cutting back on your school schedule for a while to get caught up. If school is just overwhelming to you—don't give up. You can always change your goals and get your degree a little later than originally planned.

After all, you've waited this long to get started; one or two more semesters added to your schedule to make the workload more reasonable probably won't make the degree any less valuable. If you already have a light courseload, go back to Chapter Two and evaluate your goals, motivations, and interest in college. Why waste your time if college isn't a priority to you? You don't have to go to college—it is a matter of choice and motivation. Either get motivated or quit pretending. Being able to choose is one of the nice things about living in this country.

Sometimes courses or assignments may seem pointless, juvenile, or irrelevant.
When given a dumb assignment, it's usually easier to work through it than to argue with the teacher making the assignment. Sometimes really dumb assignments turn into important assignments, but you may not realize that until you review the class using the clarity of hindsight. On other occasions, you may be assigned a truly pointless task or paper (at least from your point of view). As an adult going back to school, you may have a major knowledge advantage over the younger students that the assignment was intended for. If this is the situation, either do the work and forget about it, or politely discuss the matter with the professor and see if you can take on something more challenging and appropriate. If the professor resists this suggestion, then just do it—and do a better job of choosing teachers in your next course.

There will be at least one class in which you arbitrarily are given a B or C, instead of the A you thought you deserved.
Grades are important, but the grade in one course isn't a reliable evaluation of you as a person or even an indicator of your intelligence or ability. Some instructors are entirely arbitrary about grades. Some are fair. Some are easy graders. Some are hard. It hasn't changed since you were last in school. Sometimes you can make a case for yourself with an open-minded instructor. By all means try if you think you can support the grade change with your work in the class. In cases where you were obviously discriminated against for some reason (it does occasionally happen, even in the best schools), there is usually a well-defined grievance process for getting the grade changed (outlined in the catalog or another official document available from the administration). In cases where the instructor appears to grade arbitrarily, you will have to live with the grade—and try to do a better job next time of matching your work to the instructor's expectations.

You will experience stress as you try to juggle your priorities and meet your obligations.
Working, attending college, juggling family obligations, and trying to keep healthy and get enough sleep may make you feel worn thin. If you feel worn out for a few days during a particularly busy period but recover quickly, then you are probably okay. But if the feeling persists over several weeks or months, you may be either overdoing it or in need of medical attention. Getting an education is not worth having a heart attack. As explained previously, one powerful tool for com-

bating the worn-out feeling it to get a scheduling book or computer and carefully schedule and track your time by the hour. By using a few minutes a week to schedule activities, you benefit from being able to get all that information and pressure out of your head and onto paper or a computer screen, where it belongs. A schedule also shows you what you should be doing when. This is a powerful tool for keeping you from overworking because as part of the scheduling process, you can add time for relaxation and recovery from the busy periods and days. It's also important to understand that stress is not always a bad thing. In moderation, stress motivates us and moves us toward achieving our goals. Without stress, there is no priority—and without priorities, we can't accomplish our goals.

Sometimes you will feel lonely, as if you are the only person in the world with so much to do and so much to learn.

First, remember that there are millions of working adults studying tonight, just like you. All of them feel lonely and isolated sometimes. You may feel left out or deprived when you hear coworkers talking of going out for dinner or sitting around watching a great movie on the VCR. When you have to spend half the night studying for a mid-term, pangs of envy pound inside you. The best defense against this problem is to meet other people like yourself at school and have a cup of coffee with them while discussing how to manage school and work. With a few friends that are working and attending college as you are, you will no longer feel lonely. Use your friends and network to keep yourself focused on your goal. Think how much better you'll feel when you are graduating and your friends are still sitting in front of the TV.

In spite of your planning and concern, sometimes your family and friends will fail to understand your educational priorities.

This is a common problem. You may be trying hard to juggle everything, work, school and family, but a family member or friend still accuses you of ignoring him or her. Listen carefully to what your family members have to say. If it seems valid and you really do need to spend more time with a family member such as a child or spouse, promise that next semester, you will take one class fewer and try to fit the person into your busy schedule. Taking a child to your classes a few times can convince him or her that you really are working hard, not just ignoring them.

At least one emotional crisis will develop during the time you are trying to complete your degree.

At the risk of sounding negative, you can expect at least one emotional crisis to occur while you're in school. This may be related to going to college, or it may stem from another source, including but not limited to friends, family, and your job. What you must do is to cope with the crisis and not let it make you fall too far behind in school or provide a convenient excuse for quitting your degree program. If the crisis is severe, and you really can't pick up the pieces and go back to work, find out what your college's "Incomplete" policy is. Most schools allow you to take a grade of Incomplete and make up the work later, usually within a period of time such as a year or two. Sometimes sympathetic instructors will work personally with you to figure out how to catch up on the work. Talk with a counselor if the problem is severe. This is another time your support group will come in handy too—your mentor or study group will be invaluable in getting you through the hard times. Whatever you do, don't quit school; you've put too much effort in to let real life get in the way.

Not all college instructors or professors are good teachers.

When instructors aren't good, it's up to you to either find another instructor or learn something in spite of yours. The focus of many universities is research, not necessarily teaching. Even in schools with practitioner-based faculty or in adult-oriented schools, you will find bad teachers who may or may not have lots of good experience. Ultimately, it is you who are responsible for what you learn. Good instructors make it easier to learn, but it is possible to learn without any instructor at all. If you want to learn, you can find something in everybody even if the person is boring, monatonic, or highly opinionated.

Some close-minded instructors will expect you to agree with them and will penalize you for disagreeing.

Thankfully, most instructors are not this way. If you find one who is, you can learn from the biases of the instructor. Concentrate on ideas and topics in the course that interest you but are not in conflict with the instructor's point of view. And never openly confront one of these instructors in class. Don't pretend to agree; just don't disagree. Remember, part of college always involves jumping through hoops—and dealing with jerks is one of the real-life hoops we all have to deal with. You know that already from your life experience. Why should college be any different? (Well, you could argue that the world should change—and we agree. But, remember: You can do only what you can do. Don't let one person get between you and your degree. You have the rest of your life to change the world.) If the person is intolerable, change classes if you can. If this can't be done for some reason, just grin and bear it. You don't have to marry the close-minded bigot—you just have to get through the course.

In the last ten chapters, we hope, we have given you enough advice, motivation, and options to get through to graduation day. Remember: Persistence pays. Stick with college and keep your goals in mind. All obstacles can be overcome. Keep persistence in mind and that sheepskin will be yours in less time than you believed possible.

One last thing we recommend to everyone: *Attend your graduation.* You deserve to feel the sense of personal satisfaction, accomplishment, and pride that only your own graduation ceremony can provide—and besides, everyone has to look silly sometime!

The college graduation ceremony is one of the few remaining decorous rites of passage in Western culture. A rite of passage is an event which symbolizes that you have made a successful transition from one stage of life to another. Elaborate rites of passage are used in primitive societies to mark the transformation of child into responsible adult. Your graduation is an event that marks your transformation from "uneducated student" to "graduated/educated scholar."

Although you feel ridiculous parading around in an odd looking cap and bilious gown, do it anyway. Participate in the ceremony. Bring friends and family. Have a festive party afterwards. Take plenty of pictures to remember the event. You made it through—this is the moment you have worked so hard to achieve. Enjoy it—because the event will pass quickly and be gone forever.

In the next chapter, we will get you to look beyond your graduation, to the time when your college work is done and your role as student is finished. How will *you* take advantage of that degree now that it's yours?

Chapter Eleven

After Graduation Day: Putting Your Degree to Work

Close your eyes for a minute and imagine yourself only months away from graduation. You are about ready to write your last paper or take your last exam. The degree is in sight. A major educational goal is about to be achieved. Now what do you see?

Do you feel the euphoria that goes along with success and graduation? You anticipate recognition, self-esteem, and immediate financial rewards. You see a better job, a richer life, prestige, and recognition.

We hate to burst the bubble—but that's probably not what will happen the day after graduation. Sure, you will feel good about your accomplishments, and you'll have a sense of relief that the program is done (for now). But if you expect immediate wealth and unbridled happiness, you're letting yourself in for a letdown. Unrealistic goals before graduation often result in a postpartum depression or a feeling of buyer's remorse after the degree is attained.

Your education won't make your life much different unless you proactively put your college experience to work. While your friends and coworkers may congratulate you at graduation time, in order to put your degree to work for you, you must promote your new status to, as advertising agencies put it, "build awareness." And the best way to build awareness is to build it over a period of time with gentle persistence.

Thus, it is as important to have a plan for action *after* attaining the degree as it is to have one before starting school. The first section of this chapter will show you how to modify the objectives assembled before beginning college to aid you at the end of your college career. Your post-graduation planning should commence about six months to one year before your intended graduation date so that you can ready yourself for the transition from adult student to degreed adult.

The second section of this chapter explains how to complete the college process and put your degree to work to improve your life and career. It also explains how to switch out of student mode and avoid a common trap: staying in college just to stay in college.

There is much more to attending college than just getting a better job or otherwise advancing professionally, although this chapter primarily focuses on improvements in your career as a measurable benefit of completing college. As explained earlier in this book, completing college is personally fulfilling because you have learned more about yourself, your subject of study, and the world around you. Because these benefits are impossible to specify, we will primarily focus in this chapter on improving your material life.

Changing Your Attitudes and Behaviors to Reflect Your New Educational Level

While almost everyone has met what can only be described as a pompous jerk who, after having completed an advanced degree, suddenly began looking down on "lesser" peers, your behavior after obtaining your new degree should not change much as far as outsiders can perceive. It *can* change, however, in one positive and significant way: Whereas before graduation you may have felt and acted unsure of your knowledge and position, after graduation you can become an authority with coworkers on the subject matter you studied in college. (Don't overdo it, though.) You also can adopt a new attitude of self-assurance befitting the fact that you've succeeded in going back to college and sticking with it through graduation—an enviable achievement to your less educated coworkers.

Step 1. Plan for Life and Career after College

Much like the plan you assembled before initiating your college program, planning for graduation and post-graduation is very important. Proper planning helps you make the transition more smoothly and provides you with a clear direction for putting your degree to work. It also keeps you focused on the objectives you originally set forth to achieve by attending college. If your college program has taken several years (many do), you may long ago have forgotten your original motivation for starting school. A plan helps you keep centered on those goals and helps keep you motivated to graduate rather than lingering in school taking unnecessary classes.

The best plans are written plans. Few people are really good at keeping a comprehensive plan in their head and sticking to it. Attempting to memorize a plan may result in your forgetting one or more steps. And while you are still attending classes, you need as much brainpower as possible to cope with your studies and the normal activities that fill your life. Your written plan should provide a series of steps for managing your new status and using it to your best advantage. It should also create a logical transition from college student to "civilian life." Without proper planning, you may suddenly be forced into a transition from hardly enough extra time to grab dinner between work and evening classes to a feeling of emptiness and too much time on your hands.

Your plan should include four elements. We will detail each element in the first section of this chapter so that you understand what each element is and why it's important to you.

The before-graduation elements of your plan include:

1. Modifying your original goals to match your current needs.
2. Understanding and calibrating your after-graduation expectations.

3. Investigating the options open to you.

The after-graduation element of your plan includes:

4. Evaluating your success in applying a new degree to your career objectives

This plan should be assembled in a notebook or in a personal planner such as a Harper House *DayRunner* so that it can be referred to and updated as required. For the more tangible elements, dates and schedules can be assigned. For difficult-to-quantify components where no date can be set, instead choose a date on which to look back and review the item. For example, one of your goals may be to achieve a better position, promotion, or raise in pay, but such activities usually happen on an employer's schedule rather than yours. But, there's no reason not to set up your plan so that you review this goal six months after graduation to ensure that it has happened or to make alternate arrangements if it hasn't.

Before-Graduation Plan Elements
The elements in this section of the plan are intended to get you ready for your new role before you actually graduate. Because some of these items take a moderate amount of thinking and investigation, putting the effort in before you graduate makes your after-graduation actions clearer and keeps you focused and motivated to complete your program.

Modifying Your Original Goals to Match Your Current Needs
The first item of any plan based on a past plan is to integrate your original objectives with your current ones. To begin this phase of planning, copy the original goals from the plan you used to choose a school and program and list them in the new plan. Copy all of them, even if they no longer seem related to your current situation. (If you have been attending college for two or three years, some of the objectives you set down before starting your program may seem only distantly important.)
Then, on the next page, rewrite the goals to better reflect your current situation—being careful not to delete ones that now appear lofty or unreachable. Consider scrapping goals that have become totally irrelevant, although first attempt to rephrase them if the words need a little change. Put a large check mark by any that you have already achieved. For the remaining goals, place a tentative date next to them to indicate when you plan to achieve that goal. If any of the goals appear too vague to assign a date to consider rewriting them to make them more achievable. For example, a goal of "Make more money after graduation" should be restated as, "Improve salary position from $25,000 a year to at least $40,000 a year within six months of graduation."

Understanding and Calibrating Your After-Graduation Expectations
Once you have clarified your objectives, you need to calibrate your thinking to real-world facts. The best time to do this is early—before you graduate—to

avoid the risk of feeling deflated when pie-in-the-sky expectations come down to earth. With a set of realistic expectations laid out before graduation, you will have a better understanding of what to expect afterward.

The way we recommend calibrating expectations is reviewing your objectives and then writing a scenario that best describes what you expect for specific periods following graduation. One of these usually takes the form of a paragraph that describes your position relative to the date of graduation. Here's an example:

One Month after Graduation

I plan to be working at the same job, but lobbying for a promotion or transfer based on my new degree. I will apply for my professional certificate to be able to take on new responsibilities. (Teaching and many other professional positions require certification that can't be applied for until after graduation.) I will take a one-week vacation during this month to celebrate completing my degree.

Six Months after Graduation

I plan to have a new job with either my present employer or a new one. By this time, I also plan to begin looking for a larger home that my improved salary will allow me to purchase.

One Year after Graduation

I plan to have moved into a new home, and I will have decided whether I need an advanced degree. We will be expecting our second child during this period as well, now that we have a larger living space.

Once you have graduated, reread these expectations regularly to keep focused on your plans and not feel disappointed that graduation has not instantly transformed you into the happiest and most beautiful person on the planet. These goals can also be reviewed with your spouse and family (if you have one) to make sure that they understand what you are working toward and buy into it.

Investigating the Options Open to You

Unless your objective is to remain in the same job after graduation, it is important to be aware of career options open to you after graduation. You may have had a very exact career objective in mind when you began college, but once you have almost completed your degree, it's a good idea to reconsider your purpose, if only as an exercise in "what-if." With the passage of time, some options no longer may be viable, and new options may present themselves. If your degree has taken several years to achieve, career possibilities may have changed considerably during that time. You may have matured personally and become a different person during the time spent in college, as well.

This is a good time to reevaluate what you can use your degree for and add this information to your plan. Start by copying all of the options that were available when you began your program, then crossing out those that are no longer possible or of interest to you. Then add the new ones you discover as you come across them. If you work in a large company, for example, a variety of new positions may be available through transfers. If your career move probably means changing companies as well as jobs, then look for outside possibilities and don't necessarily limit those possibilities to your present city or area. A new degree may be more marketable elsewhere.

This should be done over several months until you have added as many options as you can find through personal contacts and research. With the new skills acquired through college, you may find career options open to you that you did not know existed when you originally assembled your plan.

Once you feel that you have a fairly complete list of career options, redraft them on another page, putting the one you like most on top, then listing the remainder in order of preference. Establishing the kind of career move *you'd like to make* will help narrow your job search criteria and possibly get you a position doing the kind of job you like doing.

After-Graduation Plan Elements

You may want to begin this plan before graduation and then come back to it several months or a year after graduation. In this section of the plan, you restate your most important objective (or maybe objectives) and then measure your success in achieving it or them. The purpose of this section is to give you a measuring stick to track the most important element in your plan for success. Unfortunately, once you graduate and lose the disciplined sense of attending college while managing the other activities of your life, it's easy to let your major objective slip away because work or family or much-needed time off get in the way. By coming back to the most important objective in your plan, you can either put a big check mark by the objective and say, "I accomplished that months ago!" or ask yourself why you have not achieved this key goal.

If the latter is the case, carefully review the work you put into the before-graduation plan elements to refocus your thinking along the lines you originally intended. Remember, your degree won't work for you unless you put it to work. If your objective was to obtain a promotion within your current company, the time that elapses between graduation and the first six months afterward might be the time to receive the promotion. After that period, your boss or manager could forget about your Herculean effort to better yourself and promote you if and when he or she gets around to it. If the purpose of getting your degree was to get a new or better job, wallowing less than happily in the position you held before graduation will continue unless you act *now*. Reviewing a major unrealized objective and realizing that you've been letting your competitive advantage go unrecognized is the best way to put your college work to use.

Step 2. Let Employers Know What You've Accomplished

There are several employer-targeted promotional actions you should take once you have your sheepskin, particularly if you plan to remain with your present company. While your employer may be well aware of your college program and pending graduation (your company may be footing the bill), it sometimes takes carefully orchestrated prodding to get your new status reflected in your job title or paycheck.

Set a Date and Stick with It

To reinforce the fact that you will be graduating, choose a realistic graduation date and stick with it. That way, your employer will have a firm handle on the date and can take appropriate measures to recognize your new status. If you name several dates as you find new requirements that must be met before graduation, when the big day truly arrives your boss may assume that it is another tentative date and ignore it.

Talk to Your Boss

A couple of months before graduation, have a talk with your boss and candidly ask him or her about your future after graduation. Do not hint that you may leave the company if your achievement goes unrecognized. Your boss will get the message. Make this a warm, friendly talk, and speak enthusiastically about your future and the future success of the company. In many companies, this kind of meeting is best held over lunch.

Have a Party

In many companies, if you are well-liked (and -known), your fellow employees will hold an informal graduation party for you. This event serves to put your employer on notice that, yes, you really do have a diploma and you're ready for new challenges. If no party materializes or if you work for a company where such events rarely happen, invite your boss and coworkers out to lunch or for drinks to celebrate graduation.

Send Out Thank-You Cards

If your employer paid for your books or tuition, send a thank-you card for that support. Send these cards to people you know in the personnel office who may have coordinated your financing. In some companies acquiring a degree means an automatic pay raise or a change in status to the "management track," and this is handled by the personnel department. Even if your boss or managers did not financially support your college effort, send them a thank-you card anyway, acknowledging their support through this tough period. Not only does this put them on notice, but they will certainly appreciate the gesture.

Take on New Challenges

Jump on new challenges to show your employer that you are ready for change. Next time a project comes along that is beyond your normal responsibilities, jump at the chance to prove to your boss how you've changed and how your new schooling has made you ready for a new level of responsibility. In this way, you make yourself a more salable commodity that the boss won't want to risk losing, while showcasing your new skills at the same time. If your job is one where you won't be aware of higher-level projects until after someone else has taken them on, take your boss aside and explain that next time a hot project comes along, you'd like your chance to prove that you can handle a new level of sophistication in your work.

What If It Doesn't Work?

If none of these "awareness-building programs" appear to have any effect, then it may be time to quietly look for another job that takes advantage of your degree and new skills before the newness of your graduation has worn off. If you find a job that represents a promotion and/or pay increase with another company, before accepting the job and giving notice, discuss the matter with your current employer and explain that unless he or she can provide you with a promotion or suitable compensation, you plan to give notice and take the other job.

If your employer recognizes your contribution and the company is doing well, he or she may make you a suitable offer. It is standard procedure for your present employer to match the higher salary offered by another company. If, however, your company remains inflexible and is willing to let you go, then you probably have left an organization where you had a dim future for promotion anyway. Some companies are extremely slow to promote from within, instead hiring outsiders for senior jobs and assignments.

Some jobs are difficult to get promoted from as well. If you work in the mailroom of a major company and complete an MBA, it's unlikely that you will be promoted from your present job to a white-collar executive position. In such cases, you simply may need to look for work elsewhere to get your achievement recognized. Otherwise, you may settle for running the mail room with little possibility of leaving it for a more senior job—ever.

A risky approach (we don't recommend it because it can backfire, although we have used it successfully ourselves to get promoted): If you are a very important employee (not just in your mind, but in the mind of your employer), let a rumor get started that you plan to take a more senior job with better pay at a competing company. When your present employers hear the rumor, they may try to keep you by meeting your terms instead of losing you to the made-up job offer.

What Do You Have to Sell to Employers?

As a recent (or soon-to-be) graduate, you offer a unique set of skills often prized by employers. These skills are not available from most job applicants—young college graduates have little practical work experience and do not know how to handle many tasks that require thinking on their feet. They also know little of how organizations really work. Older applicants don't have the benefit of your newly acquired college experience and may lack a degree like yours. You have several assets that most other job applicants lack:

1. You have the benefit of having held other "serious" jobs—something that few young college graduates have.
2. You have the benefit of life experience that makes it much easier to transfer your college learning to tangible abilities and skills.
3. You know how organizations work inside and how to get things done.
4. You are a mature person who has already jumped life's hurdles for at least several years and know what is expected of you at work.
5. You have demonstrated that you have the "stick-with-it" skills to get a degree as an adult student. That shows a tenacity that is found in the most dedicated and hardworking employees—exactly the people most employers love to hire and keep.

With these skills, you look good to a potential employer. If you bring to the interview some of the same enthusiasm and humor that got you through college, you have a much better than average chance of being offered a job—even one where many people are competing for the same position. Why? Because where is an employer going to find someone with your life experience, obvious "can-do" attitude, and the flexibility and foresight required to make it through college and receive a degree?

An Educated Job Applicant's Problem

While, fortunately, these people are few and far between, there is one kind of boss who will neither promote you from within his or her company nor offer you a job if you apply. This is the kind of undereducated person who resents your newly acquired education. Particularly a problem for applicants who have completed advanced degrees, this kind of boss probably didn't complete college (some didn't complete high school), and he or she is uncomfortably aware that the lack of a degree is holding up his or her career advancement. In return, this boss will get back at the educated by stifling their careers wherever possible or by offering a job to someone who also lacks an education.

These people often are difficult to recognize, but you can get an idea of their position by casually asking them about their education during an interview. If this causes a tightening of the lips from internal anger or frustration or a sudden change of subject, then be careful of proudly discussing your newly acquired degree. Or if you are working inside a company and asking the firm to pay part of your college expenses, a boss who attempts to explain why college is a waste of time may actually be an undereducated person resentful of people with degrees. Beware that, should you start or complete school, this person may no longer support your efforts on behalf of the company. The unusually immature ones may work quietly to remove you from their department because you represent a perceived threat to their authority.

Step 3. Put Together a Resume that Reflects Your New Status

Again, unless you plan to remain in your present position, once you have narrowed your choices (or if you have decided to advance in your present field but possibly with another employer), you need to assemble a new resume. If graduation means that you want to pursue a more senior job than your present one, you may need an entirely new resume, making you appear more senior on paper. Or if you are considering several new kinds of jobs, make up a resume specifically for each job, carefully tailoring your present skills to each kind of job you are applying for.

Of course, you will proudly add your new schooling to the resume, but you must handle this addition carefully. Most employers look first at your job history and then at your education. So, instead of trumpeting your new degree in large type at the top of your resume, add a section toward the bottom called "Education" and show your degree there. This is not to downplay the effort you have put into getting a degree, but instead to make it part of the complete package of skills and experience an employer receives when he or she interviews and hires you. Remember, on paper your education reinforces your skills and experience. The experience won't reinforce your education.

When Should You Assemble a Resume?
Once you are in sight of graduation (generally at about six months before completing the final elements in your program), you can begin to use a revised resume that claims your degree. Instead of making it sound like you've graduated, let the dates tell your story for you. If your graduation day will be June 1993 and it's now December 1992, show your education like this:

Education
    June 1993 — MS, Nursing, University of Miami
           Miami, Florida
    1987 — BS, Nursing, with Honors, San Bernadino State College
           San Bernadino, CA

This way, employers clearly can see that you are close to your degree and ready for a new challenge commensurate with your new skills. Once you have graduated, you can remove the month from the listing, but if you have a stack of resumes with the month already printed on them, it won't hurt to leave it on. This "after-the-fact" reminder tells employees that you are a recent graduate. They may be surprised by your level of enterprise and be interested in hiring an obviously dedicated and tenacious person.

Delete Now-Irrelevant Educational Accomplishments
If you have just completed your first college degree, be it an A.A. or a B.A., and you have old educational information on your resume, this is the time to delete it. Once you have achieved a degree from a college, delete high school graduation information—it detracts from your new status. If you are one of the many students who previously showed a patchwork of college credits from college programs you never completed in an effort to demonstrate that you had attended college, delete

these as well unless they are from a very prestigious college or university or if they have a direct bearing on the job you are looking for. For example, if you took engineering classes at MIT but finally completed your engineering degree at San Jose State University, leave a mention of MIT on your resume. However, if you took engineering courses at Podunk U. but completed your engineering degree at MIT, delete the reference to Podunk U., because it detracts from the important achievement. Keep in mind that showing on your resume that you attended several colleges without completing a degree not only takes up valuable space on the page, but may leave employers wondering why you moved around so much or didn't complete your degree sooner.

How Do I Deal with My Mediocre Grades When I'm Looking for a New Job?

If you achieved a *B+* average or better, by all means put this on your resume. If that puts you on your school's Dean's List or you graduated with Honors, put that on as well. But if you were an unexceptional student who still managed to graduate, keep in mind that most employers don't look at your grades. While they may check the grades of a young graduate whose work experience is limited to flipping hamburgers, grades are usually not an important part of the selection process. Instead, employers are concerned only that you actually graduated. While some may verify your degree, they rarely check your grade point average.

If you are applying to a company that *does* check scholastic achievement (reportedly Coca-Cola and a few other companies do), the person who hires you and who will be your primary boss usually has the final say, no matter what the personnel department says. If the topic comes up (don't volunteer such information), be straightforward and explain how as a working adult you had to juggle college, a full-time job with overtime, and your family life. Boast that even against all odds, you worked hard just to get through school and succeeded. Of course, if you lack one of these suggested components for a sob story, by all means dream up another one as a replacement. Remember, even with mediocre grades, you managed to *finish college on your own*—and that's a significant achievement in itself!

Don't Educate Yourself Out of the Job Market

While for most jobs a bachelor's degree brings faster promotion or better pay, there are some jobs where an advanced degree sometimes alienates employers. Though important to certain kinds of education-, scientific-, or engineering-oriented positions, the most difficult-to-sell degree is also the most advanced degree—the doctorate. While this degree is a requirement if you plan to teach at the university level, it makes some employers nervous for several reasons.

As mentioned earlier in the chapter, some employers personally lacking degrees are intimidated by as little as an A.A. degree from a community college. While these people are (fortunately) comparatively rare, a doctorate carries much more weight and therefore is that much more intimidating to a larger number of employers. Employers may also have another problem with advanced degrees: In many larger companies advanced degree holders are automatically entitled to a higher salary than their bachelor-degreed counterparts. This strains department budgets, and an employer may feel that your degree isn't useful enough to the business to justify a larger salary.

While this kind of attitude is certainly discriminatory, some employers have had bad experiences with employees holding doctorates. This is in part because getting a doctorate from an accredited university requires a considerable buy-in by the student to the mechanics and culture of academe. Even away from the university, the academic habits often persist. In the faster-paced world of business, the careful, ponderous academic attitude is often a liability, rather than a boon.

If you plan to work in business, consider limiting your studies to the bachelor's or master's degree level, or complete your doctorate if possible, but keep it quiet. Refrain from asking coworkers and managers to call you doctor (unless you are an M.D.), and consider leaving the Ph.D. off your business cards unless you work in an educational, scientific, or engineering position.

Step 4. Cut the Ties with School

Giving up college may be even more difficult than starting a college program and acquiring an attitude that allows you to juggle a job, a family, and attend class. Depending on the kind of program and school you attended, this can be a difficult period if you enjoyed the comfort of attending classes with friends and meeting new people. Or if your program was a somewhat impersonal distance-education program, it may be a relief to know that you don't need to head into the office at home and turn on the computer for a long session on line.

If you were closely tied into a college environment, life may seem a little pale without the familiar hustle and bustle of the campus. Suddenly, upon graduation, instructors who spent much of their time talking with you and helping you with your studies become disinterested, and your friends who are still attending classes have less in common with you. If you have completed all the classwork and other requirements for graduation, you may feel tempted to squeeze in a few more classes before cutting the umbilical cord. Or if you are already a graduate, you find yourself applying for a graduate degree without weighing the merits of such a program—just to keep in contact with college and your college buddies.

If you find yourself longing to keep going to school, consider these points:

- If you have a job and family that require a large time and emotional commitment from you, school really may be a way of avoiding your less-interesting commitments.
- You really may be ready for the greater challenge of using your new skills and degree to get a better job, but by staying in school, you can avoid the risk of failure because you can tell yourself that you're still going to college.

If either of these points seems applicable, then you need to take stock of what you are doing and get on with your life instead of becoming a permanent student.

How to Cut the Ties

Giving up college doesn't mean giving up the parts of it you enjoyed the most. The challenge of learning and exploring can be continued by attending classes part time without a definite degree program in mind. Community college classes provide an avenue for inexpensively exploring new subject matter and access to expensive studio facilities for learning computers, fine arts, dance, and physical fitness.

The close community of certain colleges may be unique, but it is available at the community college, and the friends you make in school can become friends out of school as well. It is difficult to replace the wooded quiet of some campuses. But at most colleges—even if you are no longer a student—you can get a Pepsi and sit on benches under the trees and listen to the birds without actually being enrolled. Your old school chums may happen by to chat with you on such excursions.

You also can become a graduate student without a declared major at many schools. This allows you almost all of the advantages of being a regular, full-time student, but provides the freedom to take classes across a broad spectrum of majors without having a specific degree in mind. For classes where there are more students than space, being a graduate student usually gives you enrollment priority over the undergraduates. And at expensive, private colleges, taking just a few units costs much less than full-time attendance. While some public colleges and universities frown on undirected graduates dabbling at an advanced degree (their viewpoint, not yours), the majority are just happy to have you enrolled because it improves the college's "body count" for state and federal funding purposes.

If the feeling of emptiness persists, see a doctor. It may be that you have set yourself up for such big expectations that you have become depressed as a result. A little depression goes a long way toward making what you accomplished appear unimportant and your self-esteem nonexistent. Fortunately, there are often easy ways of overcoming this enfeebling illness.

Graduate ASAP to Reduce the Risk that You Won't Finish

Your goal should always be to graduate as quickly as possible. If you are an adult student, a lot can happen to prevent you from ever finishing your degree. The longer you stay in college, the more you risk an event or life change forcing you to drop out without completing your degree. You may get married or divorced, change jobs, move to another city, lose an important family member, or simply lose interest because of too many other personal obligations.

Avoid taking on a slightly more advanced degree that takes longer to complete but buys you very little career-wise. For example, art students can elect to take a B.F.A. degree instead of a B.A. degree. Taking the more advanced degree requires them to take another 30 semester units before completing the program. Once they reach the B.A. point, they still can't graduate until they complete the credit requirements for a B.F.A., which takes approximately another year to finish.

Unexpected real-life interruptions may derail such a program, leaving almost enough credits for a B.F.A., but not quite the right classwork for the B.A.

Instead, carefully fine-tune your college program to reduce the risk that you will put several years into it without getting your degree. Be wary of college counselors who try to sell you on such a program. While they may have valid arguments why a more comprehensive program makes sense, many times they are simply looking to keep you enrolled longer or to build enrollment in a degree program that other students rightfully have sidestepped.

The School Trap

While we are the last people to discourage anyone considering going to college or completing a second or third degree, there is a trap that you can fall into that your professors may set for you. When you are studying for a degree that you plan to use to change careers or lifestyles, it's easy to convince yourself that once graduation is imminent, you really aren't ready to make the change you have been working toward. You will convince yourself (with your teacher's help) that more college is required before taking the big step forward.

This is really a two-pronged problem. First, by continuing in college you do not need to immediately face the challenge and fear of rejection of applying your new skills in the job market. Second, your professors have an interest in keeping you in college. Not only may they personally like you and the enthusiasm you bring to their department, but by keeping you and many other students like you enrolled, they have better job security.

Do You Really Need Another Degree?

Before embarking on an advanced degree, you must weigh the need for it carefully. You may simply be falling into the school trap. Unless your intended plan of study originally included completing more than one degree, you should take at least a one-year hiatus between finishing one degree and beginning another. This year gives you time to put the degree already achieved to work, and it provides time to weigh the pros and cons of an advanced degree program carefully to avoid several years of unnecessary and potentially expensive college. If you have a family, a one-year vacation from college gives you time to spend with them instead of being buried in books and studying.

You must ask yourself the following questions to better understand your motives:

- What is the real reason that I want to start an advanced degree?
- Is there any reason to undertake a time-consuming program, such as a chance at a better job?
- Will my life benefit, either spiritually or materially, from such a program?

Put your answers down on paper and review them over a period of weeks to see if they ring true. If you can't come up with a legitimate reason to begin an advanced degree program or a use for the resulting degree, then you may be stuck in the school trap.

In this chapter you have learned how to successfully complete the transition from student to graduate and have seen how to avoid the trap of staying in school just to stay in school. Using the advice in this chapter, you should be able to effectively apply your newly won degree to move on or up in your career—or to benefit from your education in other ways. Holding a degree opens doors to new and better jobs not only because you have acquired new skills, but also because employers seek applicants with a degree for many positions. Holding a degree makes you feel more confident in yourself as well, and it puts you on equal footing with other people you work with and for. And it gives you a unique kind of satisfaction: you have passed a major hurdle in life—getting a college education and a college degree! You're ready to reap the benefits because you earned the right to enjoy them. Congratulations.

Sources and References for Adult College Students

Books and Publications

We recommend the following books and publications as general references. These lists are not comprehensive but are intended to get you started in your search for information on programs and services. Most of these books can be ordered by your local bookstore, and many are available in public and college libraries or from school counselors. Books without publication dates are updated regularly—ask your bookstore or librarian about the most recent editions.

College and University Guides

Abroad and Beyond, Cambridge University Press, 1988 (a guide to study abroad)

Bear's Guide to Earning Non-Traditional College Degrees by John Bear, Ph.D., Ten Speed Press, Berkeley, California

Campus-Free College Degrees by Marcie Kisner Thorson, Bob Adams, Inc., Holbrook, Massachusetts

Peterson's Guide to Four-Year Colleges, Peterson's Guides, Princeton, New Jersey

Peterson's Guide to Graduate and Professional Programs, Peterson's Guides, Princeton, New Jersey

Peterson's Guide to Two-Year Colleges, Peterson's Guides, Princeton, New Jersey

Study Abroad: The Astute Students Guide by David Judkins, Williamson Publishing, Charlotte, Vermont, 1992

Career Development and Job Search

300 New Ways to Get a Better Job by Eleanor Baldwin, Bob Adams, Inc., Holbrook, Massachusetts, 1990

Careers and the College Grad ed. by Diane Ranno, Bob Adams, Inc., Holbrook, Massachusetts

Careers and the Engineer ed. by Diane Ranno, Bob Adams, Inc., Holbrook, Massachusetts

Careers and the MBA ed. by Diane Ranno, Bob Adams, Inc., Holbrook, Massachusetts

Career Development, Prentice-Hall, Englewood Cliffs, New Jersey, 1989

The Elements of Job Hunting: Everything You Need to Know to Land a Great Job by

John Noble, Bob Adams, Inc., Holbrook, Massachusetts, 1992

The Job Bank Series (National and State Editions), Bob Adams, Inc., Holbrook, Massachusetts

Retirement Careers: Combining the Best of Work and Leisure by DaLoss L. Marsh, Williamson Publishing, Charlotte, Vermont, 1992

The Right Move: How to Find the Perfect Job by Michael Zey, Ballantine Books, New York, 1987

What Color Is Your Parachute? by Richard N. Bolles, Ten Speed Press, Berkeley, California

Financial Aid, Grants, and Scholarships

Better Late Than Never: Financial Aid for Reentry Women Seeking Education and Training, Women's Equity Action League, Washington, D.C.

The College Blue Book: Scholarships, Fellowships, Grants, and Loans, Macmillan, New York

The College Cost Book, College Board

Earn and Learn, Cooperative Education Opportunities Offered by the Federal Government: Sponsors, Occupational Fields, and Participating Colleges, Octameron Press, Alexandria, Virginia

Foundation Grants to Individuals, The Foundation Center, New York.

How the Military Will Help You Pay for College by Don M. Betterton, Peterson's Guides, Princeton, New Jersey, 1990

Opportunities for Research and Study by Patricia Dineen, National Council for Research on Women, Washington, D.C.

Peterson's College Money Handbook, Peterson's Guides, Princeton, New Jersey

Peterson's Financial Aid Services, Peterson's Guides, Princeton, New Jersey

Study Techniques

The Words You Should Know by David Olsen, Bob Adams, Inc., Holbrook, Massachusetts

Improve Your Memory by Ron Frey, Career Press, 1992

Instant Recall: Tapping Your Hidden Memory Power by Jeff Budworth, Bob Adams, Inc., Holbrook, Massachusetts

Study Skills: For Those Adults Returning to School by Jerold W. Apps, McGraw-Hill, Inc., New York, 1978 (out of print, but available in many libraries)

Study Tips: How to Study Effectively and Get Better Grades, Barron's Educational Series, Barron's, Hauppauge, New York

Taking Tests by Ron Fry, Career Press, 1992

Touch Type Your Computer in 4 Hours and Keep Your Eyes Free by Frank Donnelly, DDC, c/o Bob Adams, Inc., Holbrook, Massachusetts

Standardized Examinations

Barron's, Peterson's, Lovejoy's, and other major college-guide publishers all provide

COLLEGE AFTER 30

annual guides for taking the SAT, GED, GRE, GMAT, LSAT, and other standardized examinations. These books are updated regularly and available in almost any bookstore. To get information on standardized examinations themselves and exam dates, write to the following:

Testing Agencies

CLEP Examinations, GMAT (Graduate Management Admission Test), GRE (Graduate Record Examination), SAT (Scholastic Aptitude Test)
Educational Testing Service
P.O. Box 6000
Princeton, NJ 80541
(609) 771-7595

PEP Examinations, ACT Examination, and others
American College Testing Program
P.O. Box 168
Iowa City, IA 52243

GED
General Educational Development Testing Service
One Dupont Circle
Washington, DC 20036

Test Preparation Services

The Princeton Review
Princeton Review sessions take place in dozens of locations around the country. They provide services to improve test scores on standardized admissions examinations. To find a location near you, call (800) 333-0369.

Kaplan Study Centers
Listed in the telephone books of most major cities under Kaplan, Stanley H. Educational Center.

Associations and Organizations

Academic Credit for Life Experience

For information on the process approved by the American Council of Education for gaining academic credit for learning outside the classroom, write or call:

American Council on Education
Program on Noncollegiate Sponsored Instruction
One Dupont Circle
Washington, D.C. 20036
(202) 939-9433

Ask for information on the PONSI process for acceptance of college credit.

Alternative Education

The Association for Experiential Education
C.U. Box 249
Boulder, CO 80309

(303) 492-1547

Distance Education

The National Distance Learning Center
(NDLC)
Jeff Sun, Director
Owensboro, KY
(502) 686-4556

NDLC provides an online database for
more than 400 distance learning
programs. To test the database, set your
modem for communications as follows:
Baud Rate: 300 to 2400
Bits per Character: 8

Stop Bits: 1
Parity: None
Emulation: VT-100
Telephone: 1-502-686-4555
Log-in identification: ndlc

United States Distance Learning
Association (USDLA)
Box 5106
San Ramon, CA 94583
(510) 820-5562

International Study

American Institute for Foreign Study
(AIFS)
102 Greenwich Avenue
Greenwich, CT 06830
(800) 727-AIFS or (203) 869-9090

Council on International Educational
Exchange (CIEE)

205 East 42nd Street
New York, NY 10017
(212) 661-1414

Institute of International Education
809 United Nations Plaza
New York, NY 10017-3580

Literacy

Literacy Volunteers of America
5795 Widewaters Parkway
Syracuse, NY 13214
(315) 445-8000

Degree Consulting Services

If you don't want to spend the time finding adult-oriented or non-traditional schools
and programs on your own by wading through college handbooks or searching
through telephone books, we recommend the following company:

DEGREE CONSULTING SERVICES
Specialists in Non-traditional Degree
Programs
P.O. Box 3533

Santa Rosa, CA 95402
(702) 539-6466
Street Address: 538 Black Stone Court
Santa Rosa, CA 95405

Degree Consulting Services is a counseling-by-mail service founded by Dr.
John Bear, a world-renowned expert on non-traditional education and author of the
highly recommended *Bear's Guide to Earning Non-Traditional College Degrees.*
Degree Consulting Services has assisted thousands of clients to raise their educational
levels, to gain recognition for what they have learned and accomplished in their ca-

reers, and to complete the degrees they needed. The group specializes in the rapidly expanding field of non-traditional education, which now offers the bright, mature learner a way around the obstacles of work, family responsibilities, and rising tuition.

Home Study and Correspondence Schools

The National Home Study Council, a nonprofit educational association in Washington, DC, serves as a clearing house for information about home study and sponsors a nationally recognized accrediting agency.

A *Directory of Accredited Home Study Schools* is available without charge by writing to:
National Home Study Council
1601 18th St., NW
Washington, DC 20009

Accreditation Information

The Council on Postsecondary
Accreditation (COPA)
One Dupont Circle, N.W., Suite 305
Washington, DC 20036
(202) 452-1433

Accrediting Agency Evaluation Branch
Higher Education Management Services
Office of Postsecondary Education
U.S. Department of Education
Washington, DC 20202
(202) 708-7417

Government Aid for Students

Each state administers the federal loan and grant programs in addition to offering its own financial aid options for students.
For general information on federal financial aid programs, call the following number:

Federal Student Aid Information Center
(800) 333-INFO

Accredited Degree Programs for Adults

We have compiled the following list of schools to get you started in your search for a college to meet your educational goals. This section is a compendium of qualified schools or special programs that either are designed specifically for working adults or offer flexible scheduling, part-time programs, or distance-education programs. Most of the schools on this list accept credits for experience through portfolio assessments and/or examinations and feature flexible scheduling options, and many provide accelerated programs that allow adults to finish a degree in less time than at traditional schools.

Be aware that this list is not comprehensive—because new schools are adding programs or adapting them all the time. If you want to know if a specific school in your area offers alternative programs geared toward adults' learning needs, your best bet is to call the Continuing Education Department, the Academic Services Department, or the Special Programs Department at the college of interest to you or refer to one of the handbooks we discussed to get more information on specific schools and programs, or contact Degree Consulting Services, we described earlier.

ADELPHI UNIVERSITY
Admissions Office
Garden City, NY 11530
(516) 877-3033
Degrees offered: B.A., B.S., M.A., D.A., Ph.D.
Flexible scheduling, credit for prior learning, some adult oriented programs (with students averaging over 35 years of age).
Majors: Full range of majors in liberal arts and sciences, as well as degrees in business, education, social work, banking, and nursing.

THE AMERICAN COLLEGE
270 Bryn Mawr Avenue
Bryn Mawr, PA 19010
(215) 526-1478
Short residency, adult oriented, distance-education options
Degrees offered: M.S.F.S., M.S.M.

AMERICAN OPEN UNIVERSITY OF
NEW YORK INSTITUTE OF
TECHNOLOGY
P.O. Box 9029
Central Islip, NY 11722-9029
(516) 348-3300
(800) 222-6948 (outside New York)
No residency, adult oriented, distance-education options, online program.
Degree offered: B.S.
Majors: Criminal justice, community mental health, psychology, sociology.

ANTIOCH UNIVERSITY
School for Adult and Experiential Learning
800 Livermore
Yellow Springs, OH 45387
(513) 767-6325
Short-residency, adult oriented,

distance-education options, online program.
Degree offered: M.A. (individualized)
Major: Individualized by the student

ANTIOCH NEW ENGLAND
GRADUATE SCHOOL
Director of Admissions
Keene, NH 03431
(603) 357-3122
Degrees offered: M.A., M.Ed., M.S., Ph.D.
Majors: Education, human services, environmental administration, psychology, etc.

ATLANTIC UNION COLLEGE
Adult Degree Program (ADP)
South Lancaster, MA 01561
(508) 368-2300
(800) 282-2030, ext. 2300
Short-residency, adult oriented, distance-education options, online program.
Degrees offered: B.A., B.S.
Majors: Variety of liberal arts majors are offered

BEMIDJI STATE UNIVERSITY
Center for Extended Learning
1500 Birchmont Drive NE, Box 27
Bemidji, MN 56601
(218) 755-3924
No-residency/short-residency, adult oriented, distance-education options, online program.
Degrees offered: A.A., A.S., B.A., B.S.
Majors: Indian studies, political science, psychology, social work, sociology

BEREAN COLLEGE OF THE
ASSEMBLIES OF GOD
1445 Boonville Avenue
Springfield, MO 65802

(417) 862-2781
(800) 443-1083
No-residency, adult oriented,
distance-education options, online
program.
Degrees offered: A.A, B.A.
Majors: Various theological majors

BOARD OF GOVERNORS
UNIVERSITIES
Board of Governors Bachelor of Arts
Degree Program
Accredited by North Central Association
of Colleges and Schools
No-residency required, adult oriented,
distance-education options, online
program.
Degree offered: B.A.

The Board of Governors B.A. degree is
offered by the following universities:

Chicago State University
95th Street at King Drive
Chicago, IL 60628
(312) 995-2000

Eastern Illinois University
Charleston, IL 61920
(217) 581-5000

Governors State University
University Park, IL 60466
(708) 534-5000

Northeastern Illinois University
5500 North St. Louis Avenue
Chicago, IL 60625
(312) 583-4050

WESTERN ILLINOIS UNIVERSITY
Nontraditional Program
Macomb, IL 61455
(309) 298-1929
(800) 322-3902 (Illinois only)
Major: Individualized major

BRADLEY UNIVERSITY
Division of Continuing Education and
Professional Development
1501 W. Bradley Ave.
Peoria, IL 61625

(309) 677-2374
(800) 552-1697
No-residency, adult oriented,
distance-education options, online
program.
Degrees offered: M.S.E.E., M.S.M.E.
Majors: Electrical engineering

BRIGHAM YOUNG UNIVERSITY
Degrees by Independent Study
305 Harman Building
Provo, UT 84602
(801) 378-4351
Short residency
Degree offered: B.I.S.
Major: Special liberal arts program

BURLINGTON COLLEGE
Director of Admissions
95 North Avenue
Burlington, VT 05401
(802) 862-9616
Short-residency, distance-education options
Degree offered: B.A.
Major: Liberal arts and social services
majors

CALDWELL COLLEGE
9 Ryerson Avenue
Caldwell, NJ 07006
(201) 228-4424
Short-residency, adult oriented,
distance-education options.
Degrees offered: B.A., B.S.
Major: A variety of majors are offered

CALIFORNIA COLLEGE FOR
HEALTH SCIENCES
Center for Degree Studies
222 West 24th Street
National City, CA 91950
(619) 477-4800
(800) 221-7374
No-residency, adult oriented,
distance-education options
Degrees offered: B.S., M.S.
Majors: Health services, community
health administration

CALIFORNIA STATE
UNIVERSITY—DOMINGUEZ HILLS
Humanities Degree Program
1000 E. Victoria SAC2-2126
Carson, CA 90747
(310) 516-3743/3744
No-residency
Degree offered: M.A.
Majors: Humanities majors

CENTRAL MICHIGAN UNIVERSITY
Extended Degree Programs
Rowe Hall 130
Mount Pleasant, MI 48859
(517) 774-3865
(800) 950-1144
No-residency
Degree offered: B.S.
Major: Administration

CHARTER OAK COLLEGE
270 Farmington Avenue, Suite 171
Farmington, CT 06032
(203) 677-0076
No residency
Degrees offered: A.A., A.S., B.A., B.S.
Majors: Several majors available in
business, computer technology,
humanities, social sciences, natural
sciences

CITY UNIVERSITY
335 116th Ave. SE
Bellevue, WA 98004
(206) 643-2000
(800) 426-5596
No-residency, adult oriented,
distance-education options
Degrees offered: A.S., B.S., M.B.A.,
M.P.A.
Majors: Majors in business, applied
sciences, health care, criminal justice

COLORADO STATE UNIVERSITY
Colorado SURGE
Division of Continuing Education, Spruce
Hall
Fort Collins, CO 80523
(303) 491-5288
(800) 525-4950
No-residency, adult oriented,
distance-education options, online program

Degrees offered: M.S., M.B.A.
Majors: Variety of applied sciences and
business majors

COLUMBIA UNION COLLEGE
Department of External Programs
7600 Flower Avenue
Takoma Park, MD 20912
(301) 891-4165
No-residency/short residency, adult
oriented, distance-education options
Degrees offered: A.A., B.A., B.S.
Majors: Health care

DEVRY INSTITUTE OF
TECHNOLOGY
Admissions Office
Phoenix, AZ (602) 870-9222
Atlanta, GA (404) 292-7900
Chicago, IL (312) 929-8500
Columbus, OH (614) 253-7291
Irving, TX (214) 258-6767
Kansas City, MO (816) 941-0430
Lombard, IL (708) 953-1300
Los Angeles, CA (213) 699-9927
Woodbridge, NJ (201) 634-3460
Calgary, Alberta, Canada (403) 235 3450
Toronto, Ontario, Canada (416) 741 9220
Accelerated 3-year bachelor's programs,
day and evening programs
Degrees offered: B.S. programs
Majors: Accounting, computer
information systems, electronics
engineering, telecommunications
management, business operations

ECKERD COLLEGE
Program for Experienced Learners (PEL)
4200 54th Avenue South
St. Petersburg, FL 33711
(813) 864-8226
Short-residency, adult oriented,
distance-education options
Degree offered: B.A.
Majors: Business, human development,
American studies, organizational studies

THE ELECTRONIC UNIVERSITY
NETWORK
CompuLearning Systems, Inc.
245 Northpoint Street, Suite 409
San Francisco, CA 94133

(800) 22LEARN
No-residency, adult oriented,
distance-education options, online
program.
Degrees offered: M.B.A., B.S.B.A.,
B.S.G.B., A.S.M., B.A., A.A., B.S., A.S.
Majors: A variety of degrees offered

ELIZABETHTOWN COLLEGE
Center for Continuing Education
EXCEL Program
One Alpha Drive
Elizabethtown, PA 17022
(717) 367-1151
Short-residency, adult oriented,
distance-education options
Degrees offered: B.P.S., B.L.S.
Majors: Business, criminal justice, early
childhood education, human services,
medical technology, public administration

EMBRY-RIDDLE AERONAUTICAL
UNIVERSITY
Department of Independent Studies
600 S. Clyde Morris Blvd.
Daytona Beach, FL 32114-3900
(904) 226-6397
No-residency, adult oriented,
distance-education options, online
program.
Degrees offered: A.S., B.S.
Majors: Aviation-oriented majors

EMPIRE STATE COLLEGE/STATE
UNIVERSITY OF NEW YORK
Continuing Education
1 Union Avenue
Saratoga Springs, NY 12866
(518) 587-2100
No-residency, adult oriented,
distance-education options
Degrees offered: A.A., A.S., B.A., B.S.,
B.P.S., M.A.
Majors: A variety of majors are offered

FERRIS STATE UNIVERSITY
Gerholz Institute for Lifelong Learning
226 Alumni Building
901 South State Street
Big Rapids, MI 49307
(616) 592-2340
(800) 562-9130 (Michigan only)

Short-residency, adult oriented,
distance-education options
Degree offered: B.S.
Majors: Industrial and environmental
health management, variety of applied
sciences degrees

THE FIELDING INSTITUTE
2112 Santa Barbara Street
Santa Barbara, CA 93105
(805) 687-1099
Short-residency, adult oriented,
distance-education options, online
program.
Degrees offered: M.A., Ph.D., Ed.D.,
D.H.S.
Majors: Clinical psychology, human
development

GODDARD COLLEGE
Plainfield, VT 05667
(802) 454-8311
Short-residency, adult oriented,
distance-education options, online
program.
Degrees offered: B.A., M.A., M.F.A.
Majors: Business, a variety of liberal arts
majors

GRANTHAM COLLEGE OF
ENGINEERING
34641 Grantham College Road
P.O. Box 5700
Slidell, LA 70469
(504) 649-4191
(800) 955-2527
No-residency, adult oriented,
distance-education options
Degrees offered: A.S.E.T., B.S.E.T.
Majors: Engineering

GRIGGS UNIVERSITY
Collegiate Division of Home Study
International
P.O. Box 4437
Silver Spring, MD 20914
(301) 680-6570
No-residency, adult oriented,
distance-education options, online
program.
Degrees offered: A.A., B.A.
Majors: Theological majors

INDIANA INSTITUTE OF
TECHNOLOGY
Extended Studies Program
1600 East Washington Blvd.
Ft. Wayne, IN 46803
(219) 422-5561, ext. 295
(800) 288-1766 (Outside Indiana)
No-residency, adult oriented,
distance-education options, online
program.
Degrees offered: A.S., B.S.
Majors: Business and human resources
majors

INDIANA UNIVERSITY
External Degree Program
Student Union Building, Room 526
620 Union Drive
Indianapolis, IN 46202
(800) 342-5410 (Indiana only)
(800) 334-1011 (Outside Indiana)
No-residency, adult oriented,
distance-education options, online
program.
Degrees offered: A.G.S., B.G.S., A.S.L.S.
Majors: Labor studies

IOWA STATE UNIVERSITY
Off-campus Programs
College of Agriculture, 20 Curtis
Ames, IA 50011
(515) 294-9666
(800) 747-4478
Short-residency, adult oriented,
distance-education options
Degrees Offered: B.A., Master of
Agriculture
Majors: Agriculture

JOHNSON STATE COLLEGE
External Degree Program
College Hill
Johnson, VT 05656
(802) 635-2356, ext. 290
Short-residency, adult oriented,
distance-education options, online
program.
Degrees offered: B.A., B.S., B.F.A.
Majors: Several liberal arts, business, and
applied arts majors are offered

JUDSON COLLEGE
Adult Degree Program
Marion, AL 36756
(205) 683-6161
Accredited By: Southern Association of
Colleges and Schools
Degrees offered: B.A., B.S., B.H., B.S.S.,
B.N.S.
Majors: Several business, applied
sciences, liberal arts, and pre-professional
majors are offered

KANSAS STATE UNIVERSITY
Non-Traditional Study Program
Division of Continuing Education
College Court Building
Manhattan, KS 66506
(913) 532-5566
(800) 622-2578
No-residency, adult oriented,
distance-education options, online
program.
Degree offered: B.S.
Majors: Interdisciplinary social science

KELLER GRADUATE SCHOOL
Main Office:
10 S. Riverside Place
Chicago, IL 60606-3879
(312) 454-0880
(Other locations: Milwaukee, WI,
Phoenix, AZ, Kansas City, MO)
Adult-oriented
Degree offered: M.B.A.
Majors: Business, management

LESLEY COLLEGE
Intensive Residency Program
29 Everett Street
Cambridge, MA 02138
(617) 349-8478
(800) 999-1959, ext. 8478
Short-residency
Degrees offered: B.L.S., B.A., B.S., M.A.,
M.Ed.
Majors: Liberal studies, science,
behavioral science

LIBERTY UNIVERSITY
School of Lifelong Learning
P.O. Box 11803
Lynchburg, VA 24506

(804) 582-7800
(800) 446-5000
Short-residency, adult oriented,
distance-education options
Degrees offered: A.A., B.S., M.A.
Majors: Religion, business, church
administration, counseling, psychology,
general studies

LINDENWOOD COLLEGE
209 South Kingshighway
St. Charles, MO 63301
(314) 949-4952
Short-residency
Degree offered: M.S.
Majors: Valuation Sciences

LOMA LINDA UNIVERSITY
School of Public Health, Extended
Programs
Nichol Hall 1706
Loma Linda, CA 92350
(714) 824-4595
(800) 854-5661
Short-residency, adult oriented,
distance-education options, online
program.
Degree offered: M.P.H.
Majors: Public health

LOYOLA UNIVERSITY
Loyola's Institute for Ministry Extension
Program
Box 67, 6363 St. Charles Avenue
New Orleans, LA 70118
(504) 865-3728
(800) 777-5469
No-residency, adult oriented,
distance-education options
Degrees offered: M.R.E., M.P.S.
Majors: Religious education, pastoral studies

MARY BALDWIN COLLEGE
Adult Degree Program
Staunton, VA 24401
(703) 887-7003
(800) 822-2460
Short-residency, adult oriented,
distance-education options
Degree offered: B.A.
Majors: A variety of business, liberal arts,
and science degrees are offered

MARYWOOD COLLEGE
Off-Campus Degree Program
Undergraduate School
2300 Adams Avenue
Scranton, PA 18509
(800) 836-6940
Short-residency, adult oriented,
distance-education options
Degree offered: B.S.
Majors: Accounting, business
administration

METROPOLITAN STATE UNIVERSITY
700 East 7th
St. Paul, MN 55106
(612) 296-4465
Short-residency, adult oriented
Degrees offered: B.A., B.A.N., M.M.A.
Majors: Management, nursing

MIND EXTENSION UNIVERSITY
The Education Network
9697 East Mineral Avenue
Englewood, CO 80112
(800) 777-MIND
Degrees offered: Bachelor's completion
program in management, M.A. in
education, and M.B.A., through member
universities
Majors: Management, education, and
continuing education courses

MURRAY STATE UNIVERSITY
Bachelor of Independent Studies
Center for Continuing
Education/Academic Outreach
3rd Floor, Sparks Hall
Murray, KY 42071
(502) 762-4150
(800) 669-7654
Short residency
Degree offered: B.I.S.
Majors: Human services, humanities,
social sciences, natural sciences,
administrative sciences, communication

NEW COLLEGE OF HOFSTRA
UNIVERSITY
University Without Walls at New College
Hempstead, NY 11550
(516) 463-5820
Short residency

Degrees offered: B.A., B.S., M.A.
Majors: Liberal arts, interdisciplinary
studies within the liberal arts

NORTHWOOD INSTITUTE
External Plan of Study
3225 Cook Road
Midland, MI 48640
(517) 837-4411
(800) 445-5873
Short residency
Degrees offered: A.A., B.B.A.
Majors: Business, applied sciences

NOVA UNIVERSITY
3301 College Avenue
Fort Lauderdale, FL 33314
(305) 475-7300
(800) 541-6682, ext. 7501
Short-residency, adult oriented, online
programs available
Degrees offered: Bachelor's, Master's,
Doctorates
Majors: Business administration,
education, computer-based learning,
information systems, library and
information studies

OHIO UNIVERSITY
Adult Learning Services
301 Tupper Hall
Athens, OH 45701
(614) 593-2150
(800) 444-2420
No residency
Degrees offered: A.A., A.S., A.I.S.,
A.A.S., A.A.B., B.S.S.
Majors: Liberal arts, natural sciences,
applied sciences (security/safety), applied
business management

OKLAHOMA CITY UNIVERSITY
Competency-Based Degree Program
(CBDP)
2501 North Blackwelder
Oklahoma City, OK 73106
(405) 521-5265
Short residency
Degrees offered: B.A.
Majors: Liberal arts with six sub-majors

OPEN LEARNING FIRE SERVICE
PROGRAM
Federal Emergency Management Agency
(FEMA)
National Fire Academy
16825 South Seton Avenue
Emmitsburg, MD 21727
(301) 447-1127
No-residency, adult oriented,
distance-education options, online
program.
Degree offered: Bachelor's
Majors: Fire administration, fire
technology

ORAL ROBERTS UNIVERSITY
External Degree Program
ORU Center for Lifelong Education
7777 South Lewis
Tulsa, OK 74171
(918) 495-6236
(800) 678-8876
Short-residency, adult oriented,
distance-education options
Degree offered: B.S.
Majors: Church ministries, elementary
Christian school education, Christian care
and counseling, business administration

OTTAWA UNIVERSITY
Home Campus:
1001 South Cedar
Ottawa, KS 66067
(800) 447-4797
(Other campuses in Phoenix and Tempe,
AZ, and Kansas City, MO)
Traditional school since 1865 with
adult-oriented centers
Adult-oriented programs, evening and
weekend programs, individualized study
Degrees offered: B.A in many fields.,
M.A. in human resources
Majors: Human resources, business,
education, health care,
and others human services, labor
management relations, law enforcement,
public administration, psychology,
sociology, and liberal arts,
interdisciplinary program, and others

PACE UNIVERSITY
ASTEP Program
New York, NY 10038
(212) 488-1531
Residency and part-time programs, adult oriented, distance-education options, online program.
Degrees offered: Full range of traditional degrees, along with the ASTEP part-time associate degree program geared toward working adults
Majors: Full curriculum

THE PENNSYLVANIA STATE UNIVERSITY
Department of Independent Learning
128 Mitchell Building
University Park, PA 16802
(814) 865-5403
(800) 252-3592 (PA only)
(800) 458-3617 (outside PA)
No-residency, adult oriented, distance-education options
Degrees offered: Associate degrees
Majors: Liberal arts, dietetic food systems management, business administration

PRESCOTT COLLEGE
Adult Degree Program
220 Grove Avenue
Prescott, AZ 86301
(602) 776-7116
Short-residency, adult oriented, distance-education options, online program.
Degrees offered: B.A., M.A.
Majors: Teacher education, counseling/human services, management

REGIS UNIVERSITY
University Without Walls
3333 Regis Blvd.
Denver, CO 80221-1099
(303) 458-4300
(800) 727-6399
Short-residency, adult oriented, distance-education options, online program.
Degrees offered: B.A., M.A.L.S.
Majors: Education, language and communication, psychology, social science

ROGER WILLIAMS COLLEGE
The Open Program
1 Old Ferry Road
Bristol, RI 02809-2921
(401) 254-3530
Short-residency/no residency, adult oriented, distance-education options
Degrees offered: A.A., A.S., B.A., B.S., B.F.A.
Majors: Applied sciences, administration of justice, business administration, public administration

ROOSEVELT UNIVERSITY
External Degree Program, Room 124
430 South Michigan Avenue
Chicago, IL 60605
(312) 341-3866
Short-residency, adult oriented, distance-education options, online program.
Degree offered: B.G.S.
Majors: General studies

SAINT JOSEPH'S COLLEGE
External Degree Programs
Windham, ME 04062
(207) 892-7841
(800) 752-4723 (Outside Maine)
Short residency
Degrees offered: A.S., B.S.B.A., B.S.H.C.A., B.S.P.A., M.S.
Majors: Business administration, health care administration

SAINT MARY-OF-THE-WOODS COLLEGE
Women's External Degree (WED) Program
Saint Mary-of-the-Woods, IN 47876
(812) 535-5285
(800) 926-7692
Short residency
Degrees offered: A.A., A.S., B.A., B.S., B.S.W., M.A.
Majors: A variety of business and liberal arts majors in addition to paralegal studies, and theology

SAINT MARY'S COLLEGE OF
MINNESOTA
Minneapolis Graduate Center
2510 Park Avenue South
Minneapolis, MN 55404
(612) 874-9877
Short residency
Degree offered: M.A.
Majors: Human development, education

SALVE REGINA UNIVERSITY
Graduate Extension Study
100 Ochre Point Avenue
Newport, RI 02840
(401) 847-6650
(800) 637-0002
No residency
Degrees offered: M.A., M.S.
Majors: Management, management
information systems, human resources
management, liberal studies

SAYBROOK INSTITUTE
Graduate School and Research Center
1550 Sutter Street
San Francisco, CA 94109
(415) 441-5034
Short residency
Degrees offered: M.A., Ph.D.
Majors: A variety of psychology majors
are offered, health studies

SKIDMORE COLLEGE
University Without Walls
North Broadway
Saratoga Springs, NY 12866
(518) 584-5000, ext. 2295
Short residency
Degrees offered: B.A., B.S.
Majors: Full curriculum

SOUTHEASTERN COLLEGE OF THE
ASSEMBLIES OF GOD
Continuing Education Office
1000 Longfellow Blvd.
Lakeland, FL 33801
(813) 665-4404
Accredited By: Southern Association of
Colleges and Schools
No residency
Degree offered: B.A.
Majors: A variety of theological majors

SOUTHEASTERN UNIVERSITY
Distance Learning Degree Program
501 Eye Street, S.W.
Washington, DC 20024
(202) 488-8162
Short residency
Degrees offered: A.A., B.S.
Majors: Accounting, business management

SOUTHWESTERN ADVENTIST
COLLEGE
Adult Degree Program
Keene, TX 76059
(817) 556-4705
(800) 433-2240
Short residency
Degrees offered: A.S., B.A., B.S., B.B.A.
Majors: Full curriculum

SOUTHWESTERN ASSEMBLIES OF
GOD COLLEGE
1200 Sycamore
Waxahachie, TX 75165
(800) 262-7242
Short residency
Degree offered: B.C.A.
Majors: Business administration, religious
studies, a variety of pastoral studies and
pastoral administration majors

STATE UNIVERSITY SYSTEM OF
FLORIDA EXTERNAL DEGREE
PROGRAM
Bachelor of Independent Studies (BIS)
University of South Florida, HMS443
Tampa, Fl 33620
(813) 974-4058
(800) 635-1484
Short residency
Degree offered: B.I.S.
Majors: Interdisciplinary studies

STEPHENS COLLEGE WITHOUT
WALLS
Campus Box 2083
Columbia, MO 65215
(800) 388-7579
Short residency
Degrees offered: A.A., B.A., B.S.
Majors: Business, psychology, nursing,
health information management, early
childhood and elementary education

SYRACUSE UNIVERSITY
Independent Study Degree Programs
University College
610 East Fayette Street
Syracuse, NY 13244
(315) 443-3284
Short residency
Degrees offered: B.A., B.S., M.A.,
M.B.A., M.S.Sc.
Majors: Liberal studies, business
administration, criminal justice, food
systems management, graphic design,
social science

TEACHERS COLLEGE/COLUMBIA
UNIVERSITY
525 West 120th Street
Box 50
New York City, NY 10027
(212) 678-3760
Short residency
Degree offered: Ed.D.
Majors: Several education

THOMAS EDISON STATE COLLEGE
101 West State Street
Trenton, NJ 08608
(609) 984-1150
No residency
Degrees offered: A.A., A.S., B.A., B.S.
Majors: Arts, business administration,
management, natural sciences and
mathematics, applied science and
technology, radiologic technology, public
and social sciences, human services,
nursing

TRINITY COLLEGE
The Individualized Degree Program (IDP)
300 Summit Street
Hartford, CT 06106
(203) 297-2150
Short residency
Degrees offered: B.A., B.S.
Majors: Full curriculum

TROY STATE UNIVERSITY IN
MONTGOMERY
External Degree Program
P.O. Drawer 4419
Montgomery, AL 36103-4419
(205) 241-9553

Short residency
Degrees offered: A.S., B.A., B.S.
Majors: General studies, professional
studies

THE UNION INSTITUTE
440 East Macmillan Street
Cincinnati, OH 45206
(513) 861-6400
(800) 543-0366
Short-residency, adult oriented
Degrees offered: B.A., B.S., Ph.D.
Majors: Full curriculum

UNIVERSITY OF ALABAMA
New College External Degree Program
P.O. Box 870182
University, AL 35487
(205) 348-6000
Short residency
Degrees offered: B.A., B.S.
Majors: Full curriculum

UNIVERSITY OF IDAHO
Engineering Outreach
Engineering Building, Room 40
Moscow, ID 83843
(800) 632-8590 (Idaho only)
(800) 824-2889 (Outside Idaho)
Short residency
Degrees offered: M.S., M.E.
Majors: Various engineering majors,
psychology

UNIVERSITY OF IOWA
Center for Credit Programs
116 International Center
Iowa City, IA 52242
(319) 335-2575
(800) 272-6430
No residency
Degree offered: B.L.S.
Majors: Liberal studies with a choice of
sub-concentration

UNIVERSITY OF MARYLAND
UNIVERSITY COLLEGE
Open Learning Program
University Boulevard at Adelphi Road
College Park, MD 20742
(301) 985-7722
No residency

Degrees offered: B.A., B.S.
Majors: Management

UNIVERSITY OF MINNESOTA
Division of Health Services Administration
D-305, Box 97 Mayo Building
420 Delaware Street S.E.
Minneapolis, MN 55455
(612) 624-1411
Short residency
Degrees offered: M.H.A., M.P.H.
Majors: Several healthcare and nursing
majors

UNIVERSITY OF
MISSOURI-COLUMBIA
College of Agriculture
Non-traditional Study Program
126 Gentry Hall
Columbia, MO 65211
(314) 882-6287
No residency
Degree offered: B.S.
Majors: Agriculture

UNIVERSITY OF NEVADA, RENO
Division of Continuing Education
206 Middy Bighorn Building
Reno, NV 89557
(702) 784-4046
No residency
Degree offered: B.G.S.
Majors: Interdisciplinary studies

UNIVERSITY OF NORTH CAROLINA
AT CHAPEL HILL
School of Public Health
Department of Health Policy &
Administration
CB #7400, McGavran-Greenberg Hall
Chapel Hill, NC 27599
(919) 966-7364
Short residency
Degrees offered: M.P.H., M.H.A.
Majors: Public health, health
administration

UNIVERSITY OF OKLAHOMA
College of Liberal Studies
1700 Asp Avenue, Suite 226
Norman, OK 73037-0001
(405) 325-1061

(800) 522-4389 (OK only)
Short residency
Degrees offered: B.L.S., M.L.S.
Majors: Liberal studies, liberal studies
with museum concentration

UNIVERSITY OF PHOENIX
4615 East Elwood Street
P.O. Box 52069
Phoenix, AZ 85072-2069
(602) 921-8014
(800) 366-9699
Adult oriented, no residency for ACCESS
Program—you may enroll from anywhere
in the world. ACCESS offers both
correspondence and teleconference-based
courses of study. Course-based, residency
programs are also available in Phoenix,
Scottsdale, and Mesa, Arizona; San Jose,
Los Angeles, and San Diego, California;
Denver and other satellite campuses in
Colorado; Salt Lake City, Utah; Honolulu,
Hawaii; and San Juan, Puerto Rico.
Degrees offered: B.A., B.S.B.A., M.B.A.,
M.A., M.N.
Majors offered: Business administration,
management, nursing, education,
computer information systems, and a
variety of business-related certificate
programs.

Online Program Administrative Offices
101 California Street, Suite 505
San Francisco, CA 94111
(415) 956-2121
(800) 388-5463

UNIVERSITY OF PITTSBURGH
University External Studies Program
(UESP)
3808 Forbes Avenue
Pittsburgh, PA 15260
(412) 624-7210
Short residency
Degrees offered: B.A., B.S.
Majors: Economics, history, psychology

UNIVERSITY OF THE STATE OF NEW
YORK
Regents College
1450 Western Avenue
Albany, NY 12203

(518) 474-3703
No residency
Degrees offered: A.A., A.S., B.A., B.S.
Majors: Liberal arts, nursing, business, computer information systems, electronics, nuclear technology

UNIVERSITY OF
WISCONSIN-MADISON
Department of Engineering Professional Development
432 North Lake Street, Room 725
Madison, WI 53706
(608) 262-2061
(800) 462-0876
No residency
Degree offered: P.D. in Engineering
Major: Engineering

UNIVERSITY OF
WISCONSIN-PLATTEVILLE
Extended Degree Program in Business Administration
506 Pioneer Tower, 1 University Plaza
Platteville, WI 53818
(608) 342-1468
(800) 362-5460 (WI only)
No residency
Degree offered: B.S.
Major: Business administration

UNIVERSITY OF WISCONSIN-RIVER
FALLS
Extended Degree Program
College of Agriculture
River Falls, WI 54022
(715) 425-3239
(800) 228-5421
Short residency
Degree offered: B.S.
Majors: Broad area agriculture, agricultural business

UNIVERSITY OF
WISCONSIN-SUPERIOR
Extended Degree Program
1800 Grand Avenue
Superior, WI 54880
(715) 394-8488
No residency
Degrees offered: B.A., B.S.
Major: Interdisciplinary studies

UPPER IOWA UNIVERSITY
Continuing Studies
P.O. Box 1861
Fayette, IA 52142
(319) 425-5265
(800) 553-4150
Short residency
Degrees offered: A.A., B.S.
Majors: Management, accounting, marketing, public administration

VERMONT COLLEGE OF NORWICH
UNIVERSITY
College Street
Harris Hall
Montpelier, VT 05602
(802) 828-8500
(800) 336-6794
Short residency (B.A.)/no residency
(M.A.)
Degrees offered: B.A., M.A., M.F.A.
Majors: Arts, writing, fine arts

WALDEN UNIVERSITY
801 Anchor Rode Drive
Naples, FL 33940
(800) 444-6795
Short Residency
Degrees offered: Ph.D., Ed.D.
Majors: Administration/management, education, health services, human services

WEBER STATE UNIVERSITY
Outreach Education Program
School of Allied Health Sciences
Ogden, UT 84408
(801) 626-7164
(800) 848-7770
No residency
Degrees offered: A.S., B.S.
Majors: Health services administration, health services training and promotion, advance radiological sciences, advanced dental hygiene, advance respiratory therapy

WESTERN INTERNATIONAL
UNIVERSITY
Admissions Office
9215 North Black Canyon Highway
Phoenix, AZ
(602) 943-2311

FAX (602) 371-8637
Degrees offered: A.A., B.A., M.A.,
M.B.A.
Majors: Business and management

WEST VIRGINIA UNIVERSITY
REGENTS B.A. DEGREE PROGRAM
The Office of the Coordinator
206 Student Services Center
Morgantown, WV 26506
(304) 293-5441
Short residency
Degree offered: B.A.
Majors: Full curriculum

Glossary of College Jargon for Adult Students

"College speak" can make it difficult for adults returning to school who are not familiar with the jargon that college admissions officers and educators banter around. This glossary should help you understand the "language" of school, which might otherwise cause you some consternation.

AACJC — American Association of Community and Junior Colleges.

academic rank — The designated status of a faculty member or professional researcher in a college or university. Faculty members must meet academic, publication, and research criteria to be promoted from one rank to another. Academic rank is important in traditional universities, especially in graduate schools. The titles most typically used, in hierarchical order from highest to lowest academic rank, in a traditional college are

- Professor
- Associate Professor
- Assistant Professor
- Lecturer or Instructor
- Teaching Assistant or Intern

In nontraditional colleges, the system of academic rank is not always used. In these schools faculty may use titles like facilitator, mentor, or simply "member of the faculty."

academic year — Academic year is another term for *school calendar*. In the United States the traditional school year is September through May. A traditional school year at a college or university is divided into two semesters and a summer session, or three trimester terms of equal length, or three quarters and a summer session. However, many different academic year formats are now offered to accommodate adult-oriented, distance-education, accelerated and weekend courses. In addition, many institutions offer one or more summer sessions.

accreditation — A process by which colleges and universities are evaluated by an outside organization to determine whether they meet established standards of educational quality. Accreditation of colleges and universities is a voluntary process in the United States, not a governmental function. Schools go through it to be approved or recognized as meeting the standards of the regional, state, or specialized accrediting associations. The most important accreditation for colleges and universities is that of one of the six regional accreditation agencies, listed in this book. Criteria for granting accreditation usually include the content and suitability of educational programs and curriculums; the caliber of faculty and administration based on past experience, teaching ability, publications, and research; the quality of library or reference resources; classroom facilities or suitability of technologies and procedures to deliver education in nontraditional formats; access to other facilities and resources necessary to fulfill educational criteria; and quantifiable results of the school in delivering its educational objectives.

administrative rank — The designated

status of a college official who performs predominantly administrative functions (as opposed to teaching or research functions). The titles most typically used (in order of hierarchical rank and formal authority) are:

■ 1. President, Chancellor
■ 2. Vice President, Vice Chancellor*
■ 3. Dean, Provost*
■ 4. Director, Chairperson*
■ 5. Coordinator

Sometimes the added designation of associate or assistant (or occasionally deputy) is applied to the levels marked with an asterisk to create further levels of authority.

admission — Acceptance of a candidate for enrollment in a school or program, especially into a formal course of study leading to a certificate, diploma, or degree.

admissions tests, standardized — The nationally recognized tests used as part of the selective admission procedure or, by some institutions, as a device for validating nontraditional work. The major college entrance tests are the American College Testing Program examination (ACT) and the College Board's Scholastic Aptitude Test (SAT) for undergraduate programs and the Graduate Records Examination (GRE) for graduate schools. There are also the LSAT (Law School Admission Test), Millers Analogies, and other standardized tests used for specific subject areas.

adult student — A student generally age 25 or older who has had a break of several year's duration in formal schooling.

advanced placement examinations (AP) — An exam, usually taken in high school, that allows students to receive credit for college-level courses or to enroll in advanced courses without taking the introductory prerequisites.

alma mater — The school from which someone has graduated.

alumni and alumni association — Graduates of a school are the alumni. They often form associations to meet together and/or support their alma mater.

Application for Federal Student Aid — The form designed by the federal government for use in applying for the Pell Grant. May be used for the same purpose as the FAF or FFS as well as to process institutionally administered aid.

approved — A designation, used in California primarily, to indicate a school that is more than "authorized" but one step below being "accredited." "Approved" is also a general term used for almost everything that must be signed in a college by an administrator. For example you need an approved course of study, an approved schedule, approved waivers, and other approved documents.

articulation agreements — Agreements between colleges, universities and junior/community colleges regarding transfer of courses and credit.

Associate of Arts (AA) — A two-year general education degree, usually granted for 60 to 65 semester units of credit courses.

audit — To attend a credit course on a noncredit basis without being graded. More frequently done as a graduate student than as an undergraduate.

Bachelor of Arts (B.A.) — The baccalaureate degree traditionally representing four years of study in the liberal arts.

branch campus — A unit of an institution located at a place other than its main campus and offering courses for credit and programs leading to certificates, diplomas, or degrees.

bulletin — The periodic publication containing schedules and brief descriptions of the educational programs offered during a forthcoming semester or other period. Bulletin may be synonomous with "schedule" or it may be synonymous with "calendar," depending on the school.

bursar — The administrator responsible

for collection and billing of tuition and fees payable by students.

business or specialized institute (or school) — Usually a privately owned, profit-making institution of higher education with occupational programs in business fields, generally at the certificate or associate degree level, though some offer higher degrees and may be accredited.

calendar — The arrangement of the academic year. The three common types are the semester system, the quarter system, and the trimester system (see separate definitions). Bulletins often include calendars listing the beginning and ending dates of classes, recognized holidays, registration, preregistration, add/drop dates, and dates of final examinations.

career — An occupation or profession pursued over a significant number of years.

career guidance — Counseling in career concerns, administered either by a trained career counselor or self-administered using a computer career guidance system or other means such as a battery of diagnostic instruments.

catalog (sometimes called "bulletin") — The annual publication containing descriptions of the educational programs, resources, faculty backgrounds, and services provided by an institution, as well as details of the school's official regulations and policies. The catalog is an important source of information that the student should carefully review and retain for future reference.

certificate — A credential issued by an institution in recognition of completion of a curriculum in a specific skill or subject matter, but not equivalent to a degree or diploma.

class rank — The numerical position of a student in relation to others being graduated in the same class as determined by G.P.A. or other comparison of academic records.

class types — The types of classes found at most traditional colleges include *classroom, lecture hall, seminar room, laboratory, workshop,* and *studio.* Nontraditional classes, including distance-education classes, include *televised lectures, online courses, telecommunications classes, home-based classes,* and other types of classes. These nontraditional or alternative class types are being employed by an increasing number of schools to meet the needs of working adults and remote populations.

closed (closed section) — A section or course that has been filled to capacity; no further registrations will be accepted.

college — A degree-granting institution of higher education offering instruction above the level of the secondary school (high school). Sometimes a term used by institutions offering certificates or diplomas.

College Level Examination Program (CLEP) — A series of general and subject examinations for students who have gained learning in nontraditional ways (i.e., independent reading, on-the-job training, or correspondence courses).

community college — Two- and occasionally four-year colleges started in the 1960s by cities and counties whose purpose was to create equal opportunity for higher education for all members of the community. They are less expensive and less competitive than other colleges, but offer comparable education. They also offer extensive vocational opportunities not available at traditional four-year institutions.

concentration — An area of specialization within a major. (See major and minor.)

concurrent enrollment — Enrolling at two colleges at the same time. Most schools have policies limiting concurrent enrollment.

consortia — The plural form of *consortium.*

consortium — A group of educational or

other institutions associated to serve their common interests. Attending an institution that belongs to a consortium provides certain benefits such as shared library privileges, an opportunity to take courses at other member institutions, and additional social and cultural opportunities.

continuing education — The programs or departments that provide ongoing education for people who have completed or withdrawn from full-time secondary or postsecondary school programs. Most major colleges have a "continuing education department" that services the needs of part-time, working-adult students.

continuing education unit (CEU) — A nationally recognized unit used to quantify the type, quality, and duration of noncredit course work that one has satisfactorily completed on the job, in seminars, or through other documented experiences. One CEU is equal to about ten class hours completed in a course. CEUs may be accepted by some schools to satisfy degree or certificate program requirements.

conversion factor — The equation to convert credits or units from one school to another. This should be documented in the school catalog.

cooperative education — The integration of classroom work and practical experience or employment in business, industry, government, or other agencies through contractual agreement between the educational institution and the outside agency.

core curriculum — Established by the school, a group of required courses that all candidates for a given certificate diploma or degree must complete.

correspondence education — Courses taken, usually through the mail, at a distance from the source; involves transmitting written and sometimes audio study material and examinations. Also called *distance-learning*.

counseling — The giving of advice, opinion, or instruction with the intent of affecting the beliefs, behavior, or course of action of another person. Career, academic, financial aid, and personal counseling are the most common types involving adult students.

course — An organized series of instructional and learning activities dealing with a subject.

course outline — See *syllabus*.

credit — A unit of academic award applicable toward a degree, certificate, or diploma offered by an institution of higher education.

credit hour — See *semester hour*.

curriculum (program) — The formal educational requirements necessary to qualify for a degree, diploma, or certificate. May include general education, specialized study in depth, or both.

dean — An official presiding over the faculty of an institution, an area of study, or a particular group of students.

dean's list — Common designation for the published list of undergraduate students who have achieved an honors grade average for the term.

degree — Title bestowed as official recognition for the completion of a specified curriculum or, in the case of an honorary degree, for a certain attainment. (See also associate, baccalaureate, master's, and doctoral degrees.)

department — A unit of the school's faculty organized to provide courses of study in a specific discipline such as English, mathematics, or business.

diagnostic instrument — A device or test, usually written, which helps reveal individual strengths and weaknesses in particular areas and thus enables individuals to take informed courses of action.

diploma — An academic award granted for

completion of a curriculum other than one leading to a degree or certificate. In Canada, a diploma often represents the equivalent of an associate degree in the United States.

division — A group of related academic disciplines (such as the social sciences, the arts, the humanities, and the natural sciences). Sometimes also an administrative unit of an institution.

doctoral degree (doctorate) — Any academic degree carrying the title of "doctor." The doctorate is the highest academic degree in a given discipline or profession, generally requiring three or more years of graduate work and completion of a course of study culminating in the preparation of a dissertation approved by a faculty committee.

double major (dual major) — Official recognition that a student is pursuing or has satisfied the minimum requirements for majors in two disciplines of study.

drop — To disenroll from a course or to decrease one's course load for a term by one or more courses. There is usually a specified deadline called the "drop date."

drop date — The deadline by which a student may choose, without academic penalty, to decrease his or her course load for a particular term.

education — The procedure or result of acquiring knowledge and developing the powers of reasoning and judgment. Education is a lifelong process.

elective — A course selected at the discretion of the student which is not part of the core requirements for a degree.

enrollment — The act of registering for a course or program of study. (Also see admission, matriculation.)

entrance examination — A standardized examination taken to gain entrance to an educational institution, usually prepared and administered by a testing agency or testing service.

experiential learning — Knowledge acquired through life experience, for which academic credit may be granted in some schools.

extension center — A site other than the main campus or office of an institution or any of its permanent branch campuses at which courses are offered for the convenience of students. It may be an office downtown or a classroom in another school or some other temporary facility used for a particular course.

external degree — An academic award earned through any of the following: extrainstitutional learning, credit by examination, special experiential-learning programs, self-directed study, or satisfactory completion of campus or off-campus courses. In some programs the learning is attained in circumstances outside of the sponsorship or supervision of the awarding institution. Generally credit is granted for documented learning from such sources as work and life experience and noncollegiate courses previously completed.

4-2 transferring — Going from a four-year college to a two-year college while still an undergraduate.

4-2-4 transferring — Going from a four-year college to a two-year college and then returning to a four-year school.

faculty rank — See *academic rank.*

FAF — See *Financial Aid Form.*

Family Financial Statement (FFS) — A form designed by the American College Testing Program (ACT) to provide information for determining a student's eligibility for financial aid. At most schools, completing the FFS (or FAF Application for Federal Student Aid) is usually the first step in applying for financial aid.

fees — Charges assessed in addition to tuition to cover costs of operation and administration of the school, required course materials and equipment, or student services (such as application fees, library fees, lab fees, and student activity fees).

fellowship — A financial gift or award to a student, usually given for support of graduate study. The recipient is not usually required to demonstrate financial need, but must meet academic selection criteria. The award is designed to support study activities and/or provide for educational and living expenses.

final examination — A test given at the end of a course. The final exam may be cumulative (covering the entire course) or noncumulative (including questions only on material since the midterm or last major exam).

financial aid — Any source of monetary assistance sponsored by federal, state, or local governments or provided by educational institutions, business institutions, or private agencies so students can meet the costs of attending school. Financial aid options include loans, grants, and work-study programs.

Financial Aid Form (FAF) — This form, designed by the College Board, is used for the same purpose as the Family Financial Statement (FFS).

financial need — The difference between your cost of going to a particular school and the money you (and your spouse, if you have one) can provide for your college costs.

full-time — Status of a student who takes at least 12 credits (or some other number defined by the school) during an academic term. For financial aid purposes, 6 credits might be considered full-time during the summer, for example. Non-traditional schools establish other standards to meet financial aid criteria.

General Educational Development (GED) tests — See *high school equivalency examinations*.

grade-point average (GPA) or quality-point index (QPI) — A system of measuring students' average grades for academic rating purposes. Points are given for each credit of course work undertaken based on the grade earned.

graduate degree — Any academic degree conferred by a graduate division or the graduate school of an institution of higher education (such as M.A., M.S., Ph.D., Ed.D.). Also includes professional degrees (such as the M.D., D.D.S., or J.D.), which are conferred by professional rather than graduate schools.

graduate school — An institution of higher education which offers study beyond the baccalaureate level. If the study is in a technical or professional area, such as medicine, law, or engineering, the term *professional school* may be used.

graduate study — A program of study beyond the bachelor's degree.

graduation — A formal procedure, often including a ceremony, for awarding an academic degree or certificate.

graduation requirements — A specified group of minimum achievements, courses, or other procedures needed for a student to qualify for a certificate, diploma, or degree. For a bachelor's degree, for example, a college might require the following: (1) successful completion of 126 credits, at least 25 of which must be earned in residence; (2) a cumulative grade-point average of 2.0 or better; (3) completion of all specified courses in the core curriculum and major area of concentration; and (4) payment of all tuition and fees as required.

grant — A gift of money to a student with no requirement of repayment or of services to be rendered. Also called a *scholarship*.

Guaranteed Student Loan (GSL) — A program of the federal government that provides for low-interest deferred-payment loans for students attending eligible institutions of higher education in the United States and abroad, as well as thousands of vocational, technical, business, and trade schools.

guest semester — see *visiting students program.*

gut course (slang) — A course requiring relatively little effort to complete.

higher education — Education undertaken beyond high school (secondary school). Also called *postsecondary education.*

high school equivalency examinations — Examinations approved by a state or authorized agency intended to provide an appraisal of a student's achievement in the subject areas usually required for high school graduation. The General Educational Development (GED) tests, the most widely recognized high school equivalency examinations, are administered by the department of education in states, commonwealths, and territories of the United States and in Canadian provinces.

honors — Recognition of academic excellence achieved by a student. At the undergraduate level, one of the following Latin terms traditionally designates graduation with honors: *cum laude* (with honors), *magna cum laude* (with high honors), and *summa cum laude* (with highest honors). At the graduate level, one term only, *graduation with distinction*, is generally used.

honors program — A particularly challenging program offered to students who have demonstrated superior academic ability. Students who succeed in satisfying the stringent requirements of an honors program are generally graduated with honors.

incomplete — A temporary designation assigned to a student's record for a course in which the student was unable for a valid reason to take the final exam or complete a required course assignment. The student must make arrangements with the course instructor to make up the exam or submit the missing assignment within a certain time pe-

riod (determined by school policy) to have the incomplete changed to a regular grade.

independent study — Study undertaken without the immediate assistance of an instructor. The study may, however, be formally guided at a distance through correspondence, telephone, and other contacts.

information and guidance system — A computer-assisted method for imparting career and/or academic information and guidance.

institutional aid form — The school's own form of application for financial aid. Students usually must complete both the institutional aid form and the FFS, FAF, or Application for Federal Student Aid to receive financial aid.

intercampus transferring (or intrauniversity transferring) — Going from one campus to another within the same university, or transferring from one college to another on the same campus.

interdisciplinary — Including two or more academic disciplines.

intersession — The period between academic terms during which short, intensive courses may be scheduled to satisfy the special interests of groups of students or to provide an additional opportunity for acceleration of progress. Many schools use the "4-1-4" plan, that is, a four-month term in the fall (September to December), one month of school during what normally is the intersession break (January), and a four-month term in the spring (February to May).

junior college — A college granting the Associate of Arts Degree.

liberal arts — The broad scope of academic disciplines encompassed by the humanities, the arts, the social sciences, and the natural sciences (generally exclusive of professional fields of study).

load (credit, course) — The credit hours or

courses required for graduation divided by the number of semesters or terms normally required for graduation determines the normal full-time load. A heavier than normal load is usually permitted when a student demonstrates exceptional academic ability. A lighter than normal course load for a full-time student may require special permission.

loan, student — See *Guaranteed Student Loan* and *National Direct Student Loan.*

lower-division courses — Introductory-level courses, usually taken during the first two years of college study.

major — A student's primary area of concentration. Can be in a specific discipline or some combination of disciplines (a combined major). Usually one-quarter to one-half of the student's degree program must be taken in the major.

master's degree — A degree granted for completing a one- to two-year, full-time course of study usually encompassing 30 to 60 semester credits beyond the baccalaureate degree.

matriculation — Registration following acceptance of an individual in a certificate, diploma, or degree program. Not generally used in referring to enrollment in individual courses. (Also see *admission, enrollment.*)

mid-year admissions — The policy of accepting students for the spring semester. Most schools have two separate deadlines (fall and spring); others have only a fall deadline but will admit students for both the spring and fall semesters.

minor — A secondary concentration in a specific discipline or field of study, usually requiring about half the number of credits required for a major.

NCAA — National Collegiate Athletic Association.

National Direct Student Loan (NDSL) — A low-interest loan available through joint sponsorship of the federal government and the individual postsecondary institution.

need-blind admissions — The policy of accepting students without regard to financial need. In other words, the admissions office reviews an applicant's folder without examining his or her financial situation.

noncollegiate instruction — Instruction offered by an institution, agency, or organization other than one engaged primarily in higher education.

nonmatriculated — Status of a student who has been admitted to a school and allowed to take courses on either a credit or noncredit basis but not as an official certificate, diploma, or degree candidate. Nonmatriculated students are often referred to as "special students." Students may be able to take courses and accumulate credits toward a credential while matriculation is pending due to some unfulfilled admissions requirement.

non-traditional higher education — Off-campus education, pursued at a distance from an institution, and involving significant independent study.

occupational education — Education designed to impart sufficient knowledge and skills to enable a person to acquire at least an entry-level job in a trade, technical, or other skills-oriented field. Also called *vocational education.*

Open admissions — A policy whereby a two-year college accepts all applicants who have a high school diploma or its equivalent.

part-time — Status of a student who takes fewer than 12 credits (or some other specified amount) during a conventional academic term.

pass-fail option — A provision enabling a student to take a course with annotation of having passed or failed, rather than receiving a letter grade. Pass-fail is sometimes excluded in computing a student's grade point average (GPA).

Pell Grant — A federal grant for the support of undergraduate study. Eligibility requires attendance at an approved institution on at least a half-time basis and demonstrated financial need.

Pell Grant Application — See *Application for Federal Student Aid.*

percentile — A measure of the relative standing of a student among all students in the same category. Scoring at the 70th percentile on the verbal portion of a standard graduate school admission exam, for example, means that only 30 percent of all students who took the same exam in the current testing group scored higher in verbal skills than the individual scoring 70.

postgraduate study — Usually taken to mean study beyond the master's degree but below the doctorate. For the completion of a postgraduate program, a certificate of advanced graduate study, an advanced professional certificate, or a diploma of advanced graduate study may be awarded.

postsecondary education — See *higher education.*

preregistration — The plan by which students select and are assigned courses for a succeeding term well in advance of the official opening date of registration for the term.

prerequisite — A course that must be taken, or a requirement that must be satisfied, before a student will be permitted to take a more advanced course in the same field of study.

primary sources — Anything published by a school or any person directly affiliated with a school. A written primary source includes school newspapers, magazines, alumni publications, academic journals, and admissions brochures.

probation, academic — A warning (as opposed to a penalty) resulting from unsatisfactory scholarship, that provides an opportunity to improve. Academic probation usually involves the compulsory reduction of the academic load, interviews for diagnosis of difficulties, and academic counseling.

professional degree — The first degree satisfying completion of the minimum academic requirements for practice of a profession. Includes certain bachelor's, master's, and doctoral degrees.

proficiency examination — A test taken by a student to demonstrate competence in the subject matter of a course in order to receive equivalent credit for that course.

program (curriculum) — The formal educational requirements necessary to qualify for a degree, diploma, or certificate. May include general education or specialized study in a particular field, or both.

projected or planned academic program — A list of courses that you plan to take at your new school and the semesters in which you plan to take them.

provisional registration — Permission to attend classes pending the adjustment of standing.

quality-point index (QPI) — See *grade-point average (GPA).*

quarter — A period of about 10 weeks representing one-fourth of a school year (as compared to a semester or trimester, which is usually about 16 weeks in length).

rank — See *class rank, academic rank,* and *administrative rank.*

"reach or fall" plan — The traditional approach to college applications in which one applies to many schools, including several "reaches" and "safeties."

reasons for applying — These are your reasons for choosing a particular school. In order to be valid they must be academic reasons, and in order to be compelling they must be specific and demonstrate exactly why you have chosen the school.

reasons for leaving — These are your personal reasons for deciding to transfer. They can range from academic and social problems to dissatisfaction with the weather.

registrar — The college administrator responsible for supervising course and program admissions and enrollments, academic recording, and certification.

registration — Official enrollment in a course or program or approval of a student's curriculum.

residence — Pursuit of full- or part-time study in classes on campus. At some institutions it means living in the school's dormitories.

residency requirement — The number of terms a student must spend at one school in order to earn a degree. Calculated in semesters, quarters, or credit hours.

reverse transferring — Enrolling in a junior college after receiving a bachelor's degree from a four-year school (not to be confused with *4-2 transferring*).

rolling admissions — A policy whereby a college gives an admissions decision as soon as possible after an application is completed. Applications are accepted throughout the year and there is no set notification deadline.

ROTC — Many colleges have units of the Reserve Officer's Training Corps that offer two- and four-year programs of military training culminating in an officer's commission. In some colleges, credit for courses can be applied toward a degree. Not appropriate for adult students beyond service age.

satellite center — Same as *branch campus*.

schedule, class — The list of courses and sections offered, together with the names of the instructors and the days, hours, and places of meeting.

schedule — See also *bulletin*. A list of all courses available in a given semester at a school.

scholarship — A gift of money to a student, ordinarily for the support of undergraduate study. It is granted in recognition of academic or other distinction and may require that the recipient be in need of financial assistance. The donor may specify particular conditions or restrictions in addition to demonstrated financial need.

school — Loosely, any educational institution. Also, a division of a university organized to provide training in a professional field (such as school of business, school of nursing).

secondary sources — Any research or information source not directly related to a school, such as magazine articles, guidance counselors, and college guidebooks.

section — A division of a course into two or more classes, each having the same subject matter, but not necessarily taught by the same instructor, or at the same hour.

semester — Traditionally half an academic year, usually about 16–17 weeks, beginning in August/September or January/February.

semester hour — A unit representing one hour of classroom instruction per week for a semester of not less than 15 weeks. One credit, point, or other academic unit is traditionally granted for the successful completion of each semester hour. This basic measure must be adjusted proportionately to translate the value of academic calendars and formats of study other than that of the traditional two-semester academic year (this includes summer sessions and independent study).

suggested course equivalency chart — A list of all courses taken at one school and equivalent courses at another. Prepared by the student to facilitate the arrangement of transfer credit.

summer session — A session not a part of

the academic year (September through May).

Supplemental Educational Opportunity Grant (SEOG) — A federally funded grant administered by the school for undergraduate students who have exceptional financial need not entirely satisfied by the Pell Grant.

survey course — A course designed to provide a general overview of an area of study. Completed by a student either prior to undertaking specialized work in a given field, or to provide broad, general concepts about an area in which one does not plan to specialize.

syllabus — A sequential outline of topics to be covered by the instructor and assignments to be completed by the students during a course.

target school — The school to which you want to transfer.

tenure — The institutional designation that serves to identify the status of the employee with respect to permanence of position. A faculty member on tenure normally cannot be discharged except for extreme reasons such as moral turpitude or the financial exigency of the institution.

term — The period of time that a course runs with specific beginning and ending dates. Usually a semester, trimester, or quarter.

trade or technical institute (or school) — An institution of higher education offering occupational programs in trade and technical fields, usually granting certificates but not degrees, and subject to accreditation by the National Association of Trade and Technical Schools.

traditional higher education — On-campus education involving classroom work and direct contact with instructors.

transcript — The official record of a student's academic performance.

transfer — Admission to a new school with acceptance of previously earned credits toward the degree, diploma, certificate, or program requirements of the new school.

transfer coordinator — Admissions officer responsible for handling transfer applications.

transfer credit packet — All validation materials sent to the admissions office during the reapplication process. Includes Suggested Course Equivalency Chart, Projected Academic Program, course syllabi, and cover letter.

transfer student — A student who has attended another college for any period from a single term up to three years.

transfer student's rights — A statement adopted by the National Association of College Admissions Counselors to help all transfer students understand their responsibilities and rights during the admissions process.

transferable credits — Credits accepted by your transfer school that will count toward graduation.

trimester — A period of about 16 weeks representing one-third of a school year. A school using the trimester system is on a normal academic schedule during the summer months when schools operating on a traditional semester system would be closed except for summer session courses. Two trimesters constitute an academic year.

tuition — The amount of money charged to students for instructional services. Tuition may be charged on a per-term, per-course, or per-credit basis. Fees (see definition) may also be charged to students.

undergraduate study — Study at the associate or baccalaureate level.

university — A higher education institution that confers graduate as well as undergraduate degrees in various fields of study. A university has at least two colleges or professional schools granting doctorates and sponsoring research at an advanced level.

upper-division courses — Advanced courses usually taken as part of a student's major during the last years of college study.

validation materials — Written documentation of completed course work used to obtain transfer credit (i.e., syllabi, course catalogues, and letters from professors).

Veterans Administration (VA) educational benefits — Benefits paid for student financial assistance at approved postsecondary educational institutions for three types of beneficiaries: (1) surviving spouse and children, (2) discharged veterans, and (3) active armed-service employees in special programs.

visiting student program — A program which allows students to spend a semester or a year at another institution without transferring.

vocational education — See *occupational education.*

withdrawal — A release from enrollment. A student may usually withdraw from a course officially within a specified period without being graded. Withdrawal without permission usually results in a failing grade.

work study — A plan of part-time work for which a student receives pay. Usually part of the financial aid package offered to a student. May be on or off campus, usually has no relationship to the student's degree program, unlike a teaching assistantship or research assistantship.

work-study program — The federally subsidized employment and study program that funds work study opportunities.

yield — Out of the total number of students who are accepted, the percentage of students who actually matriculate.

About the Authors

With more than ten years of direct experience as teachers, advisors, and consultants for college and university programs designed for mid-career adults, Sunny and Kim Baker are well versed in the options and obstacles that pop up when adults attend college. In the last few years they have seen distance-education and adult education programs adapt, evolve, and expand to reach an ever broader range of adults who felt they would never be able to finish college. *College After 30* makes the benefits of the Bakers' experience and the insights gained from their contacts with thousands of adult college students available to even more people.

SUNNY BAKER has more than fifteen years of teaching, counseling, and curriculum development experience in colleges and universities. Ten of those years have been dedicated to educating mid-career adults at the University of Phoenix, where she is a member of the accreditation, curriculum planning, and program planning committees. She has also taught and developed special programs in adult education and distance education at Colorado Mountain College, the University of Southern California, and the British Columbia Institute of Technology. She has been a faculty advisor and taught in traditional college programs at San Jose State University, the University of British Columbia, and West Valley Community College.

In addition to her role as an adult educator, Sunny is a businessperson and former executive in major corporations. She founded Microsoft University, which offered advanced adult training programs to people using Microsoft products, and was a general manager and director of marketing for Microsoft Corporation, where her unit designed, tested, documented, promoted, and merchandised a full range of PC- and Macintosh-based applications. Sunny has held executive management and marketing positions of similar responsibility at Intel, National Semiconductor, and Tymshare.

The consulting firm and advertising agency she founded with her husband in 1983, Baker & Baker, provides marketing and management services to companies including Microsoft, Apple Computers, Rolm, Xebec, CAE Systems, and Telenet. Sunny recently directed a computer-based translation project at Arizona State University.

Sunny completed doctoral work in applied linguistics at the University of Southern California. Her master's degree in linguistics and her bachelor's degree in cultural anthropology were earned at San Jose State University.

KIM BAKER is a teacher, artist, and marketing communications professional. Currently running a successful high-technology advertising and marketing agency, in addition to teaching part-time and writing books with his wife Sunny, Kim has also worked as a creative director for advertising agencies and managed marketing communications departments for high-technology companies including Viasoft, Intel, Sydney Development, and Epic Data Systems.

As a principal in Baker and Baker, Kim has managed the production of countless marketing programs, brochures, newsletters, public relations campaigns, tradeshow booths, and annual reports for corporations, small companies, and nonprofit organizations. Kim has also taught art, computer science, and desktop publishing in adult-oriented programs in California, Colorado, and Arizona and has written curricula for the University of Phoenix and Apple Computers. Kim's paintings, which have won awards in the United States and Canada, are currently represented by The Art Collector, a gallery in San Diego, California.

Kim has a bachelor's degree in the creative arts (art, creative writing, music, and theater) and a master's degree in fine art. Both degrees were awarded by San Jose State University. He has also completed advanced graduate study at the Emily Carr College of Art and Design in British Columbia, and when he was 32 he studied computer education in the computer-based distance-learning program at Nova University.

As a team, Sunny and Kim Baker have also written books on marketing, publicity, project management and desktop publishing and even a restaurant review guide.

Other books by Sunny Baker and Kim Baker

How to Promote, Publicize, and Advertise Your Growing Business: Getting the Word Out without Spending a Fortune, John Wiley & Sons, Inc., New York.

On Time/On Budget: A Step-by-Step Guide for Managing Any Project, Prentice Hall, Englewood Cliffs, New Jersey.

Market Mapping: How to Use Revolutionary New Software to Find, Analyze, and Keep Customers, McGraw-Hill, New York.

Color Publishing on the Macintosh — From Desktop to Print Shop, Random House, New York.

Color Publishing on the PC—From Desktop to Print Shop, Random House, New York.